South Africa
The Wild Paradise

For my daughter Alizée and all other children in the world, who are our future:
"The future belongs to those who believe in the beauty of their dreams…"
ELEANOR ROOSEVELT

"Inkosi sikelel' i Africa…" (May God protect Africa…)

First published 2005 under the title:
"Paradis sauvages d'Afrique du Sud
by Kubik éditions
© Archipel studio, 2004

All rights reserved. No part of this publication may be reproduced, stored in a retrieval system, or transmitted in any form or by any means, without prior permission in writing of the copyright owner.

This edition © Kubik/RvR 2005
RvR Verlagsgesellschaft
Schulstr. 64
D-77694 Kehl
info@kubikinternational.de
www.kubikinternational.de

Design: Thomas Brisebarre

Editor: Juliette Neveux

English Edition
Produced by Silva Editions Ltd.
Project Manager: Sylvia Goulding
Translated by Rafael Pauley
Edited by Jacqueline Fortey

ISBN: 3-938265-20-5

Printed in Slovenia in September 2005

Franck Fouquet

Preface by Johnny Clegg

South Africa
The Wild Paradise

KUBIK PUBLISHING   RvR

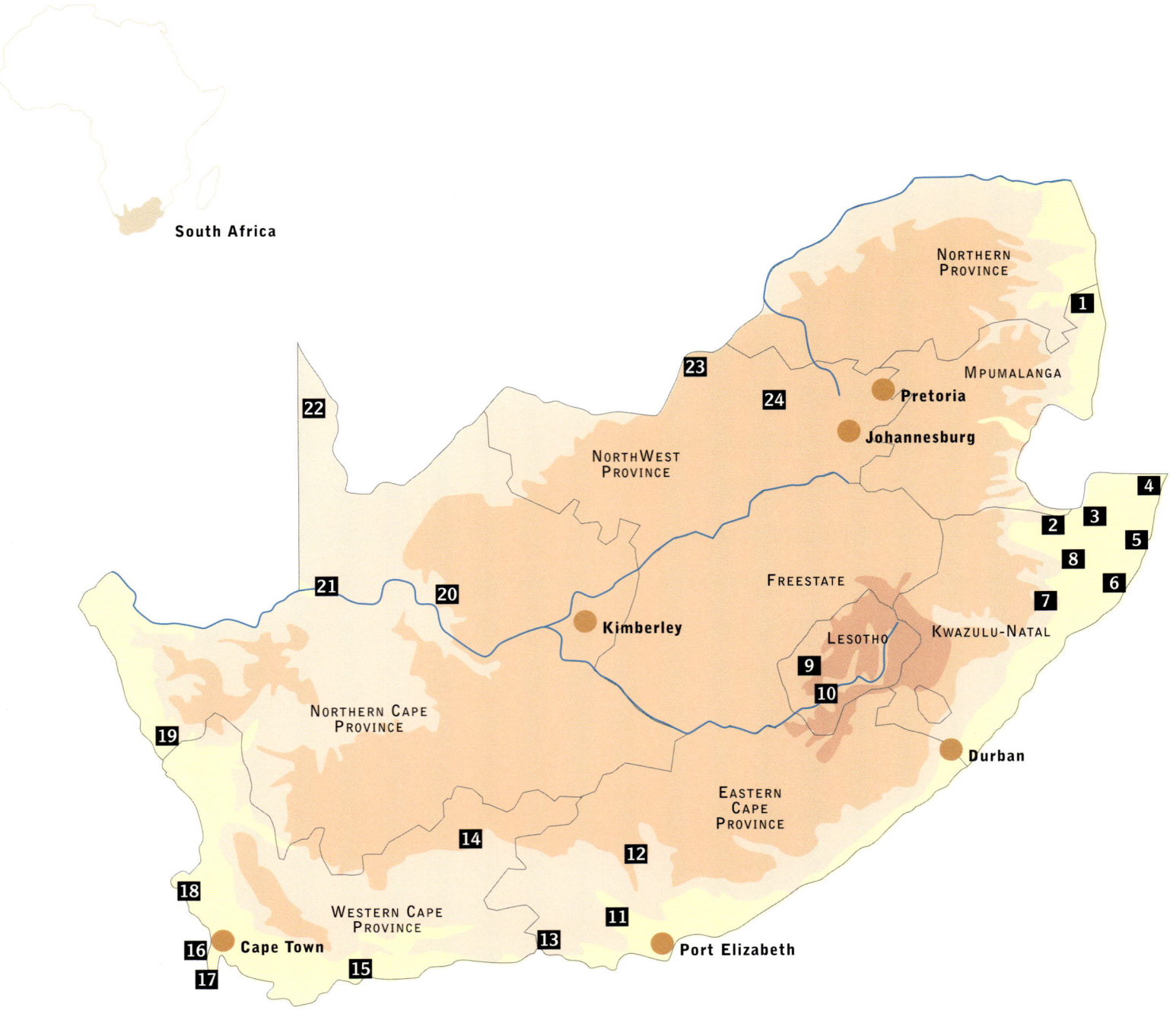

National Parks and Reserves

1. Kruger National Park
2. Ndumo Game Reserve
3. Tembe Elephant Park
4. Kosi Bay Nature Reserve
5. Sodwana Bay Nature Reserve
6. Greater St Lucia Wetland Park
7. Hluhluwe-Imfolozi National Park
8. Mkuze Game Reserve
9. Royal Natal National Park
10. uKhahlamba-Drakensberg Park
11. Addo Elephant National Park
12. Mountain Zebra National Park
13. Tsitsikamma National Park
14. Karoo National Park
15. De Hoop Nature Reserve
16. Cape Peninsula Nature Reserve
17. Cape of Good Hope Nature Reserve
18. West Coast National Park
19. Namaqua National Park
20. Witsand Nature Reserve
21. Augrabies Falls National Park
22. Kgalagadi Transfrontier Park
23. Madikwe Game Reserve
24. Pilanesberg National Park

Contents

7   Preface by Johnny Clegg

9   Introduction

Mpumalanga Province
11   Kruger National Park

Kwazulu-Natal Province
23   Ndumo Game Reserve
27   Tembe Elephant Park
33   Sodwana and Kosi Bay Nature Reserves
39   Greater St Lucia Wetland Park
45   Hluhluwe-Imfolozi National Park
55   Mkuze Game Reserve
63   Royal Natal National Park
67   uKhahlamba-Drakensberg Park

Eastern Cape Province
79   Addo Elephant National Park
87   Mountain Zebra National Park
95   Tsitsikamma National Park

Western Cape Province and Cape Peninsula
103   Karoo National Park
111   De Hoop Nature Reserve
115   Cape Peninsula Nature Reserve
121   Cape of Good Hope Nature Reserve
129   West Coast National Park

Northern Cape Province
137   Namaqua National Park
143   Witsand Nature Reserve
151   Augrabies Falls National Park
159   Kgalagadi Transfrontier Park

North West Province
167   Madikwe Game Reserve
179   Pilanesberg National Park

188   Practical Advice
189   National Parks and Reserves

Preface

The intensity of the struggle against apartheid often diverted attention away from other aspects of South Africa that are a fundamental component of its national character. The relationship between man and nature has been a powerful force in shaping indigenous African culture and, later, white settler culture, in the formative years of the country. The incredible beauty, variety and bounty of the land, its various climates, rivers, fauna and flora were assets that traditional cultures valued and thus also became part of the political struggle later on.

Within the South African psyche there is a deep and romantic connection to that magical entity called "the bush". The bush is a term that describes many things. It generally refers to that place where normal urban civilization stops and another world, which is wild, free and unconstrained, can be experienced through an incredibly diverse collection of landscapes and climates. The power of the bush is always guaranteed to redefine you, unsettling you with its sounds and its silence, with its beauty and its cruelty. The immense power of the natural environment to make you reconsider your place in the world and reconnect to fundamental natural phenomena – such as wind, fire, mountains, water, grass, wildlife, the slowing down of time and the pace of life – has had tremendous appeal to South Africans and visitors alike. There is a real sense that the landscape forces you to find the "real you", the simple you, with simple needs.

The environment encourages the social undressing of highly technical communication and sophisticated behaviour down to a bare minimum, without the loss of self. In fact, it generates a new refreshing aspect to the psyche, and this book is a particularly powerful introduction to those wonderful moments when one finds a deeper and simpler connection to the natural world that makes up South Africa. One of the key aspects of this book is that it not only presents the part of my country that is a natural Eden, but also the vast deserts, mountains and geological formations which add another layer to the understanding of this environment. The many moody and powerful landscapes contained in the photographs accurately reflect both the struggle and the victory of life in a sometimes harsh and sometimes beautiful environment.

The quality and care taken in the production of this visual narrative is a wonderful witness to my country's ongoing interaction with its natural heritage. It is therefore with great pleasure that I invite you to sample some of the best pictures I have ever seen of the many faces and moods of a wild paradise.

Johnny Clegg

Introduction

South Africa presents a paradox. While many know the political history of this nation and the names that have made it famous, few people have had the privilege of travelling around this country and discovering its nature reserves as I have done for over two years. This gigantic territory, which covers over 1.2 million square kilometres, can take pride in its variety of landscapes and climates. Due to the diversity of its ecosystems, South Africa possesses a unique wealth of wild fauna and flora.

It is a land of contrasts – vast savannah plains stretch alongside deserts, wide beaches covered with fine sand adjoin lavish jungles, rocky wave-battered coasts compete with fragrant blooming fields, snow-covered peaks tower above lodges where tourists admire herds of elephants come to water.

What these varied ecosystems have in common is their incredible beauty and the way in which they demonstrate the power of nature. How could one fail to be impressed by the landscapes of the Kalahari Desert? How could one not be overwhelmed by the magnificence of the panoramas that unfold in the heart of the Royal Natal or its formidable neighbour, the Drakensberg? How could one not feel awestruck by the force of the elements at the Cape of Good Hope? The discovery of South Africa and its landscape is an experience that stays with you forever. South Africa, a showcase of the planet's plant life, alone makes up around 10 per cent of the world's floral nature reserves, with over 20,000 individual species. As a matter of fact, the country is very proud to possess the West Cape, one of the world's six flower kingdoms, where fynbos, proteaceae and bruniaceae grow alongside no less than 8,500 other species. Another unique phenomenon is the yearly blossoming of millions of flowers that cover the semi-desert area of Namakwa (until recently called Namaqualand), in the east of the territory, which is as sudden as is it spectacular.

In this wildlife paradise, the passion of South Africans for their animals is very evident. The origins of this date back to the dawn of its history: the cave paintings left by the San 28,000 years ago demonstrate an impressive diversity of species. Much later, with the animal slaughter that followed the arrival of the Europeans, South Africa was obliged to organize the protection of its wildlife and was one of the first nations in the world to create nature reserves. Paul Kruger, the first president of the ZAR – as the first South African Republic was called – was the instigator of nature conservation politics. In 1898 he created one of the world's largest nature reserves, the renowned park which bears his name, and declared: "If I do not close this small part of the Lowveld, our grandchildren will never know what a kudu, an elk or a lion looks like…" Nowadays, as in other African countries, wildlife finds itself restricted to reserves and parks; these are, however, numerous, among the largest in the world, and contain an incredible diversity of fauna and flora.

The directors of the reserves and parks continue to assure the protection of the animals, and work for their reintroduction. South Africa is one of the rare countries to shelter such a high quantity of endangered species, and can be proud of having prevented the extinction of various species including the white rhinoceros, the black rhinoceros, the mountain zebra, the jackass penguin, the African black oystercatcher, the white-tailed gnu and many others. Of course, the Big Five are among the natural species of South Africa. The lion, the leopard, the elephant, the buffalo and the black rhinoceros, former trophies for game hunters, have become the prized game of image hunters. They are, however, not alone in producing the show in this wildlife theatre. Many other animals such as giraffes, hippopotamuses, crocodiles and herds of antelopes populate the parks and reserves. No less than 900 species of birds cross the skies over these protected areas, not to count the tens of thousands of insects, which live on the ground or in the air.

South Africa is without doubt one of the last wildlife paradises left in the world, and this book will provide you with just a hint of the treasures it has to offer.

Franck Fouquet

Mpumalanga

Kruger National Park
A national treasure

In the Lowveld region, a few hours drive from Johannesburg, lies one of the largest wildlife reserves in Africa: Kruger National Park. For myself, as for many other wildlife enthusiasts, the name in itself is symbolic. As renowned as the Masaï Mara in Kenya, or its Tanzanian neighbour, the Serengeti, Kruger is one of the oldest parks in the world. It was created in 1898 thanks to Paul Kruger, then Prime Minister of South Africa, who recognized the threat game hunting presented to the animal kingdom. Today the park is a pioneer in wildlife preservation and ecotourism. This made it the natural choice for the start of my journey.

Passing through one of the park gates, at Punda Maria, I embark upon what promises to be a delightful adventure: 1,500 lions, 8,200 elephants, 500 leopards, 5,000 giraffes, 1,800 white rhinoceroses, and many other species populate the 20,000 sq km of the reserve, which is shared between the Northern Province and the Mpumalanga. Thanks to information obtained from the park rangers, I have established a route plan: my journey begins as soon as the enormous gates, designed to protect overnight guests in the lodges and camping grounds, are opened. I follow a trail that leads me to one of the wilder sites, where I hope to capture some good images. During my visit, I am forced to admit that the old park offers scenes of unparalleled beauty. Its imposing landscapes shelter 1,200 individual animal species and I feel as emotionally attached to these historic open spaces as I would to a grandmother.

However, first impressions can be deceptive: the long ribbon of tarmac which crosses the park, and the park's rather intrusive infrastructure, can create the sensation of being in an enormous open-air zoo. In fact, although the park's main aim is conservation, its directors also try to make it accessible to the largest possible number of people and all types of vehicle. This is a good idea in principle, but watching lions wander along the tarmac was not the wildlife experience I had been hoping for. There are scenes that are somewhat reminiscent of Johannesburg in the rush-hour: an elephant strolls along the road and stops shamelessly in the middle, much like the shared taxis on the roads of the South African capital! In order to discover my corner of paradise, I have to leave the mass of tourists and traffic.

Recent agreements to extend the unfenced area of Kruger Park across the borders of Mozambique and Zimbabwe to form the Greater Limpopo Transfrontier Park should help this national treasure to regain its authenticity.

The monitor lizard, a reptile with a prehistoric past, searches the savannah for scarce food (above).

Within Kruger National Park, numerous families of hippos have chosen to live in the waters of the Oliphant River, which flows in a leisurely fashion along the Mozambique border (opposite).

The river waters of Kruger National Park flow through imposing scenery (above).

A female impala savours the skin treatment administered by an oxpecker (right).

Always on the lookout, a leopard is perched high up in a tree: this observation point dominates the river, allowing an excellent view of the animals that come to quench their thirst (opposite).

The lack of rain has caused the level of the Oliphant River to drop, yet the clouds, which are beginning to multiply over the horizon, should deposit enough to refill the park's drying watering holes (following pages).

Meeting

An elephant calf has become separated from the herd while exploring. Intrigued by the old buffalo it meets, it remains unruffled, and soon sees off the larger animal.

He has a reputation to protect as the lord of the savannah! This scene unfolds under the curious, but cautious, gaze of some vervet monkeys (following pages).

KRUGER NATIONAL PARK | 17

The southern yellow-billed hornbill, very common within Kruger National Park, spends a large part of the day on the ground, looking for morsels of food (above).

The white-fronted bee-eater is a formidable insect hunter: it runs them through using its beak as a dagger (below).

The bare branches of the trees in the Kruger National Park are one of the last refuges of the Bateleur eagle, an endangered species (right).

Bird paradise

"If I do not close this small part of the Lowveld, our grandchildren will never know what a kudu, an elk or a lion looks like...", Paul Kruger, 1898.

Kwazulu-Natal

Ndumo Game Reserve
The bird marsh

I arrive in Ndumo Game Reserve in a canoe. It is within a stone's throw of the Mozambique border and, after the rains, is often compared to a miniature Okavango. This comparison with Botswana's famous reserve, crossed by the meanders of the Okavango River where it flows into an immense delta, is not exaggerated. Drifting on the lakes fed by the waters of the Pongola and Usutu Rivers, which cross Ndumo Reserve, I reach the heart of the bird kingdom. The numerous marshes are rich in vegetation ideally suited to the 450 different species of wildfowl that live in the park. Their food supply is guaranteed by the insects that thrive in this continuously hot and humid region.

I meet other travellers who have chosen Ndumo as the final stage in their journey: they have come, as I have, to observe this land inhabited by many of East Africa's bird species. Some birds have finished their annual migration: they will not travel farther south. Due to the abundance of food provided within the park, they regain strength rapidly before setting off on the long return journey of their odyssey.

Soon the swamps will lead me to the magnificent Nyamithi Lake, with an exceptional wealth of fauna and flora, that has earned it membership of the very select list of Ramsar sites. (The Ramsar Convention is an intergovernmental treaty for the conservation of wetlands of international importance, in particular the ecosystems of water birds.)

Here, in the tranquillity of this unrivalled scenery, I have the chance to observe rare species, like the brown-headed bulbul, the fishing owl, and even the southern banded snake eagle. In order not to disturb the characters in the exceptionally beautiful drama, where the noise of a shutter can provoke flight, I leave by the wings and without images of this wild theatre.

Ndumo, which opened its gates in 1924, was created for the protection of the hippopotamus. Among the waters and marshes of the reserve, these river giants found a pleasant home, capable of providing the forty or so kilos of fodder a hippo needs every day daily. Only the many crocodiles, which, as fossil evidence shows, have haunted the waters for thousands of years, disturb the tranquillity of these heavyweights that live in family groups in the reserve's peaceful waters.

The many warm, wet areas of the Ndumo Game Reserve guarantee a rich and varied diet for the brown-headed martin fisher (above).

A large population of waterbucks live in the Ndumo Game Reserve. This antelope, which prefers wetlands, is an excellent swimmer and uses his ability to escape from predators (opposite).

The waters of the Pongola River have become a sanctuary for magnificent crocodiles, which live here in large numbers (above).

The thick undergrowth provides a hiding place for the common duiker (left).

The common zebra is very widespread all over South Africa (opposite).

Kwazulu-Natal

Tembe Elephant Park

Safe haven for pachyderms

Man can cause irreparable damage to the natural world. The examples are, unfortunately, common; many will remember the gorilla genocide, which started during the war in Rwanda. On the other hand, few know how many elephants paid the ultimate price during the Mozambique civil war. And yet, as I enter the Tembe Elephant Park, these events still remain fresh in people's memories. The last of the pachyderms to escape the battlefields were regrouped in this park, which was opened in 1983 on the Mozambique border, in a sandy setting dotted about with subtropical forests and thorns. Tembe has a mission to protect elephants from the poachers responsible for epic massacres during the general confusion of the war, providing the last remaining refuge for the numerous elephants that escaped from the Maputo reserve.

Tembe Elephant Park, which covers 300 sq km around 100 km north of Mkuze, on the Mozambique border, today shelters over 100 individuals, some of which still bear the scars of war, or were partially mutilated by land mines. Due to their painful past, some of these majestic creatures showed signs of aggression towards man – who can blame them! But, with the passage of time, new generations of these savannah giants, whilst remaining cautious, have lost the hostility of their elders.

Thanks to the observation points that the park authorities have installed at carefully chosen locations, it is possible to survey and approach the family groups that have formed on Tembe territory. I am able to witness, at close quarters, the unceasing ballet at the Mahlasela watering hole, where the elephants come to drink at the end of the morning. A little later, in the late afternoon, these everhungry creatures leave to devour the rich, green leafy plants that grow on the edges of the Mkuze swamp, surveyed by the Ponweni hide. Were I to follow them, I might chance upon one of the lion families recently arrived in the Tembe, or have a rare sighting of a leopard with its characteristic growl that occasionally pierces the silence of the reserve, or a slender antelope, a magnificent giraffe or even a grouchy warthog. If I see one of these species at the watering hole, I know they will make way for the elephants because, here at least, the pre-eminence of these giants is still respected.

Among the many species that live alongside the Tembe elephants, one can find spectacular lizards, which are able to blend almost completely into their natural surroundings (above).

After their terrible suffering, the elephants that escaped the civil war in Mozambique were finally able to find tranquillity in the Tembe Reserve, and their rehabilitation is demonstrated by the presence of young within this family. The park has guaranteed their future (opposite).

The watering holes in the Tembe Park are an ideal location for an elephant's favourite activity: bath time (above).

The park's exceptionally rich vegetation allows the elephants a sufficiently varied diet as they browse over the land (right).

A black-breasted bustard profits from the high grasses to hide from my lens (left).

Two young nyalas benefit from the elephant's absence to drink at the watering hole (below).

The twisting horns of male kudus are formidable weapons, and confer on these gracious animals an unmistakable presence (opposite).

If I come across a slender antelope, a magnificent giraffe, or even a grouchy warthog, at the watering hole, I know they will make way for the elephants because, here at least, the pre-eminence of these giant creatures is still respected.

Kwazulu-Natal

Kosi and Sodwana Bays
Paradise between land and sea

Beaches which stretch out of sight, coral banks a few hundred metres from the shore – both contribute to the idyllic atmosphere of Sodwana Bay, where diving enthusiasts from around the world come to observe the rich display of multi-coloured fish, eels, giant skate, leatherback turtles and even sharks.

Yet this diversity extends far beyond the coast. As I continue my exploration farther inland, I discover rolling moors dissected by streams, on the banks of which luxuriant vegetation floods the land with its verdant leaves, a place where the beauty of the scenery rivals the wealth of fauna and flora. The glorious calm remains undisturbed, other than by the sound of birdsong. Farther in lies the immense Lake Sibaya – the largest freshwater reservoir in South Africa – surrounded by high dunes and marshes, and difficult to reach. Luckily I have equipped myself with an all-terrain vehicle in order to explore its banks, an experience which is well worth the effort: I find hundreds of bird species, including herons, pelicans and African fish eagles which closely observe the fish-filled waters of the lake. This natural wonder has not been overlooked by Unesco, which has included the Bay of Sodwana on the list of World Heritage Sites. Its accessibility from Durban contributes to its increasing popularity.

And so, in order to escape the growing influx of tourists, I head for nearby Kosi Bay. When I reach the beaches with their immaculate white sands and I see the forests of giant fig trees, I imagine myself as Robinson Crusoe: this bay, whose very name causes the eyes of genuine nature lovers to light up, is one of the best preserved areas of South Africa. Situated on the coast of the Indian Ocean, Kosi Bay was long kept off the tourist circuit by its proximity to Mozambique, with its turbulent past. Although a direct road was recently built, the communication routes that connect the bay to the large towns are few.

Kosi Bay profits from an ecosystem that is unique in the world, made up of four lakes that are connected by a small channel, and are separated from the ocean by a wide band of dunes. One small estuary allows salt water into the northern lake, Makawulani. Depending on the strength of the tides, sea water can rise high enough to mix with the waters of the neighbouring lakes. For this reason, each lake – Makawulani, Mpungwini, Nhlange and aManzimnyama – has a constantly varying salinity. Kosi Bay reveals wild Africa, free from clichés, an Africa with the remoteness of a desert island, and yet with a vulnerability that needs protection from human activity.

Away from the beaches of Sodwana Bay, the reserve inland contains landscapes with lush natural growth (above).

As well as being a haven of rich aquatic and wildlife, Lake Sibaya is also the largest fresh-water reservoir in South Africa (opposite).

The salt-water lakes of Kosi Bay form an ecosystem that is unique on earth (following pages).

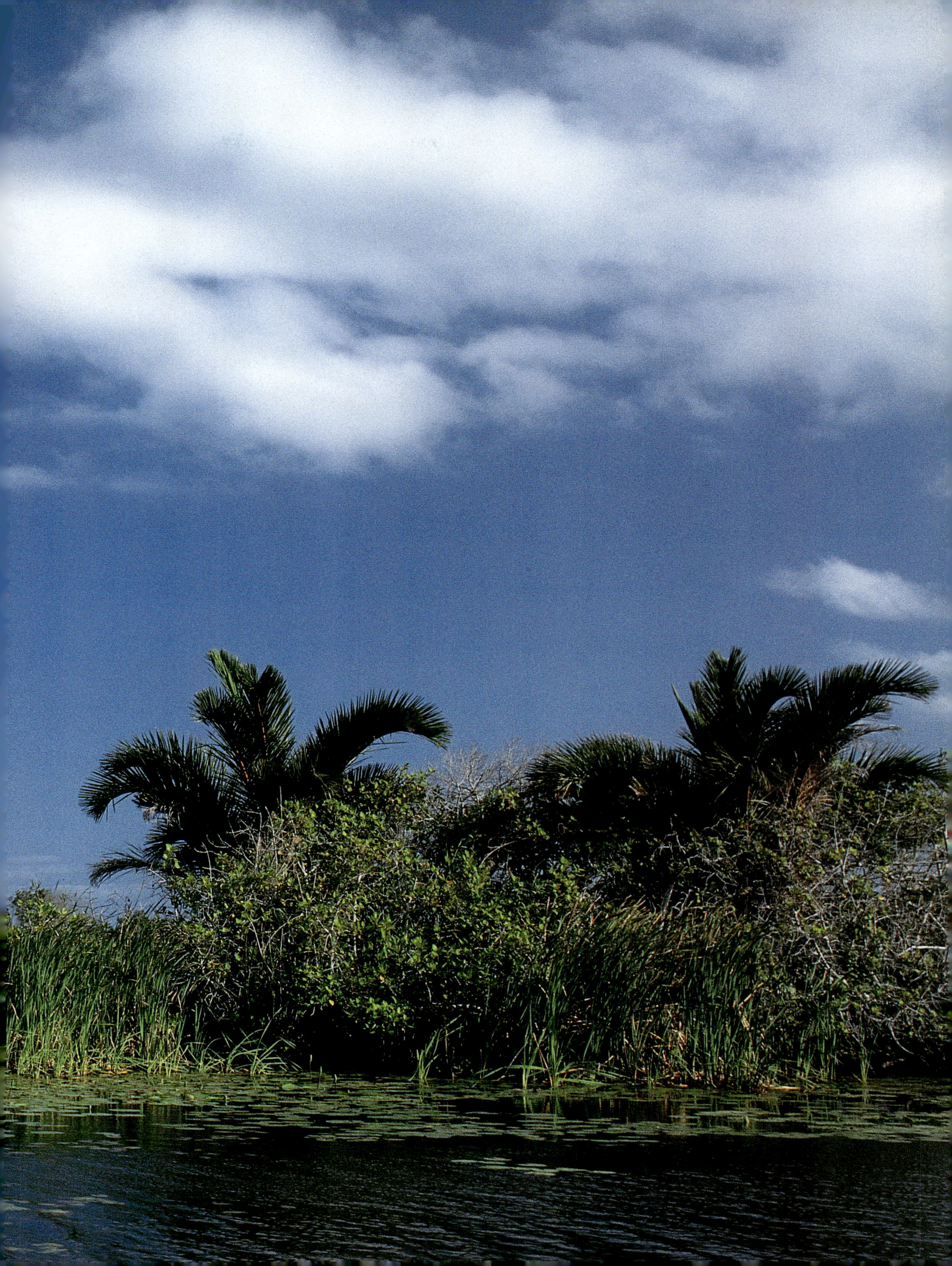

Rolling moors intersected by streams, the banks of which are flooded with luxuriant green vegetation.

On the ground, in the water or in the air, feathered creatures reign majestically over Sodwana Bay (below and opposite, top).

The fishermen of Kosi Bay have learned to profit from the area's extraordinary ecosystem. For generations they have installed keep nets, which make use of the fluctuations of the waters in the lakes, while respecting the fragile ecology: the coral creates a long corridor that leads the fish to a net from which they cannot escape. Each day the ocean forces sufficient fish into the traps to feed the community of fishermen (opposite, bottom).

KOSI AND SODWANA BAYS | 37

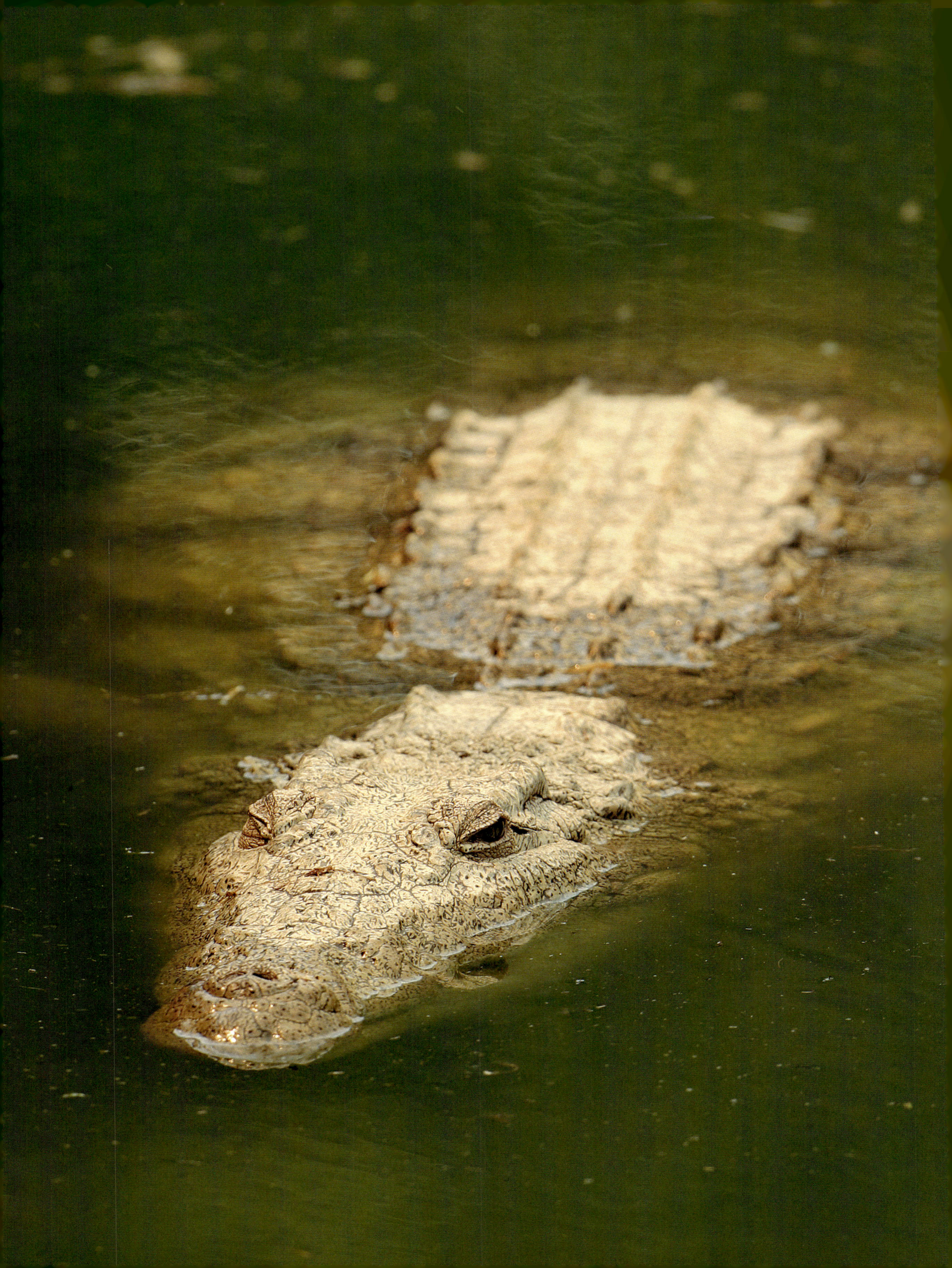

Kwazulu-Natal

Greater St Lucia Wetland Park
A sanctuary for birds

The 235,000 hectares of wetlands and lakes within the Greater St Lucia Wetland Park make this the third largest reserve in South Africa. The importance of its fauna and flora is such that Unesco added the site to the World Heritage List in 1999. A rare privilege for this vast estuary with its incredible wealth of flora and fauna.

With its coral reefs, its long sandy beaches, its reed-covered islands, its mangroves, its marshes and its wooded dunes – said to be the greenest on earth – St Lucia shelters an extraordinary number of marine species, and over 500 species of birds. The most common inhabitants are the Nile crocodile and the hippopotamus. Despite the fact that these two species are age-old rivals, they are both fond of humid areas, and reproduce with such ease in this region, due to the abundance of watering holes, that there are no less than 1,400 individuals of each species in the largest of the lakes, the one after which the park is named.

Early in the morning, before the first rays of sunlight have appeared, I surprise a herd of enormous grey hulks during their "harvest" of soft grass, in the pastures surrounding the St Lucia estuary. They are, of course, hippos. The evening before, they left the waters at nightfall, in search of food. They will not return to their cool spot until the sun is almost at its hottest. I imagine that, not far off, the enormous Nile crocodiles – claimed to be the largest on the African continent – lie in wait, hidden in the reeds, until the heat of the sun drives their prey to the waters in desperate need of drink.

Yet I came to St Lucia above all to discover its exceptional birdlife. A veritable abundance of species are to be observed: pink flamingos, terns, pelicans, herons, ducks, geese . . . With the help of a boat, I penetrate the private world of these airborne creatures, and am able to approach an African fish eagle. Perched atop a tree, he observes the surface of the water, watchful for the fleeting movement that will betray his future prey. Nearby, a goliath heron has chosen to remain immobile, his long legs firmly anchored in the water; a fish will pass too close, and its destiny will be sealed with a stroke of the beak. In a few weeks, the beaches will see a new rush of sea turtles coming to lay their eggs in the night, thus securing their survival. All these enchanting scenes confirm the importance of protecting this zone – the mission of the Greater St Lucia Wetland Park is being fulfilled.

One of the most beautiful viewpoints over Lake St Lucia is from within the luxuriant jungle (above).

Some say that the largest crocodiles in the world are to be found in the wetlands of St Lucia. The size of this lacertilian appears to prove that this is true (opposite)!

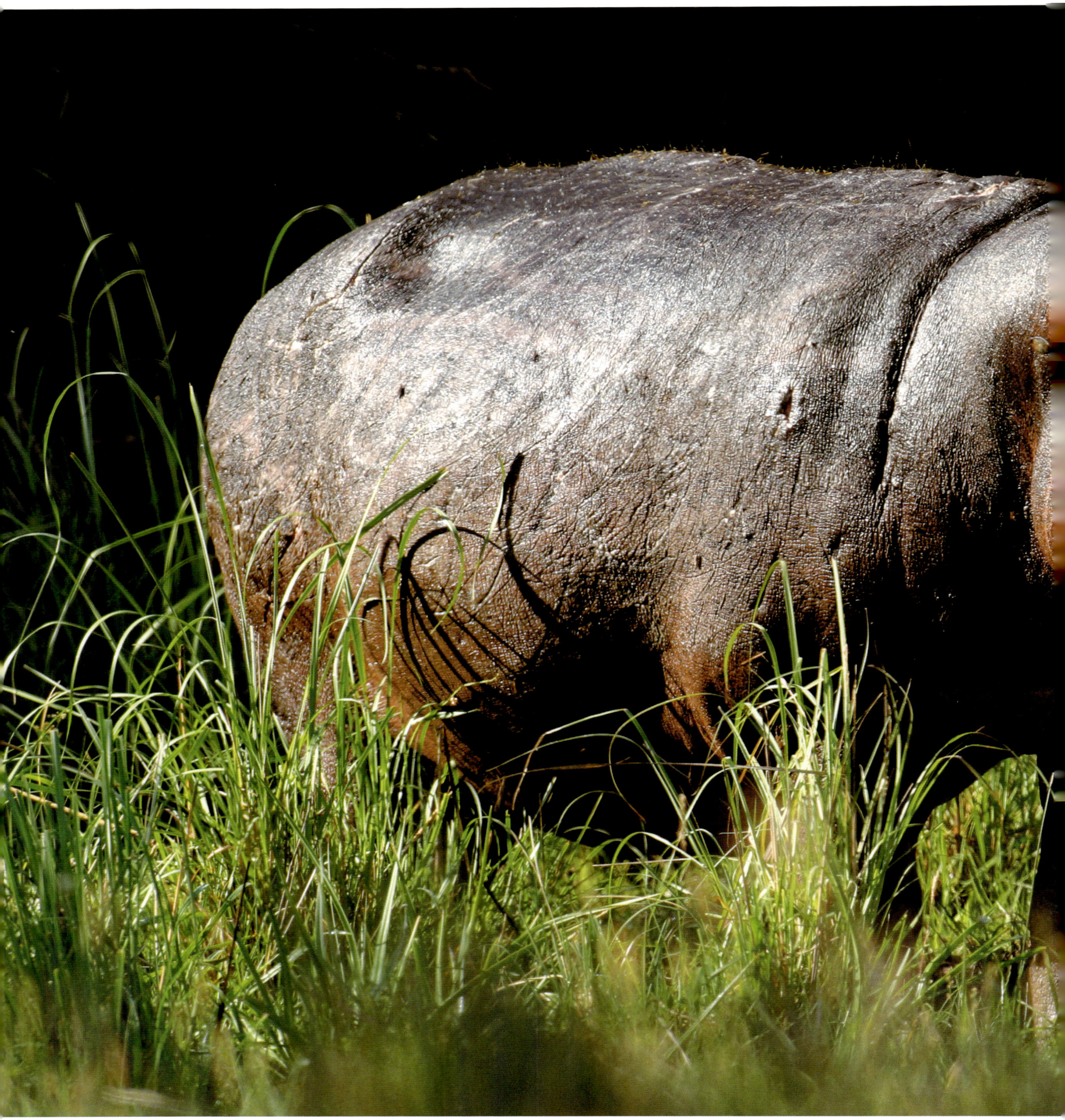

Swimming prohibited

It is best to avoid drawing attention to oneself in the waters of St Lucia. Whether it is the crocodiles (above) or the hippos (top and left), the inhabitants are generally not given to sharing.

GREATER ST LUCIA WETLAND PARK | 41

With its 235,000 hectares of wetlands and lakes, its reed-covered islands, its mangroves, its marshes and its wooded dunes, the Greater St Lucia Wetlands Park is a haven for an extraordinary number of birds.

The piercing gaze of an African fish eagle allows it to identify the smallest fish approaching the surface of the lake (above).

The marshes of St Lucia are often resplendent with magnificent water-lilies (right).

The goliath heron is very patient. It will spend hours immobile, legs in the water, waiting for a fish to forget its presence and venture within reach. The victim is then harpooned by its pointed beak (opposite).

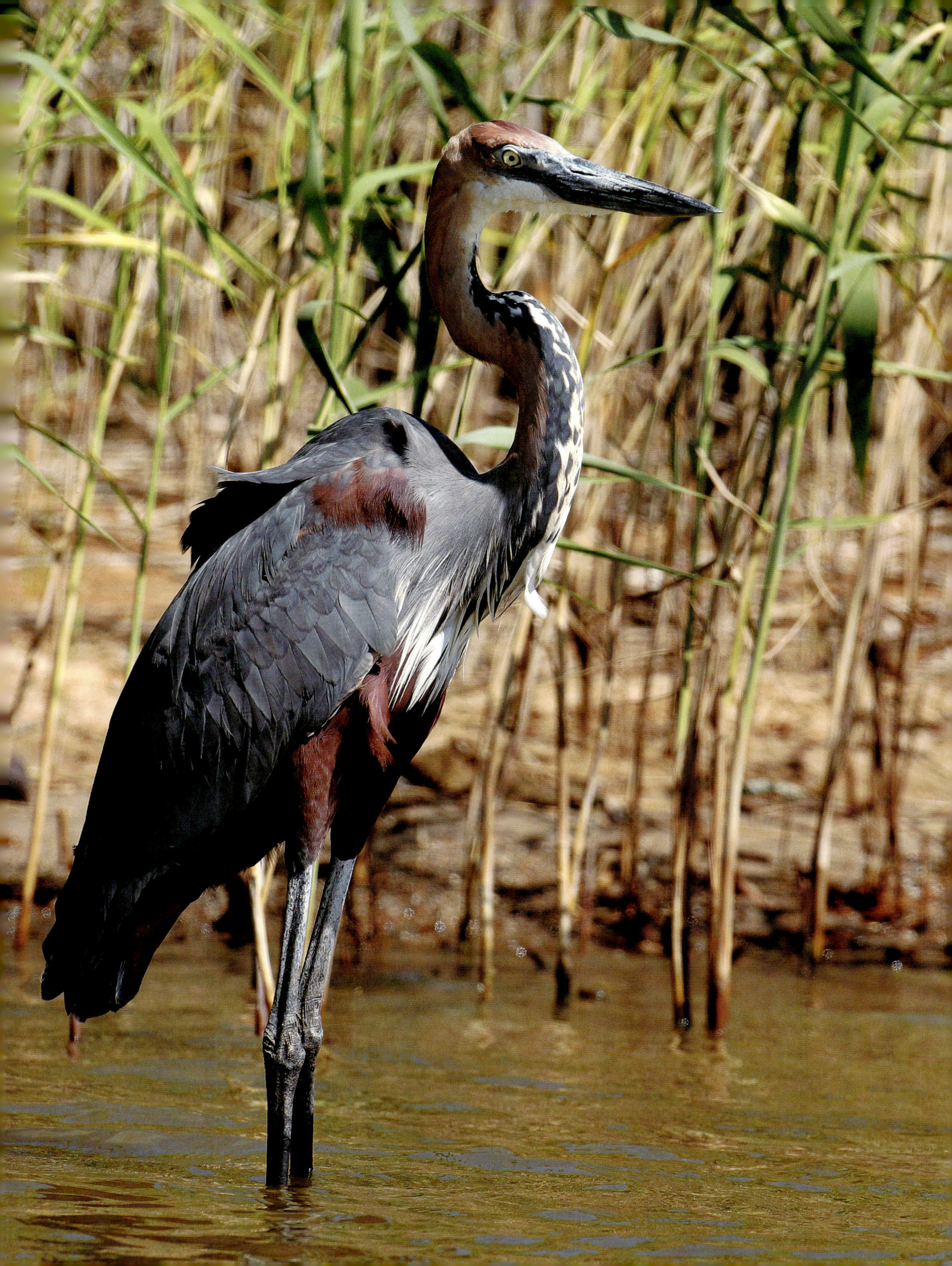

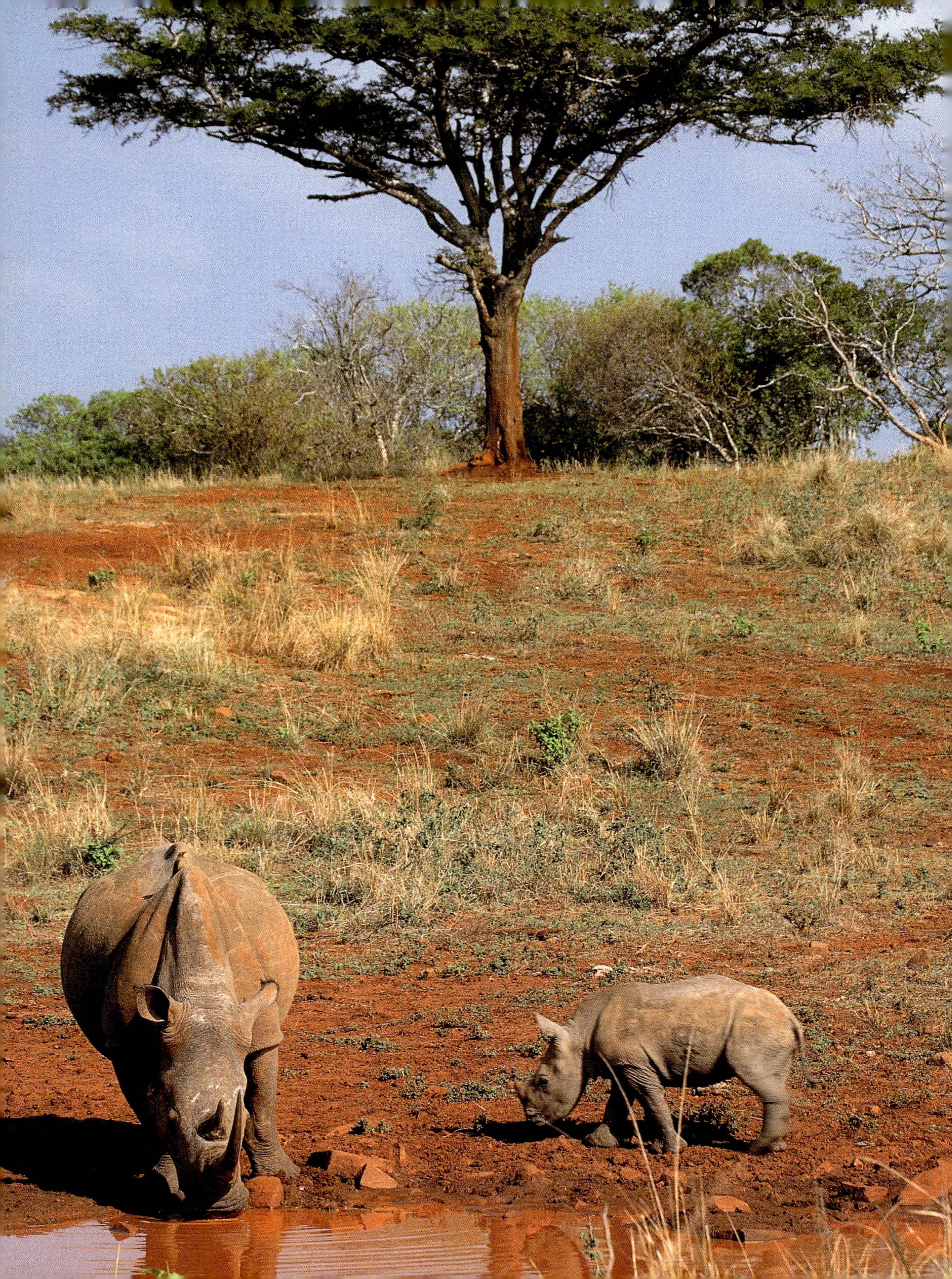

Kwazulu-Natal

Hluhluwe-Imfolozi National Park
Refuge for the white rhino

The reputation of some parks is closely linked with a specific animal. Hluhluwe-Imfolozi, situated around 200 km from Durban and one of the oldest wildlife reserves in the world, is one of these. Its creation in 1895 was brought about by the imminent extinction of the white rhinoceros. When the park opened there were only around thirty individuals left in the world, and so it was a matter of urgency that the species survival be assured. The Hluhluwe-Imfolozi has become the sanctuary, and the rhino, which can weigh over two tonnes, has found in its 96,000 hectares of park, a plot in keeping with its needs.

Today the Hluhluwe-Imfolozi even acts as a "breeding ground": white rhinos are captured in order to reintroduce them in other reserves, and thus perpetuate the species. This strategy of reintroduction was not without its difficulties, for a white rhino is not as easy to capture as a giraffe or an antelope. The incredible physical power of the animal and its relatively fragile heart pose a double challenge: it is useless to try to push a rhino into a pen with the help of vehicles! The rangers tried to put it to sleep with darts filled with a powerful anaesthetic, yet did not anticipate the incredible resistance of this savannah locomotive, which, even after having being hit by the dart, continued to run for kilometres.

Some rhinos even took refuge in thick groves where they fell asleep, but failed to wake up. Thus many paid with their lives for these attempts at capture, and it was only in 1963, with the introduction of a new tranquiliser called M99, that the capture and reintroduction of the white rhino became possible. This derivative of morphine, deadly to man, has proved itself remarkably effective on rhinos: only a few minutes after having been hit, they are on the ground. The rangers can then administer first aid and transport them to their new homes.
Thus "Operation Rhino" has allowed the reintroduction of the species in areas the inhabited in the past. Thanks to this ambitious program, the white rhino was the first species to have been withdrawn from the WWF list of animals at risk of extinction. Its cousin, the black rhino, has also profited from this success: within the vast lands of the park, it has found the refuge and peace necessary for its survival.

Today the magnificent landscape of the Hluhluwe-Imfolozi National Park, where undulating terrain and long plains of wooded savannah run side by side, shelters hundreds of white rhinos whose tranquillity proves that this imposing creature no longer has anything to fear from man.

Perched upon a branch, high in a tree, this tawny eagle emits a cry to call its kind (above).

The white rhino has become the key animal of the Hluhluwe-Imfolozi National Park. Thanks to the reserve's conservation policy, the species can now be considered saved (opposite).

In front of my lens, this gracious giraffe shows its finery: all its teeth in a row (above).

During the hot hours at the end of the day, the muddy pools are stormed by the white rhinos. The pools also provide an excellent treatment against the insects that proliferate on the animals' hides (right).

A white-breasted bee-eater, with its sharp beak and lively eyes, appears to profit from the abundant food of the park (following pages).

Mud baths ...

The vast territory of the Hluhluwe-Imfolozi National Park, refuge of the white rhino, is a peaceful haven, which has secured the survival of a species almost extinct at the end of the 19th century.

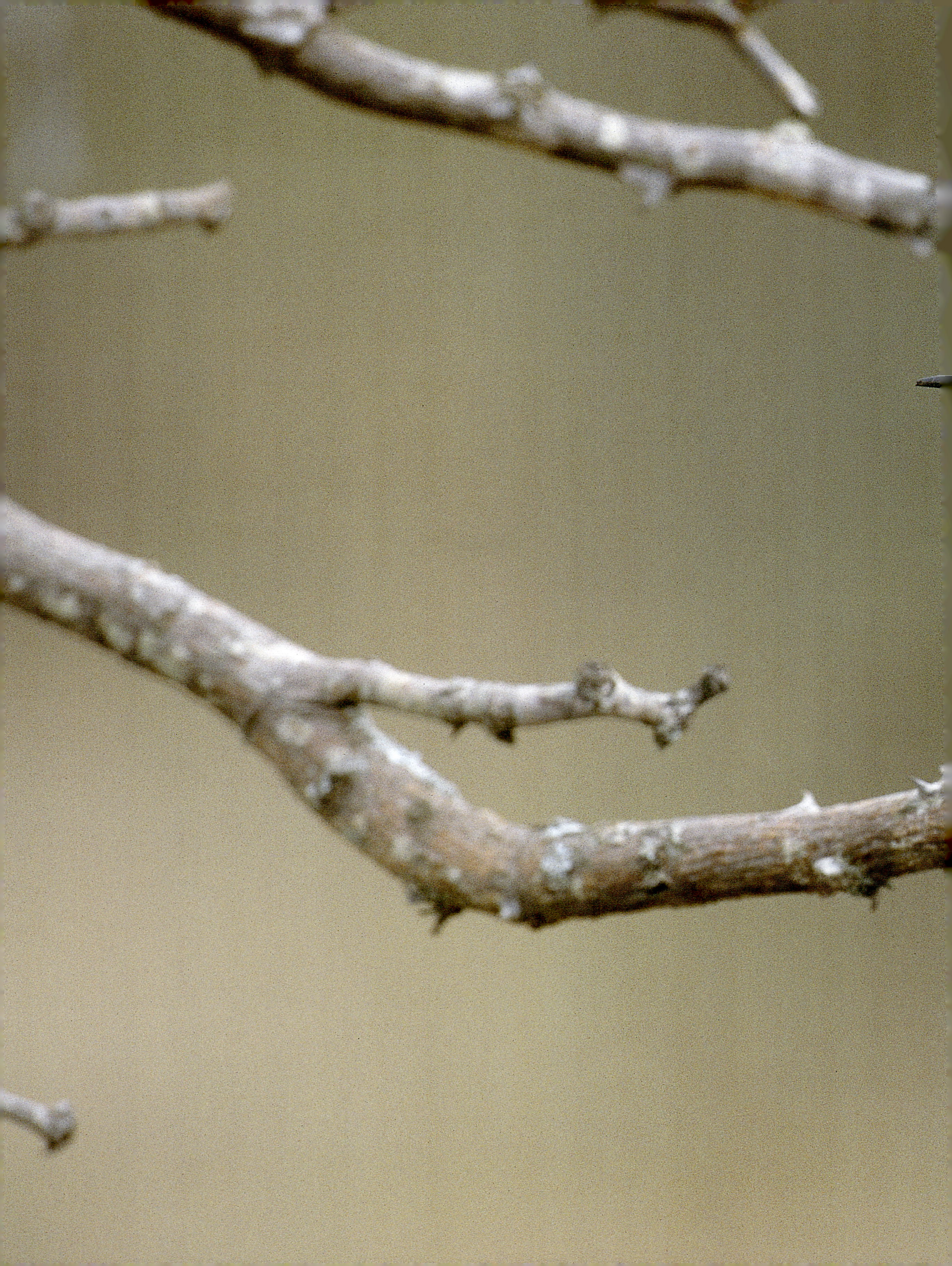

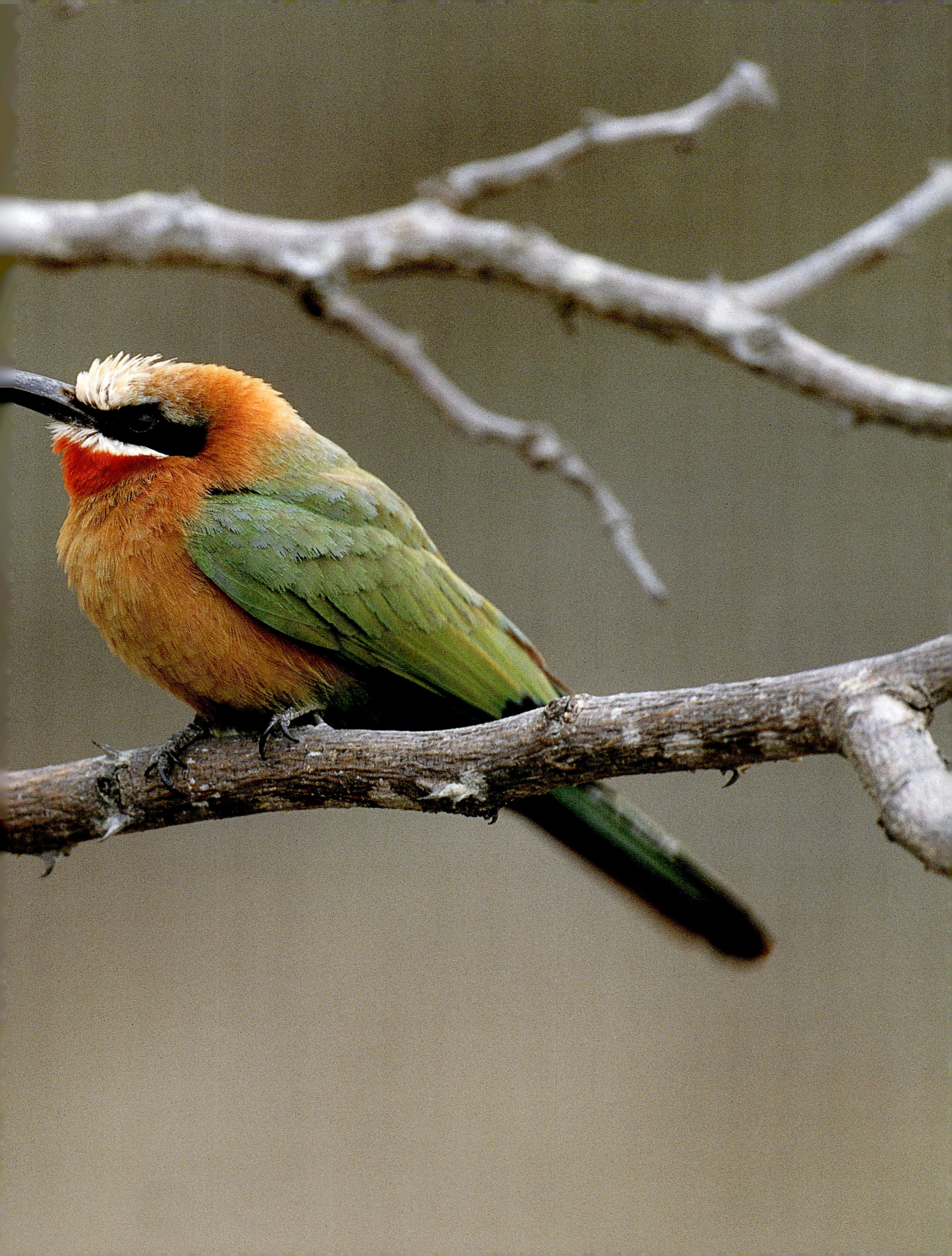

A tawny eagle has spotted its prey and, with a flap of its wings, launches its attack with impressive speed (left).

The colour green dominates the Hluhluwe-Imfolozi National Park, yet sometimes a dash of vibrant colour punctuates this verdant harmony (above).

An aerial encounter takes place around a termite mound, as the occupants leave before the first rains (opposite).

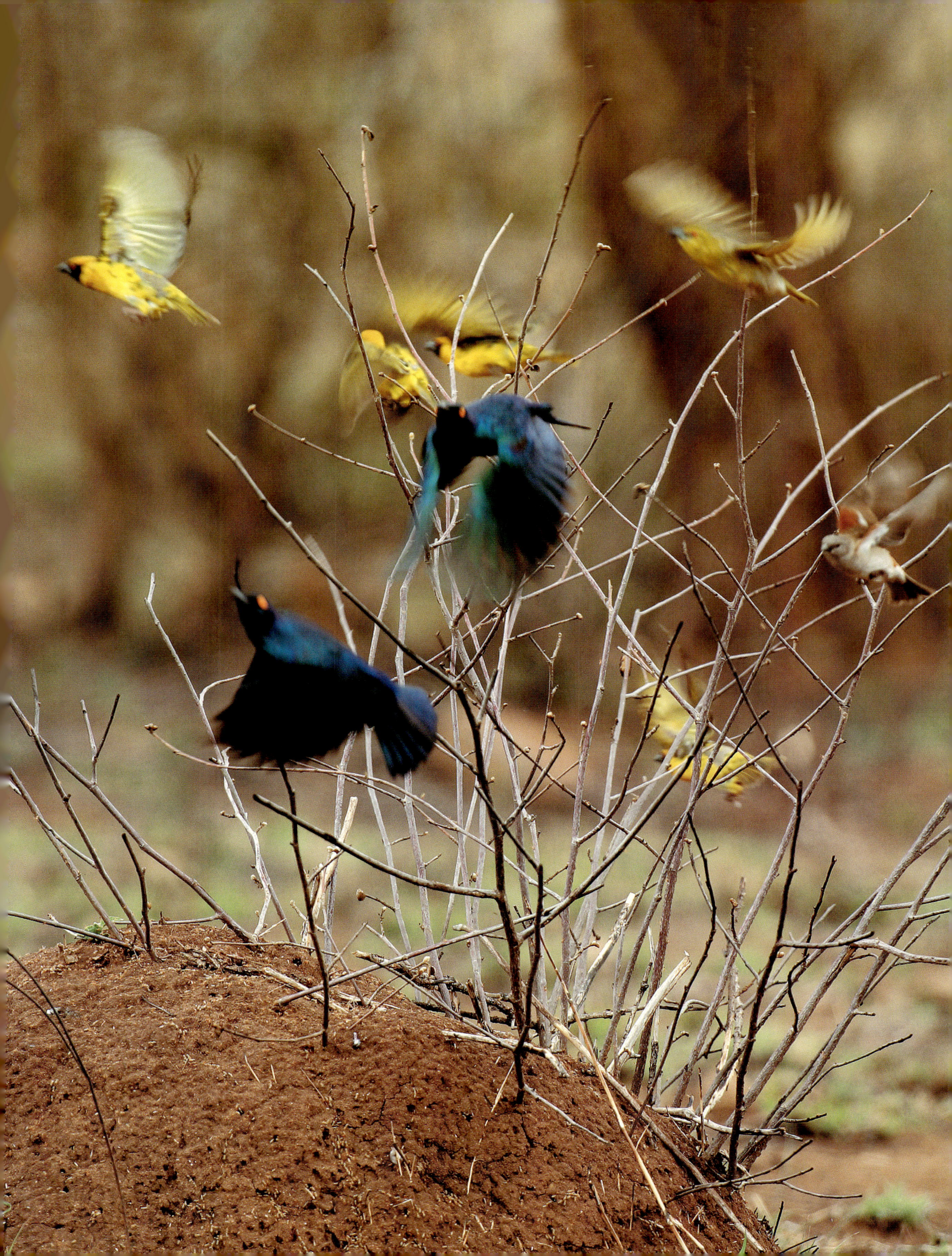

Despite its apparent placidity, the buffalo is one of the most formidable of animals (above).

The male impala expends an immense amount of effort in order to regroup his entire harem (right).

The Nzimane River, which runs dry in the arid season, waits for the next rains to refill its bed (opposite).

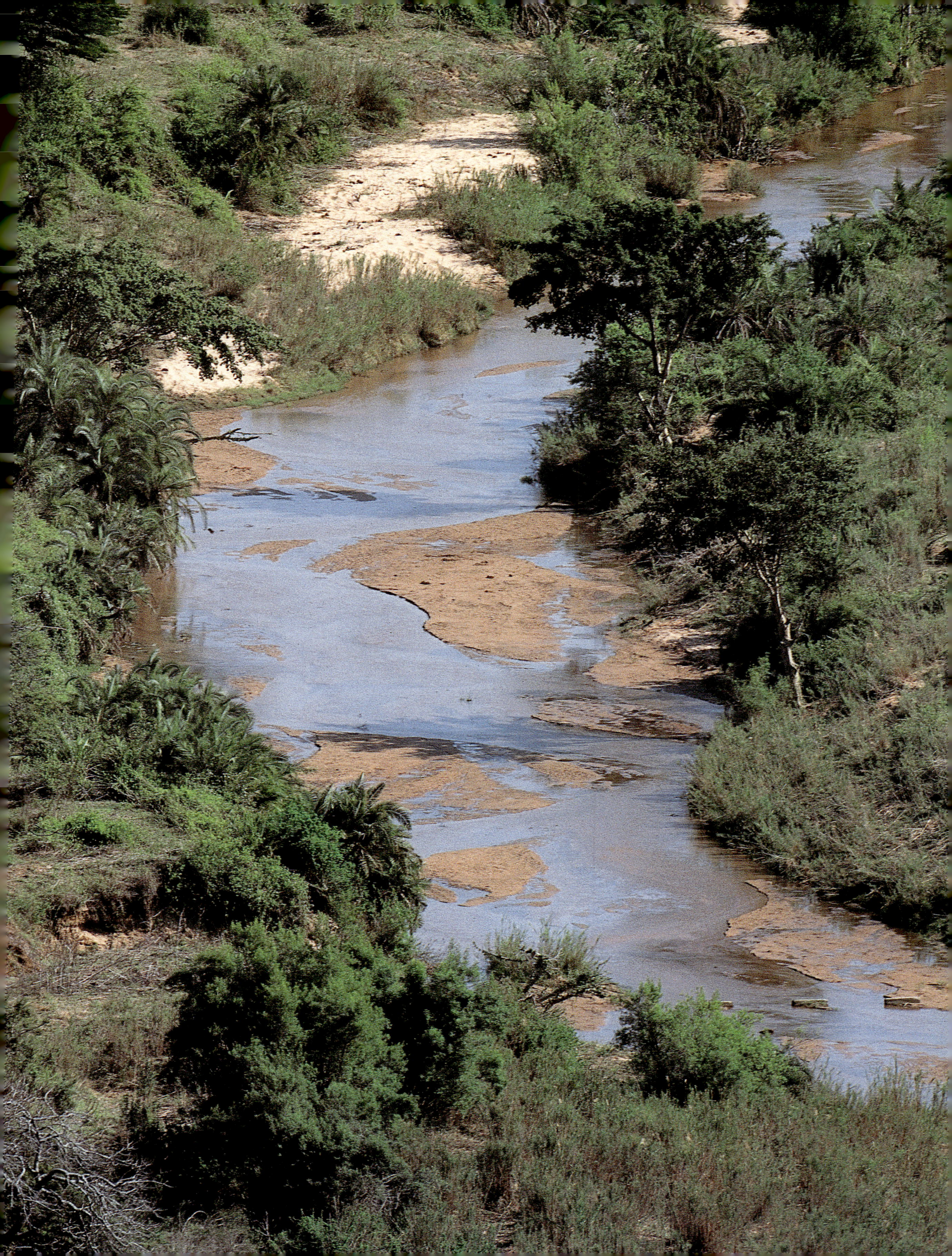

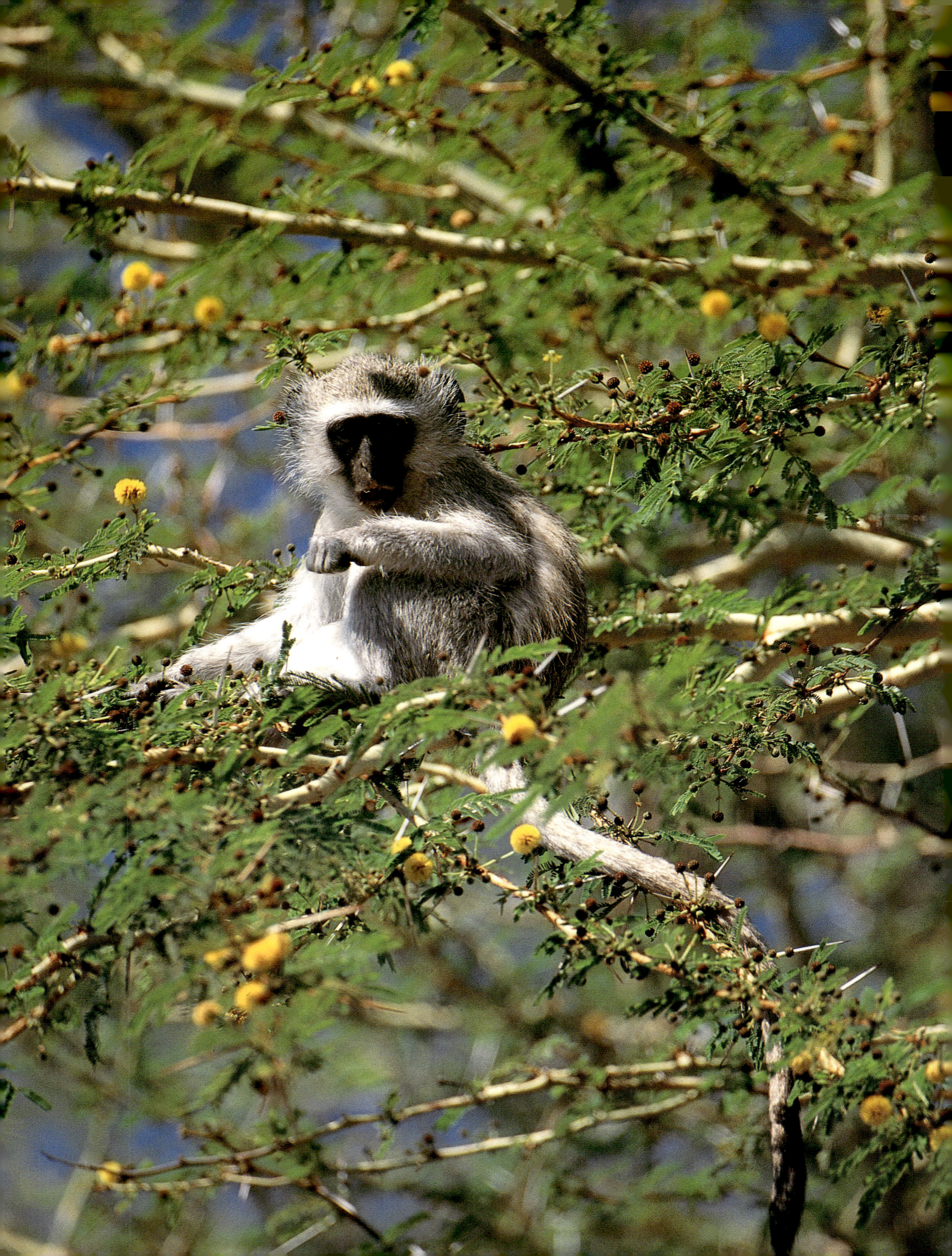

Kwazulu-Natal

Mkuze Game Reserve

A display of wildlife at the watering hole

Bordering the extensive Greater St Lucia Wetland Park, the Mkuze Game Reserve is a veritable paradise. Within this 40,000-hectare reserve, I am not obliged to travel long distances in search of wildlife – it finds me! It suffices for me to position myself near a watering hole, in one of the observation shelters installed by the park authorities.

When I arrived in the Mkuze Game Reserve, the drought had preceded me: most of the smaller watering holes had dried up. In fact, other than Lake Nsumo, which is filled by the waters of the Mkuze River that gives its name to the reserve, only two watering holes were able to withstand the arid conditions. It is in front of one of these that I decided to spend the day, in an observation post hidden by shrubs. From the hot early hours of the morning, animals come to quench their thirst in an unceasing ballet, which seems to follow the rhythm of some invisible orchestra: each species has its place, its rank and its superiority over another. No matter how thirsty one is – with some rare exceptions – one does not mix, in the small world of the Mkuze!

The gnus arrive first, trotting nonchalantly, in single file. They slake their thirst as a group and, after a few minutes, leave, as unperturbed as when they arrived. Soon the gnus are replaced by a dozen zebras. They seem worried and alert. The dominant male approaches first, followed by his entourage. Suddenly and swiftly the herd flees, escaping an invisible danger. I scan the area for a predator, but only catch sight of an old warthog with its robust defences, coming to refresh itself in its turn, closely followed by a magnificent male kudu, bearing a splendid pair of lyre-shaped horns. The ballet continues, as if to the beat of a metronome, until a small band of vervets arrives to disrupt the score. Preceded by their piercing cries, these monkeys besiege the premises and squabble, scattering a few multicoloured birds that have come to bathe. When this disruptive element is finally calmed and watered, the watering hole regains its tranquillity, and the procession of parched animals can revert to its rhythm, hardly disturbed by the few visitors who join me in the shelter.

The magnificent radiant blue plumage of the crested touraco lights up the dry branches of an old tree (above).

A vervet monkey delights in the freshly blossomed flowers on the branches of an acacia, which serve as perch and ideal observation point (opposite).

56 | SOUTH AFRICA

Abundance at the watering hole

Having gorged themselves on acacia flowers, it is time for the vervets to quench their thirst at the watering hole (opposite, top).

Soon the little monkeys give up their places to the zebras, which come to drink their fill with almost military precision (opposite, bottom)

Soon after their arrival, the gnus cause a flurry of agitation as they take over the watering hole (above). Between two baths, the hippos lounge in the sun on the banks of Lake Nsumo. By alternating bathing and sun-bathing, these "river horses" preserve their thick, but surprisingly delicate skin (following pages).

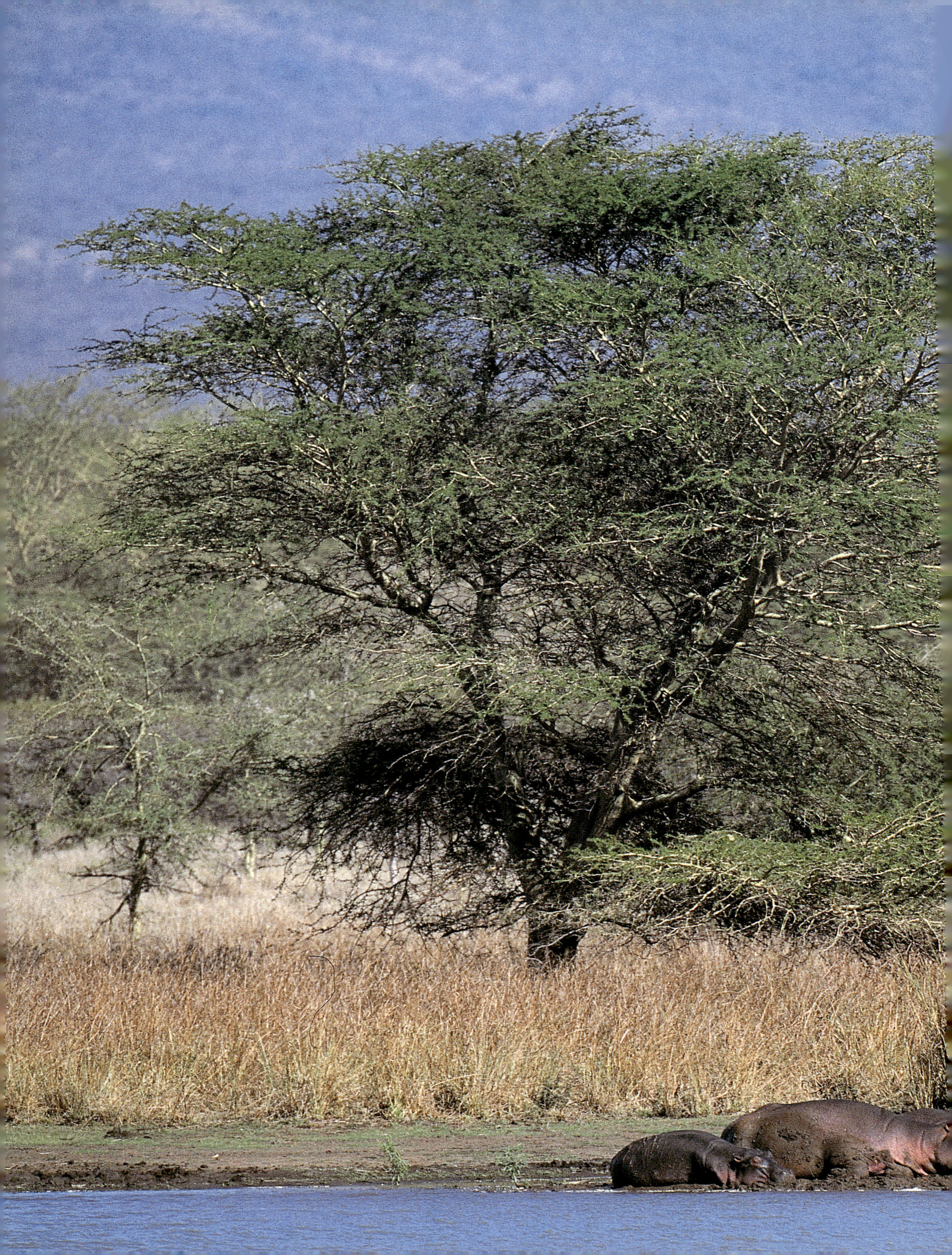

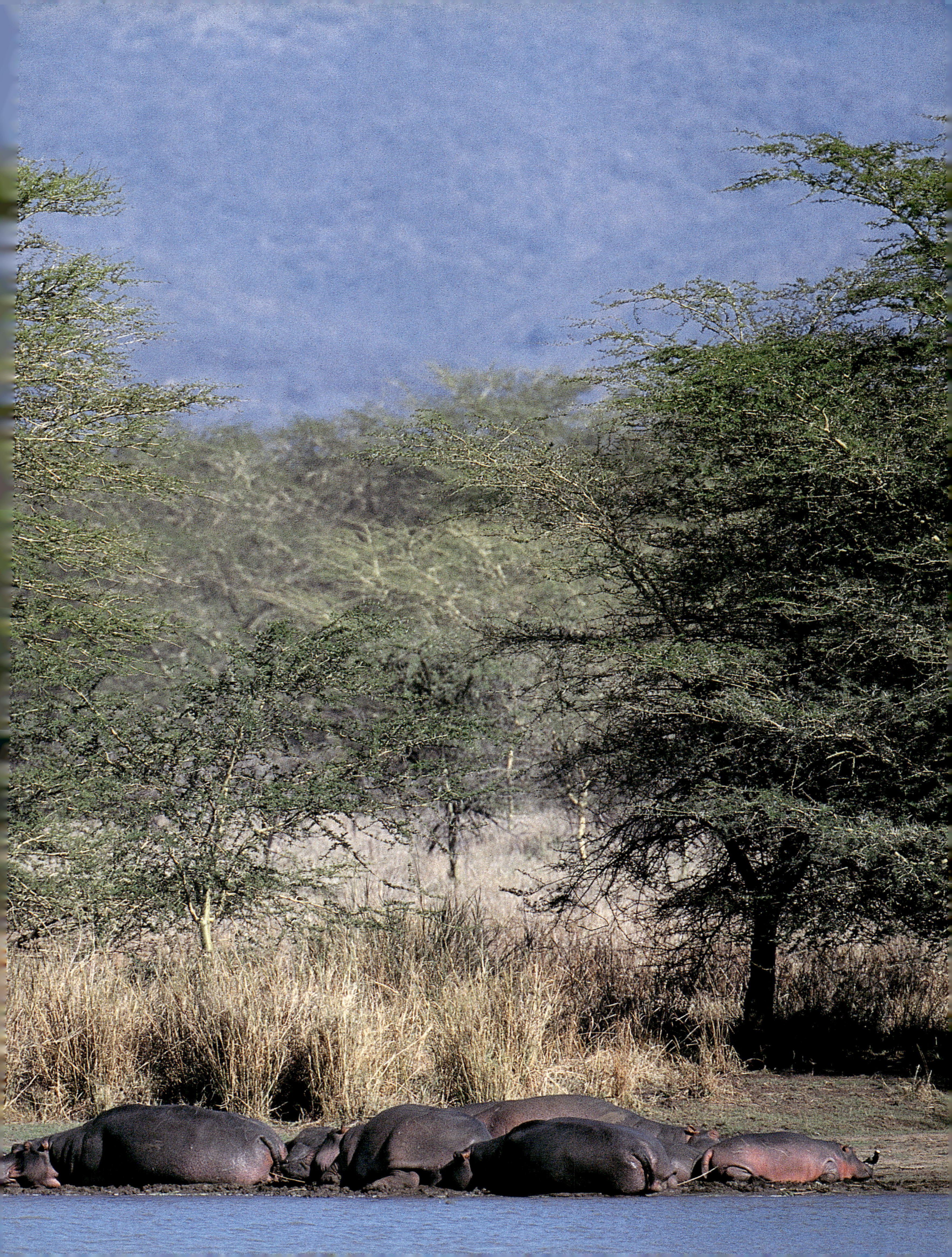

As the morning heats up, animals come to quench their thirst, in an unceasing ballet which seems to follow the rhythm of some invisible orchestra: each species has its place, its rank, its superiority over another.

A zebra, alert as always, prepares to approach the watering hole for a drink (left).

Numerous warthogs inhabit the Mkuze Game Reserve. These imposing animals breed easily within the park, due to the absence of large predators (above)

Thanks to the large number of observation points built within the reserve, it is not difficult to spot a nyala, despite the fact that it is one of Africa's rarer antelopes (opposite).

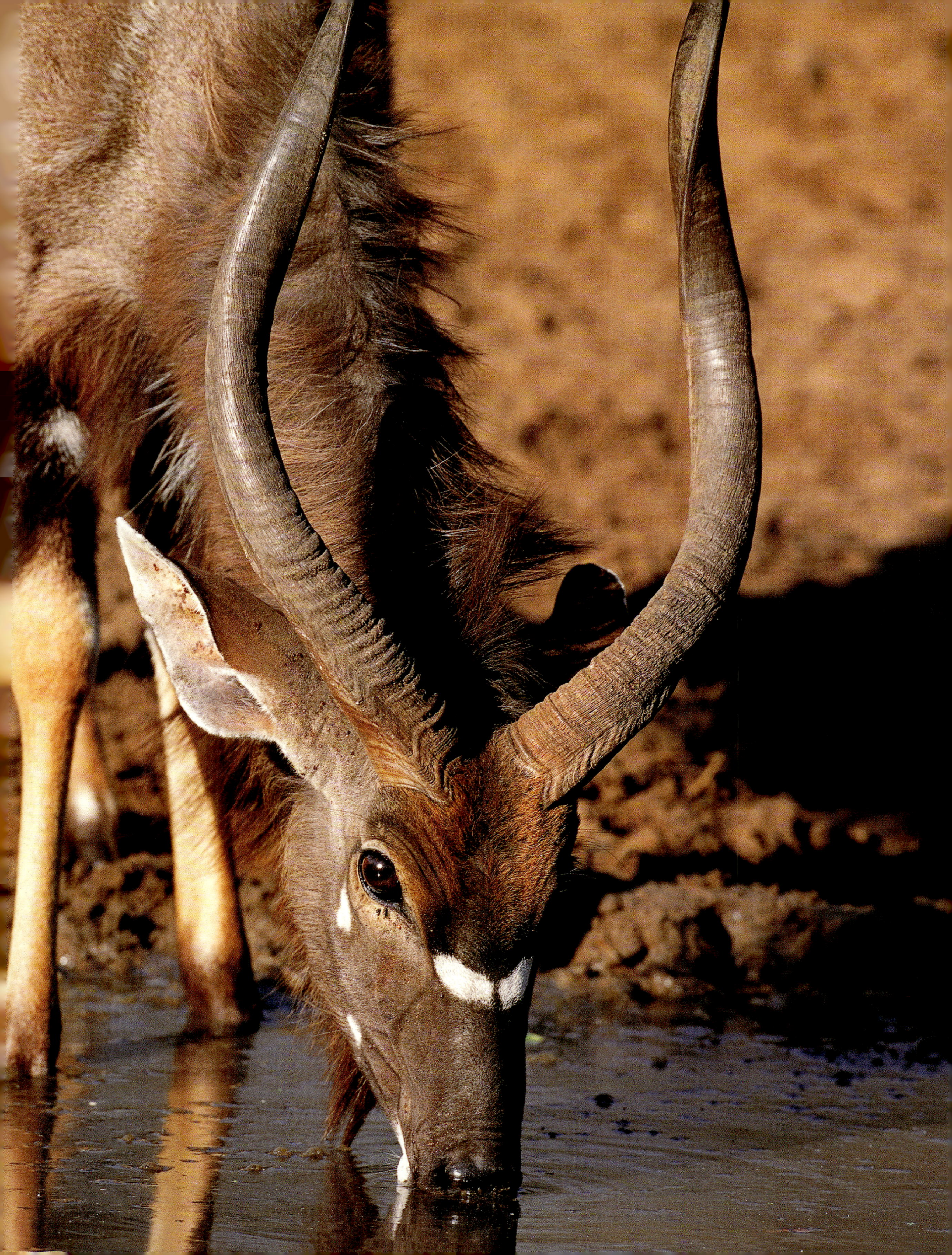

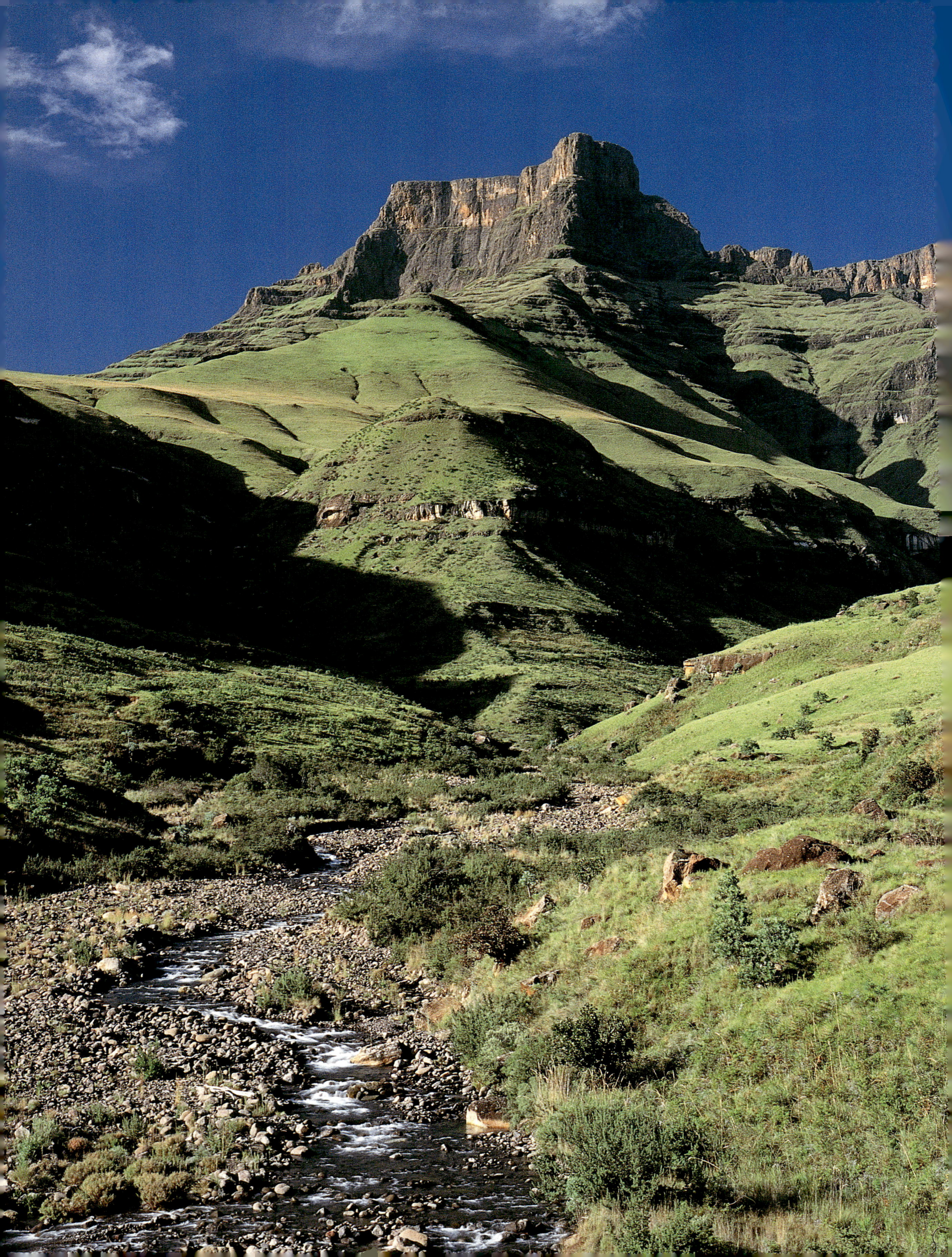

Kwazulu-Natal

Royal Natal National Park
South Africa's mountain jewel

Nestling to the north of the immense Drakensberg mountain chain and adjoining the small neighbouring country of Lesotho, the Royal Natal National Park, whose peaks reach a height of over 3,200 metres, is a little known mountain reserve. Despite the fact that it covers a little less than 8,000 hectares, the Royal Natal remains the most dazzling and appealing of South Africa's mountain parks.

In the course of my rather energetic expedition within this craggy park, I follow murmuring rivers and eventually arrive at an extraordinary basalt amphitheatre which stretches for almost 5,000 km and is 500 metres high, and which juts upwards into the deep blue sky, scraping the occasional cloud. Here, a torrent gushes forth in a series of waterfalls, cascading over five levels. Over there, crossing a thick carpet of vegetation that contains an almost infinite palette of shades of green, the waters complete their dazzling fall, and take on the calm rhythm of a river flowing through spectacular gorges.

I am alone in the vast open spaces of the park, and its majestic landscapes are breathtakingly beautiful. The Royal Natal really lives up to its name! In fact, this small national park was thus named after the British royal family paid it a visit in 1947, when the park celebrated its thirtieth birthday. According to the story, the guests found the scenery very seductive. And its peaceful atmosphere, one could add, because, although the park is inhabited by a multitude of bird species, antelopes, small rodents, and some predators, such as the caracal and the African wildcat, the wildlife is not exuberant, and encounters with animals take place discreetly.

At the end of my first, short night, I leave in order to survey another side of the park. I set off very early, well before sunrise, in order to catch on film the first gleams of light, as they caress the landscape. I climb up a steep track, encumbered by my equipment. At a sharp bend, as I begin to imagine the composition of my photographs, I feel a light breath on my neck, as if I were being closely followed. I turn around, spot a shadow on the ground and raise my eyes to the heavens: a Verreaux's eagle is gliding above me! This imposing bird of prey, in all its glory and in a silence disturbed only by the sound of air upon its wings, captures the prey that it has pinpointed: an African hare. Against the precision and speed of the predator, the victim does not stand a chance. The eagle glides off into the distance, swiftly and silently, carrying its meal in its beak.

The plantlife of Royal Natal Park is among the most luxuriant of South Africa. Where life has decided to exist, nothing can stop it, not even a boulder (above).

The vegetation, the splash of deep blue sky across the amphitheatre and the turbulent rivers create a dazzling harmony against the grandiose backdrop of the Royal Natal Park (opposite and following pages).

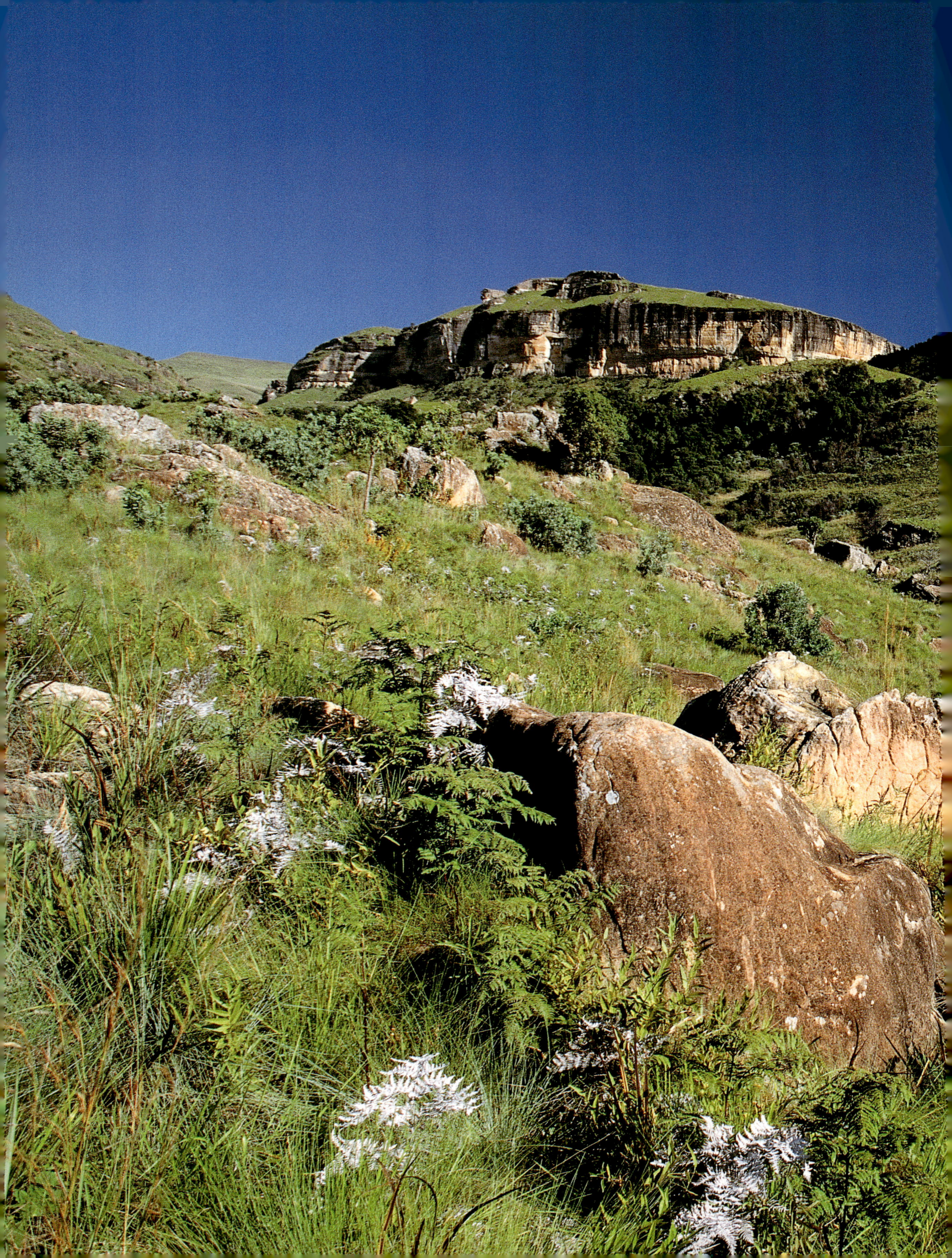

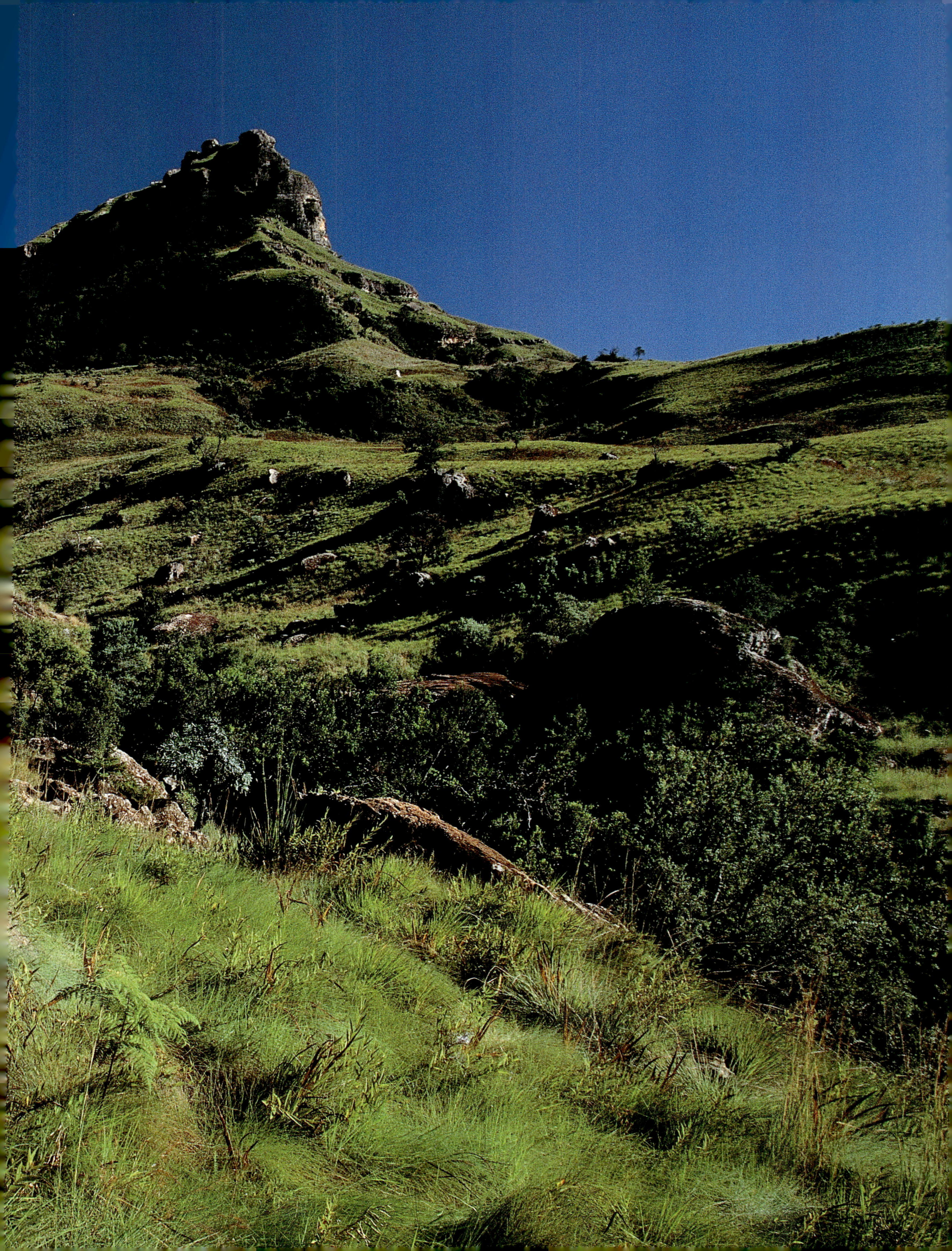

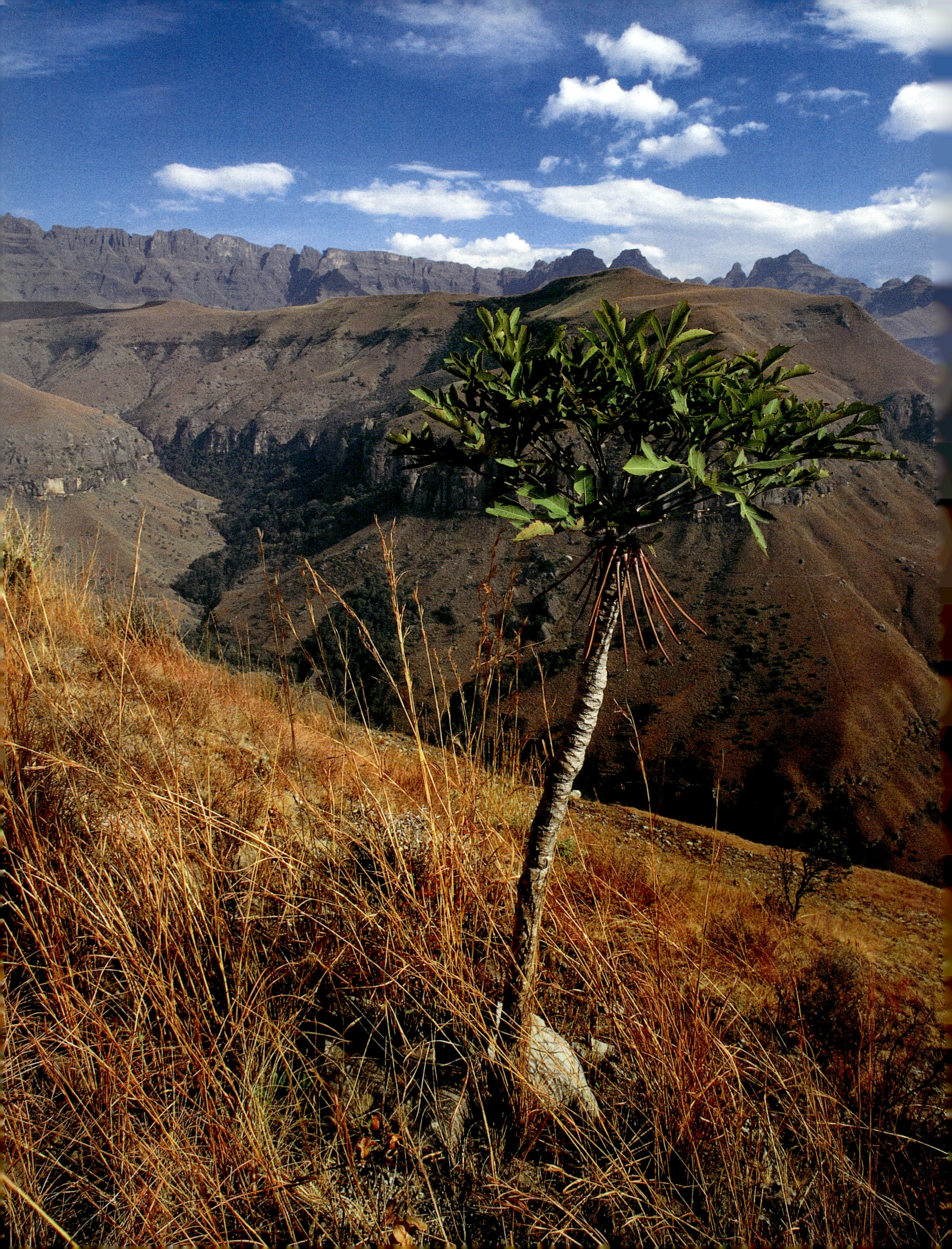

uKhahlamba-Drakensberg Park
Cathedral Peak and Giant's Castle

When one discovers the Drakensberg mountain range, one can not help but feel humbled before the power of natural forces capable of erecting, millions of years ago, this wall of rock, 400 km long, which separates the west of the Kwazulu-Natal from Lesotho, one of Southern Africa's smallest countries. Within this range, hiking takes on a surprising new dimension, as if the climb to the peak was as spiritual as it is physical. The footpaths of Drakensberg, the key features of which are Cathedral Peak and Giant's Castle, lead to summits from which I can almost touch the clouds and converse with the gods!

It is at Cathedral Peak that the expression "reach for the clouds" takes on its true meaning. To get there, I take a difficult path that overhangs vertiginous drops. At the end of the steep hairpin bends that make up this long trek, a superb panorama unfolds: Mike's Pass marks the entrance into the world of mountain lovers, who come from the four corners of the globe to take on the formidable rock faces. The only equal to the majesty of the landscape is the silence that reigns over it, and with one turn of my head I can take in the whole mountain scene, up to the neighbouring Royal Natal Park. Here man is in close harmony with nature, a harsh nature: the grass beaten by the winds, burned and yellowed by the heat of summer, did not survive the first cold spells of the southern winter.

Unfortunately, I am obliged to finish my contemplation, and think of my bivouac, because soon the sun will set and, during the night, the temperature can drop well below zero. Tomorrow I will continue on my route to Giant's Castle. Situated high in the mountains, this feature is much less steep, despite the fact that it includes the Injasuti Dom – the highest summit in South Africa – and was turned into a reserve in 1903 in order to assure the protection of the largest African antelope: the Cape eland. This impressive herbivore – the male can weigh up to 700 kilos and sometimes more – has found an ideal habitat here. Naturally fearful, the Cape eland is very hard to observe. On one of the numerous paths across the reserve, I have the chance to glimpse an eland as I round a bend. I have to be quick and quiet, because otherwise the animal will escape before I have even had the chance to approach it! Although the Cape eland is a protected species, the numerous paintings left on the cave walls by the San, attest to the importance it had for the first inhabitants of the area. I find myself imagining how life may have been, at a time when a few fur-clothed primitive people were the only ones to follow these paths at the base of the crown of South Africa.

The Drakensberg is not only a beautiful region; it is also a reservoir of plantlife. Numerous plants line the paths and display their dazzling colours to hikers, helping them forget how hard their trek is, if only for a few moments (above).

Cathedral Peak offers the most beautiful views of the Drakensberg mountain range (opposite).

The heat of summer, the absence of autumnal rainfall and the rigours of winter nights have parched the vegetation, which spreads like a brown carpet. It will not be until the first spring rains that this land will become green again (following pages).

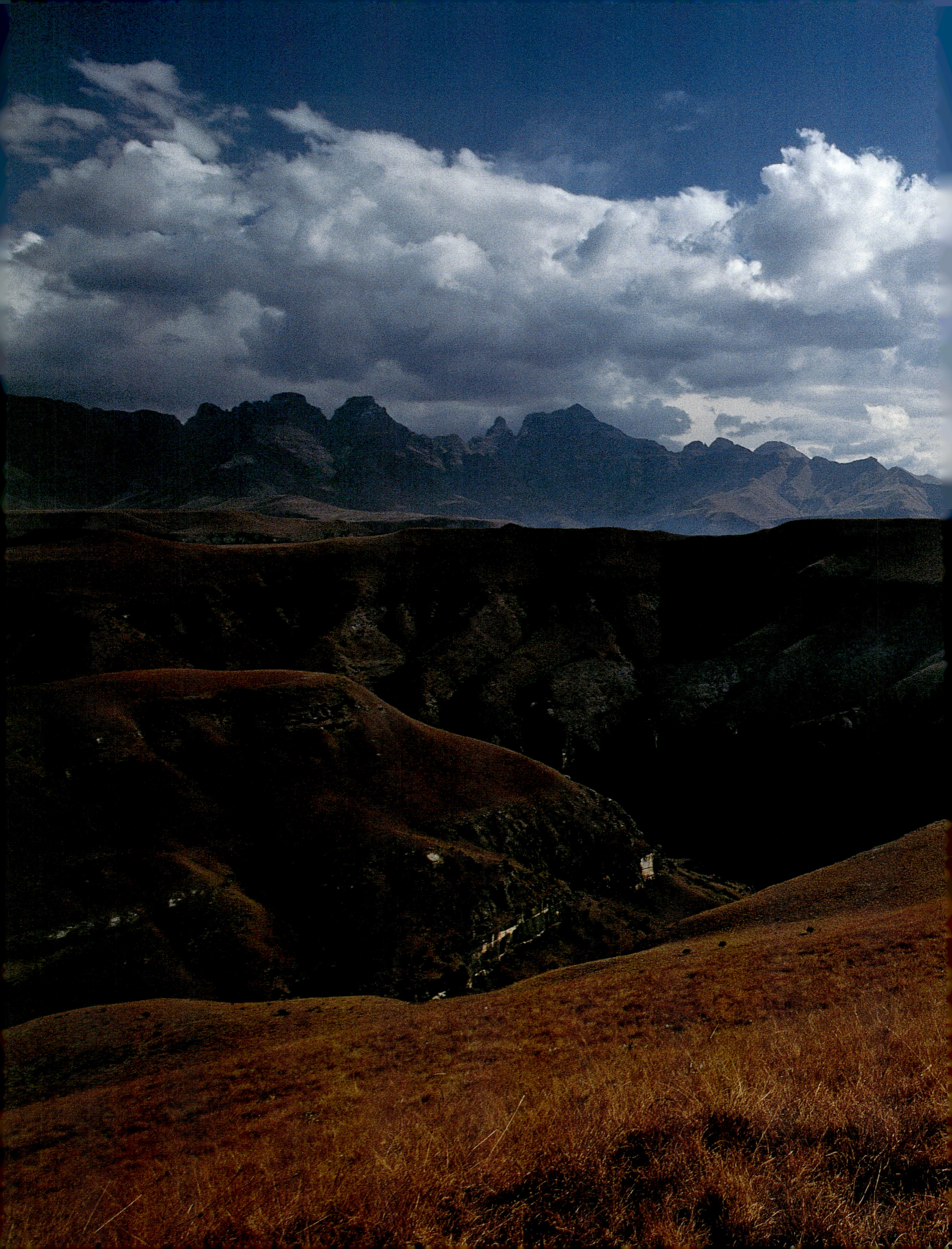

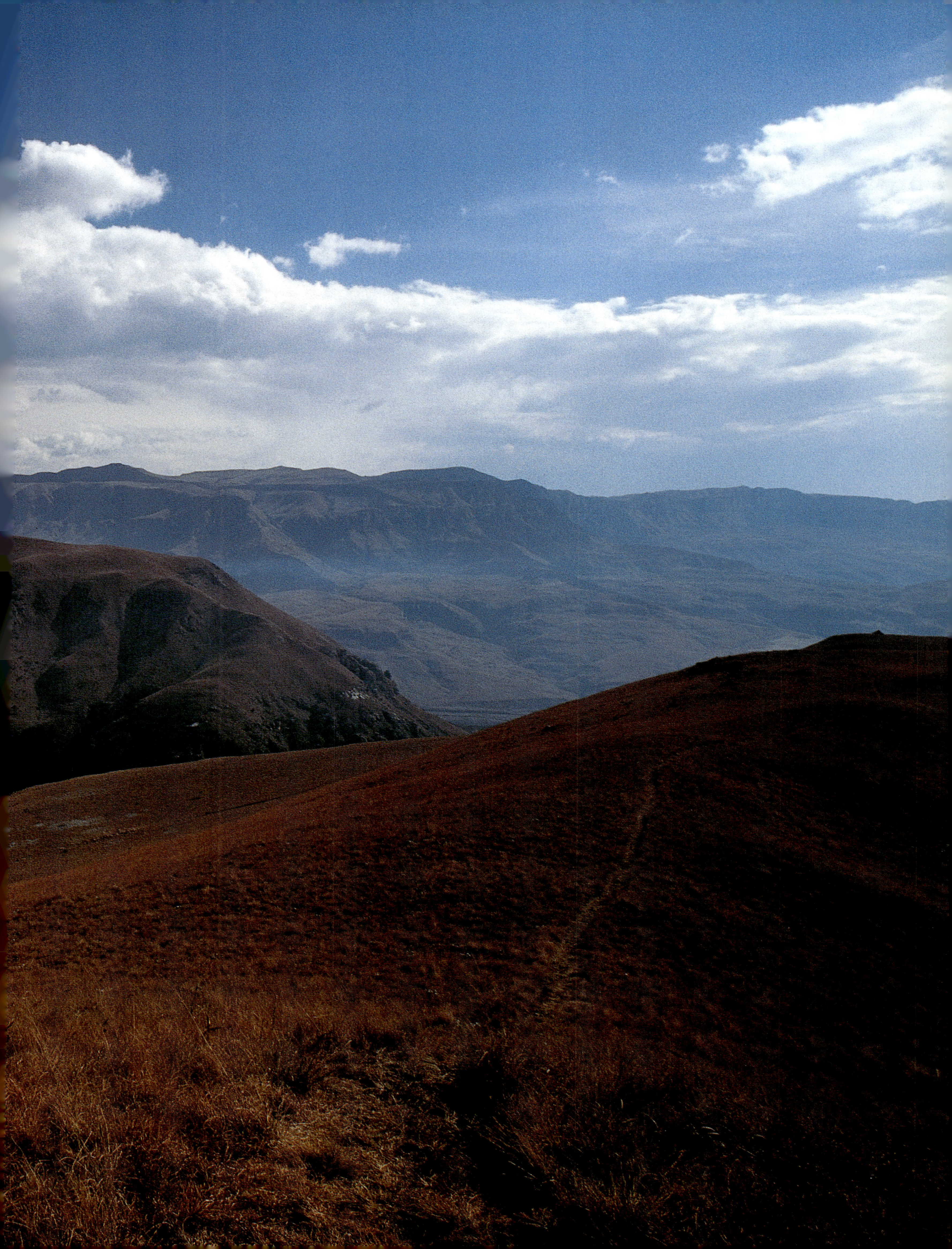

Here man is in close harmony with nature, a harsh nature: the grass beaten by the winds, burned and yellowed by the heat of summer, did not survive the first cold spells of the southern winter.

At first light, the uneven relief of Cathedral Peak takes on magnificent golden hues (above).

The Bushmen left Giant's Castle long ago. All that remains are their cave paintings, which bear witness to the relationship between this mysterious people and the wild animals (right).

UKHAHLAMBA-DRAKENSBERG PARK | 71

Contemplating the Drakensberg mountain range, one cannot help but feel humbled before the power of natural forces capable of erecting, millions of years ago, this wall of rock, 400 km long.

On the Giant's Castle highlands, the sun plays hide and seek with the mist (left).

Lichens have found a niche, here on an exposed rock face (above).

Under a deep blue sky, Drakensberg appears to be an anteroom for paradise (opposite).

The waters that cascade from the summits of Drakensberg are among the purest on the planet (following pages).

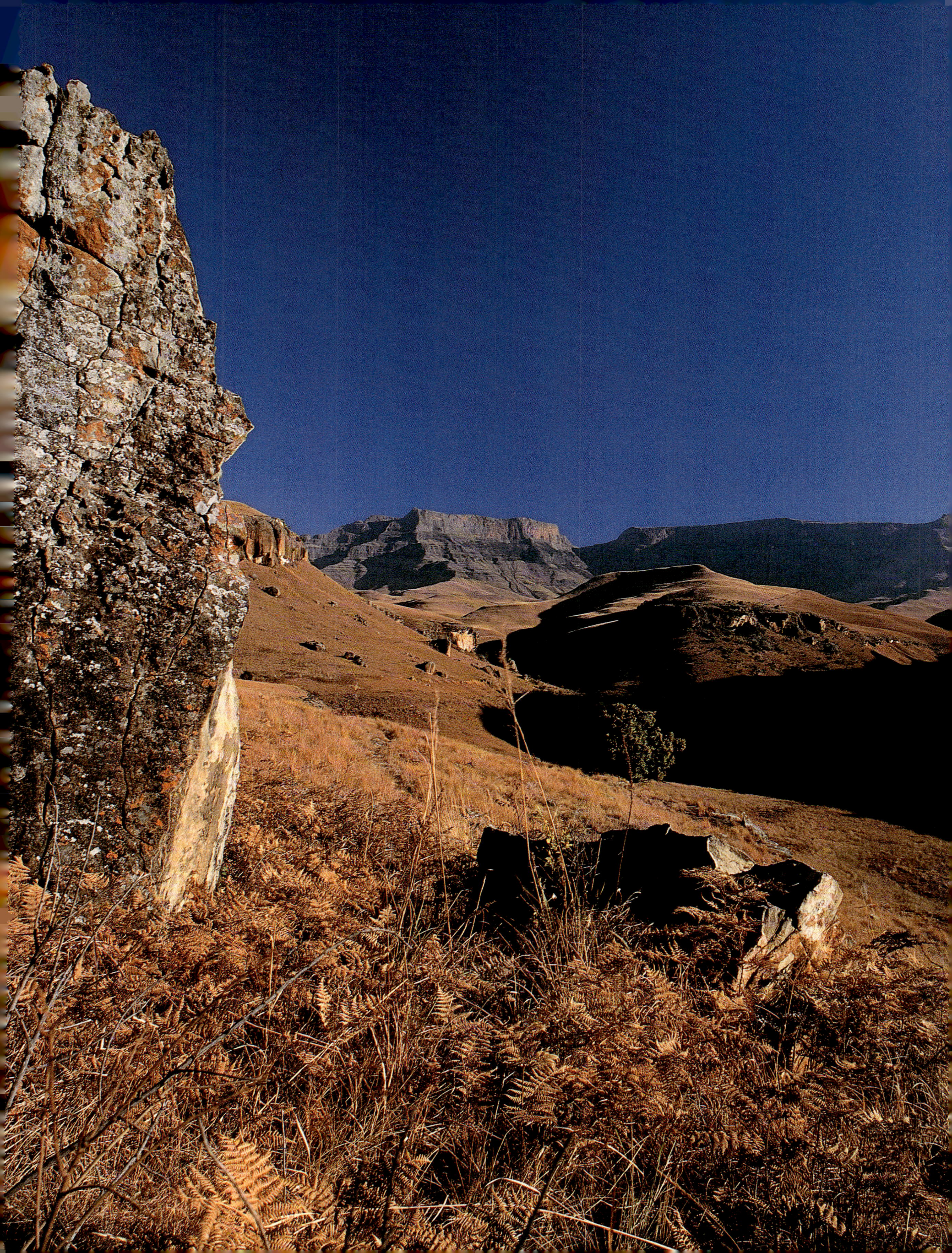

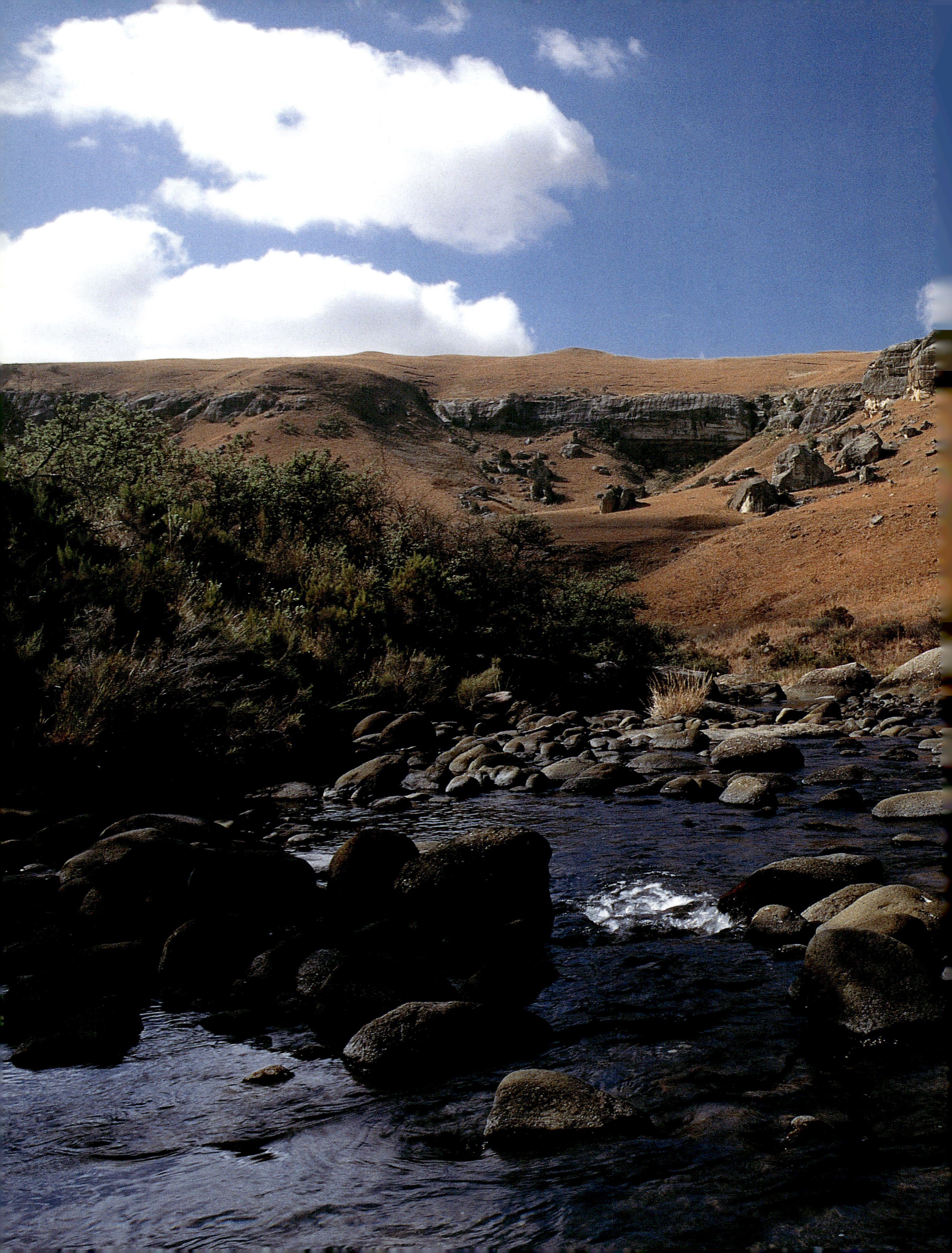

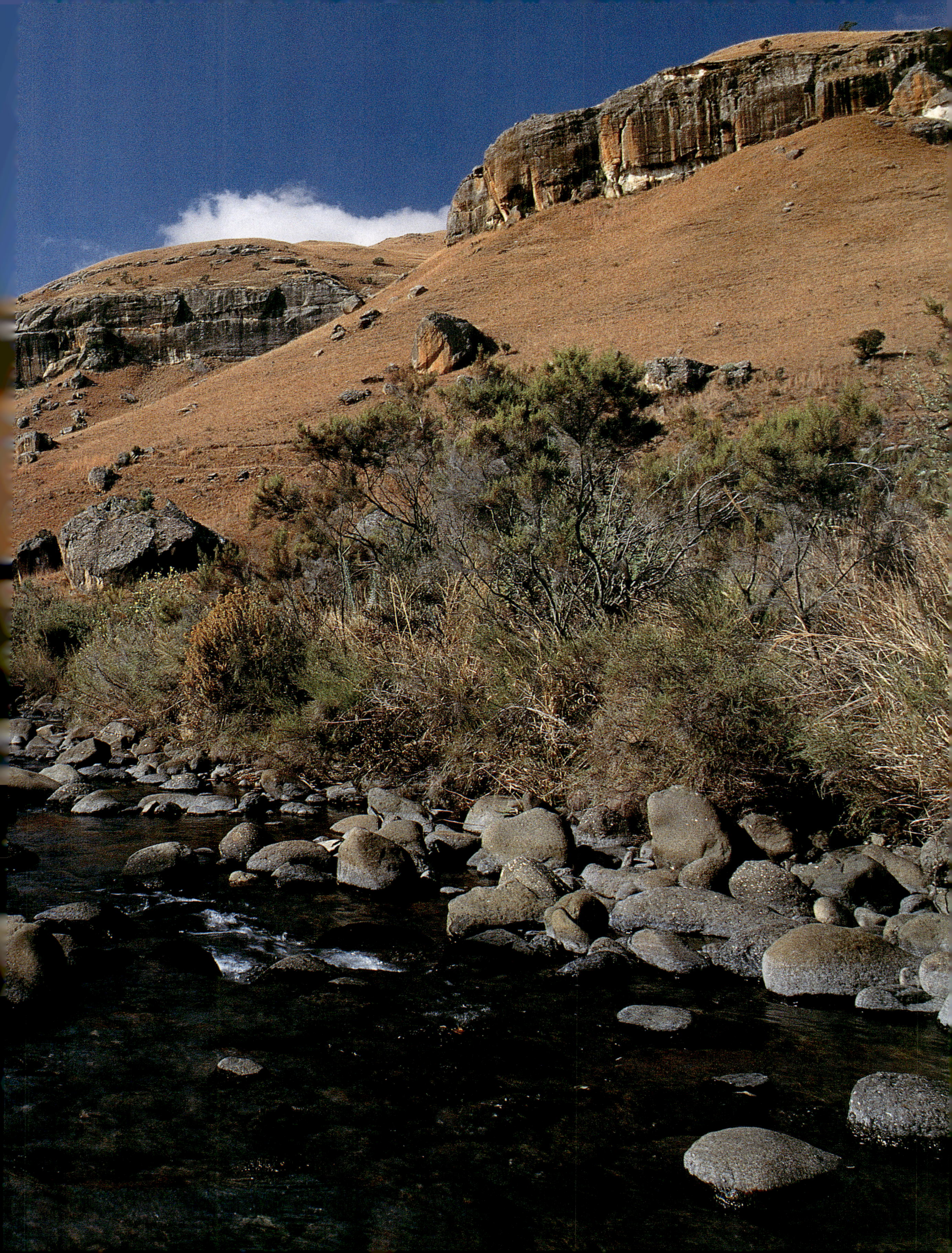

The highlands of Giant's Castle were turned into a reserve in 1903 in order to assure the protection of one of the largest African antelopes: the Cape eland.

For all I know, a herd of Cape may be hidden behind the magnificent highland scenery of Giant's Castle (above).

A few more hours would pass before my furtive meeting with more Cape elands.

Cape elands are rather fierce animals, and it is better not to disturb the creatures that have lived here so peacefully since the opening of the uKhahlamba-Drakensberg Park – the place to which they owe their survival in this part of Southern Africa (right).

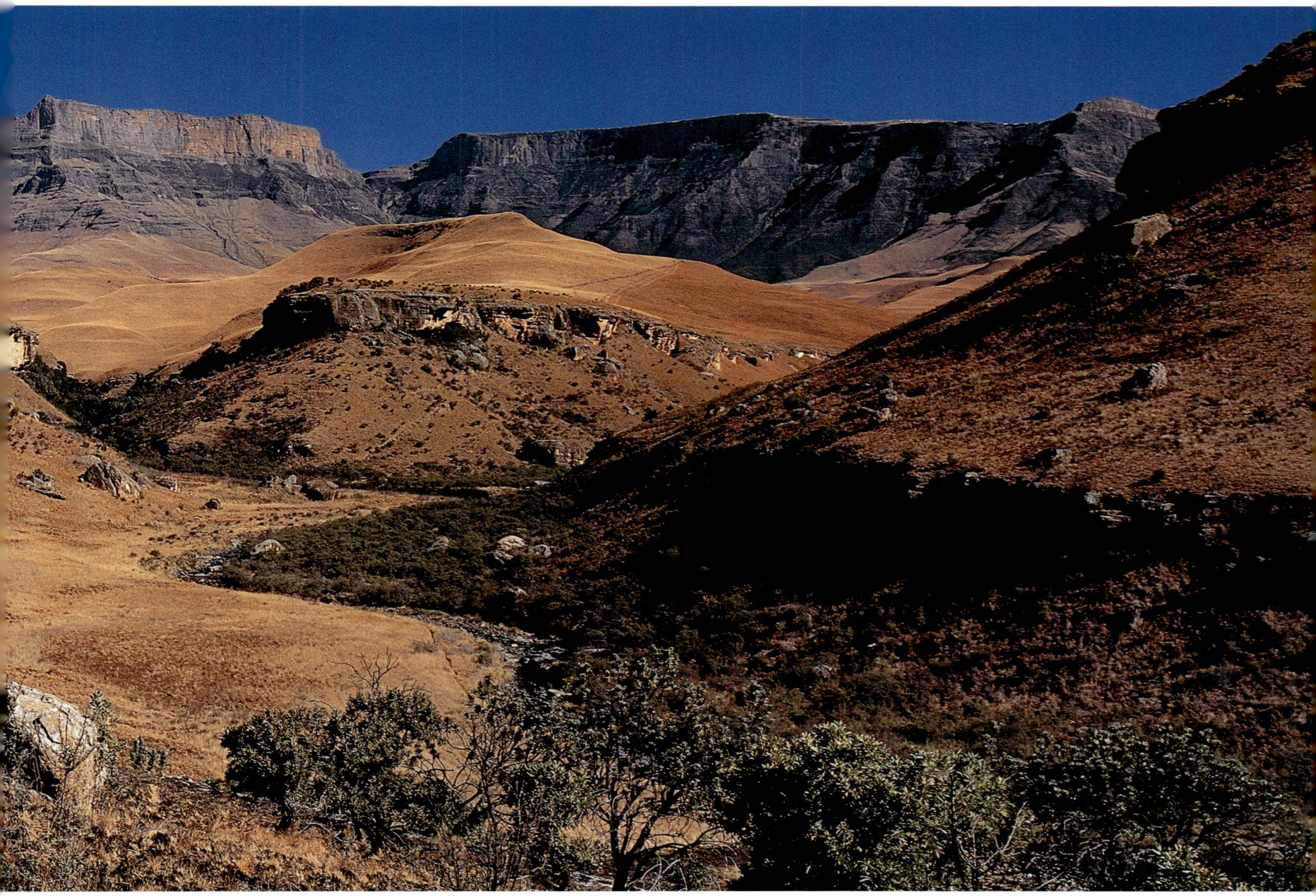

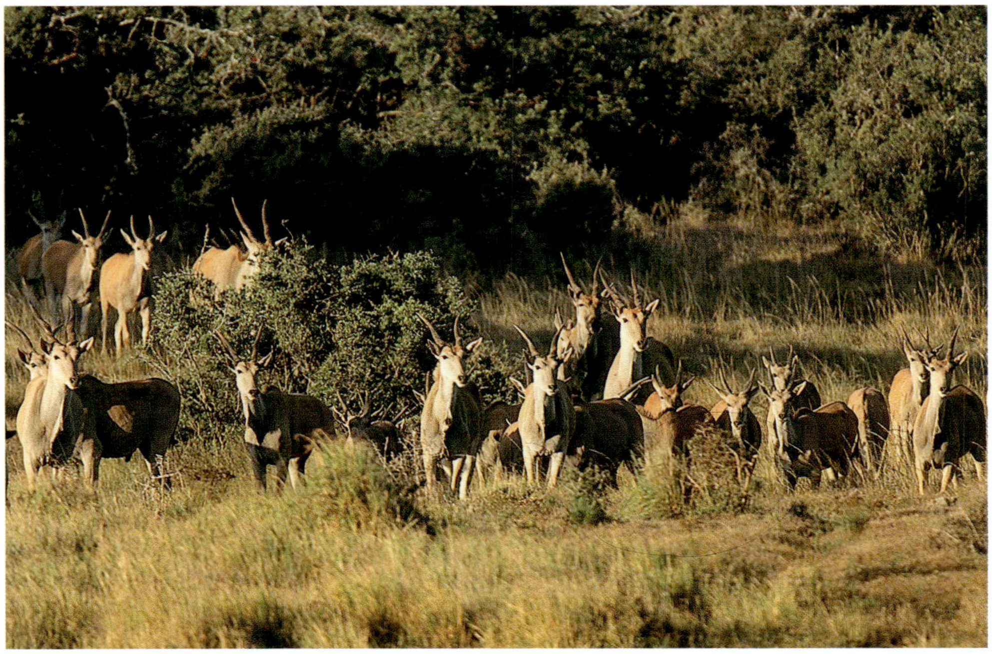

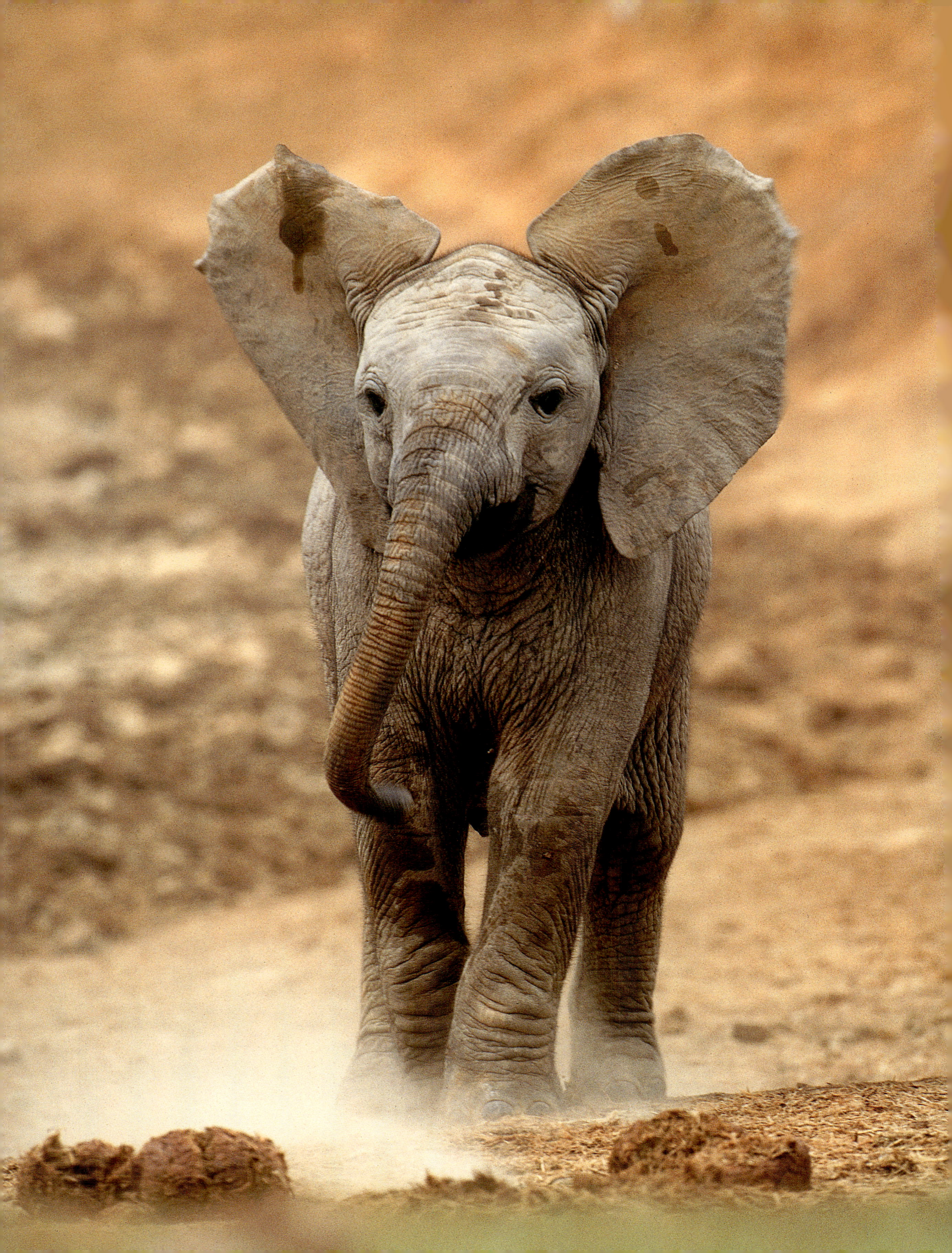

Eastern Cape

Addo Elephant National Park

Last paradise of the elephants

Since its creation in 1931, Addo Elephant Park has had the difficult task of catering for the last survivors of the massacre of the region's elephants. Situated not far from Port Elizabeth, the 12,000 hectares of today's park were the scene of violent confrontations between farmers and elephants, in the early years of the 20th century. As the farmers claimed land that had always been elephant pasture, the elephants discovered an easy source of food in these newly claimed lands. In 1919, the farmers employed a professional hunter, Major Pretorius, who set about exterminating the elephants with such zeal that there was a public outcry. Thus a few landowners decided to accommodate the last eleven surviving animals and allow them to wander free. They were the ancestors of around 350 elephants that live in the Addo Park today.

Certain males played an essential role in this spectacular repopulation of pachyderms. Among them, special tribute must be paid to Happoor, whose enthusiasm for the opposite sex contributed greatly to the expansion of the Addo elephant families. This large male, with formidable defences and a cut ear, the souvenir of a wound inflicted by a hunter, reigned alone over the territory for 18 long years, and it was not until 1968 that he was ousted by a younger male. Hunted, Happoor managed to leave the park limits, but the danger he represented to the local community forced the authorities to have him slaughtered. What a sad end for a king of the savannah!

This elephant gave his name to a watering hole situated in the south-west of the park. In the first hot hours of the morning, I had the pleasure of watching a unique display: almost a hundred individuals surged out of the wooded savannah in order to access the watering hole. For almost an hour they stayed there drinking and playing – an impressive sight, just a few metres away from my lens.

The large elephant herds have found sanctuary here. These savannah heavyweights find all the food they need in the rich plant growth of the park: they love the small greasy leaves that are found on the masses of pink-flowered spekboom (*Portulacaria afra*), and the groves of aloes and vygies. The presence of many young is evidence that the Addo elephants are in excellent health. Sometimes, in the middle of a herd, a large imposing male with large tusks breaks away from the group, as if to remind us that the shadow of Happoor still floats over the herd.

As the first rays of light illuminate the dry grass, I surprise some mongooses at the entrance to their burrow (above).

A young elephant calf, who does not appreciate my presence, charges me in order to remind me that I am on his territory (opposite).

With a heavy and majestic step, a family of elephants move towards the watering hole, which soon turns into an aquatic fun park (following pages).

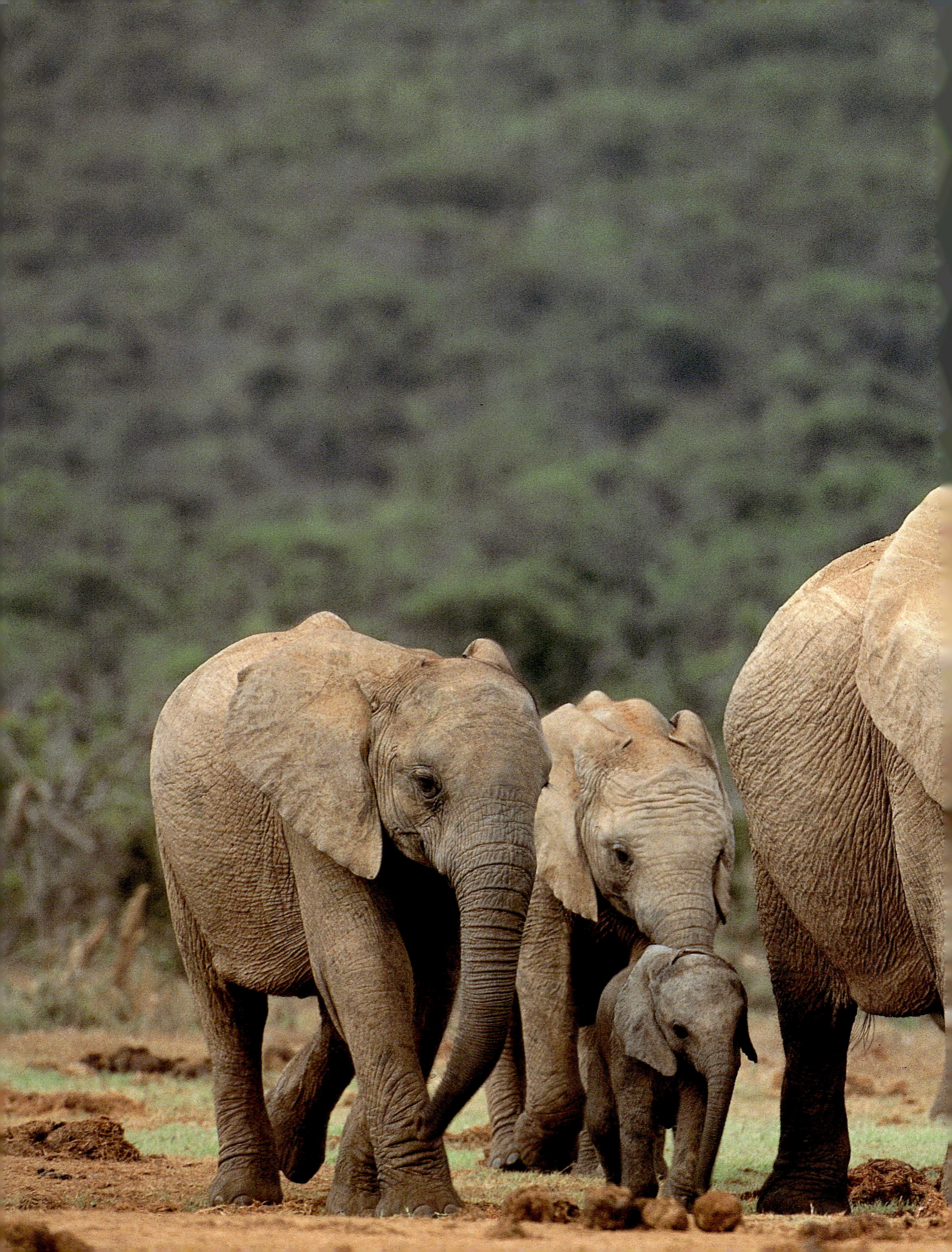

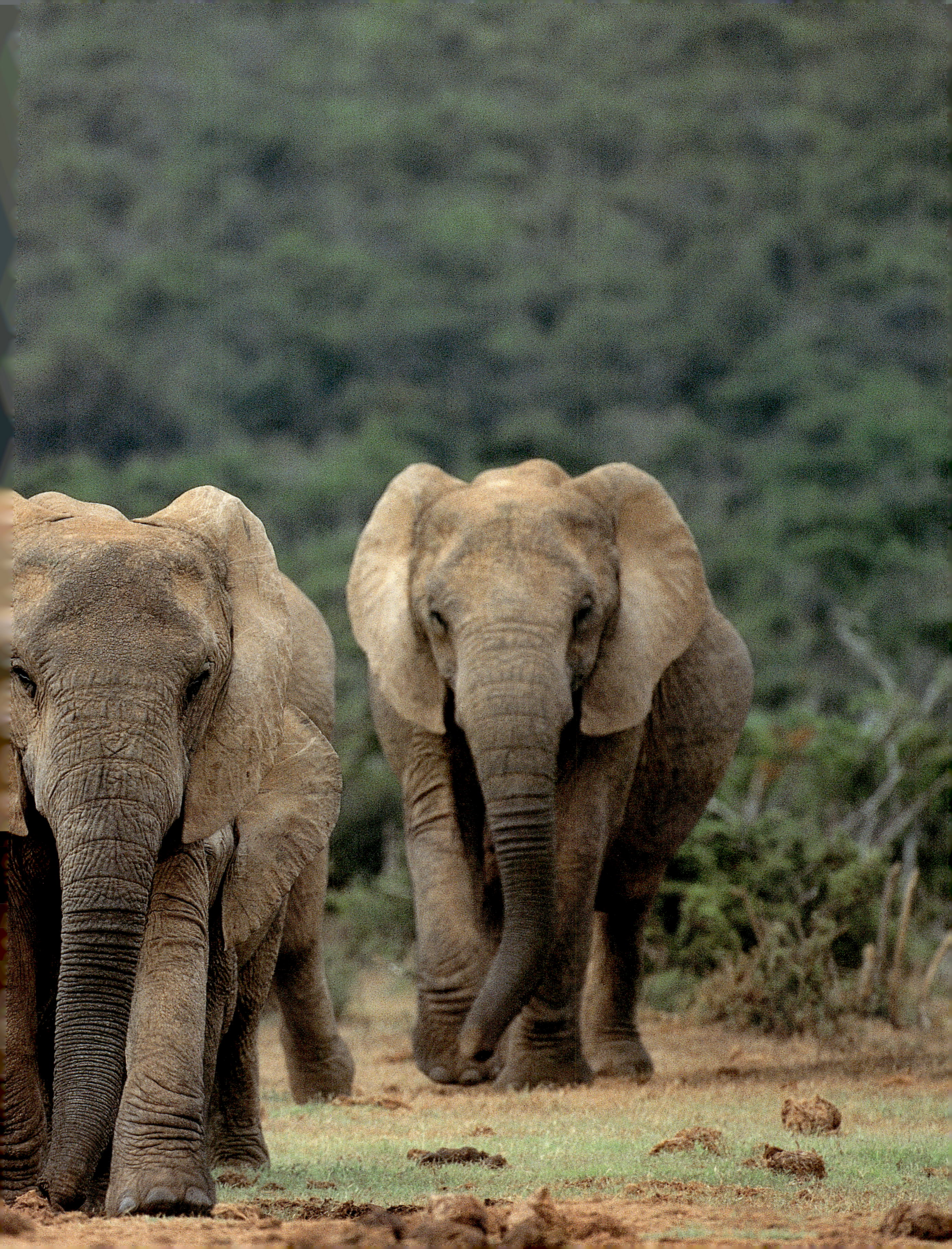

In the first hot hours of the morning, I have the pleasure of watching a unique display at the watering hole:
For almost an hour the elephants stayed there, a few metres away from my lens, drinking and playing.

For the pachyderms, the watering holes of the Addo Elephant National Park are also places for relaxation and pleasure. The elephant calves, in particular, animate the bathing time with all sorts of practical jokes (opposite and above).

An enormous foot that shows strength and delicacy (below).

Water games

ADDO ELEPHANT NATIONAL PARK | 83

In the savannah, each animal should know its place. A young warthog, which appears to have been lacking in respect for his elder, takes flight (above).

The noise of my camera shutter gave away my presence as I was observing some young jackals at the watering hole (right).

On the other hand, a large kudu remains imperturbable (opposite).

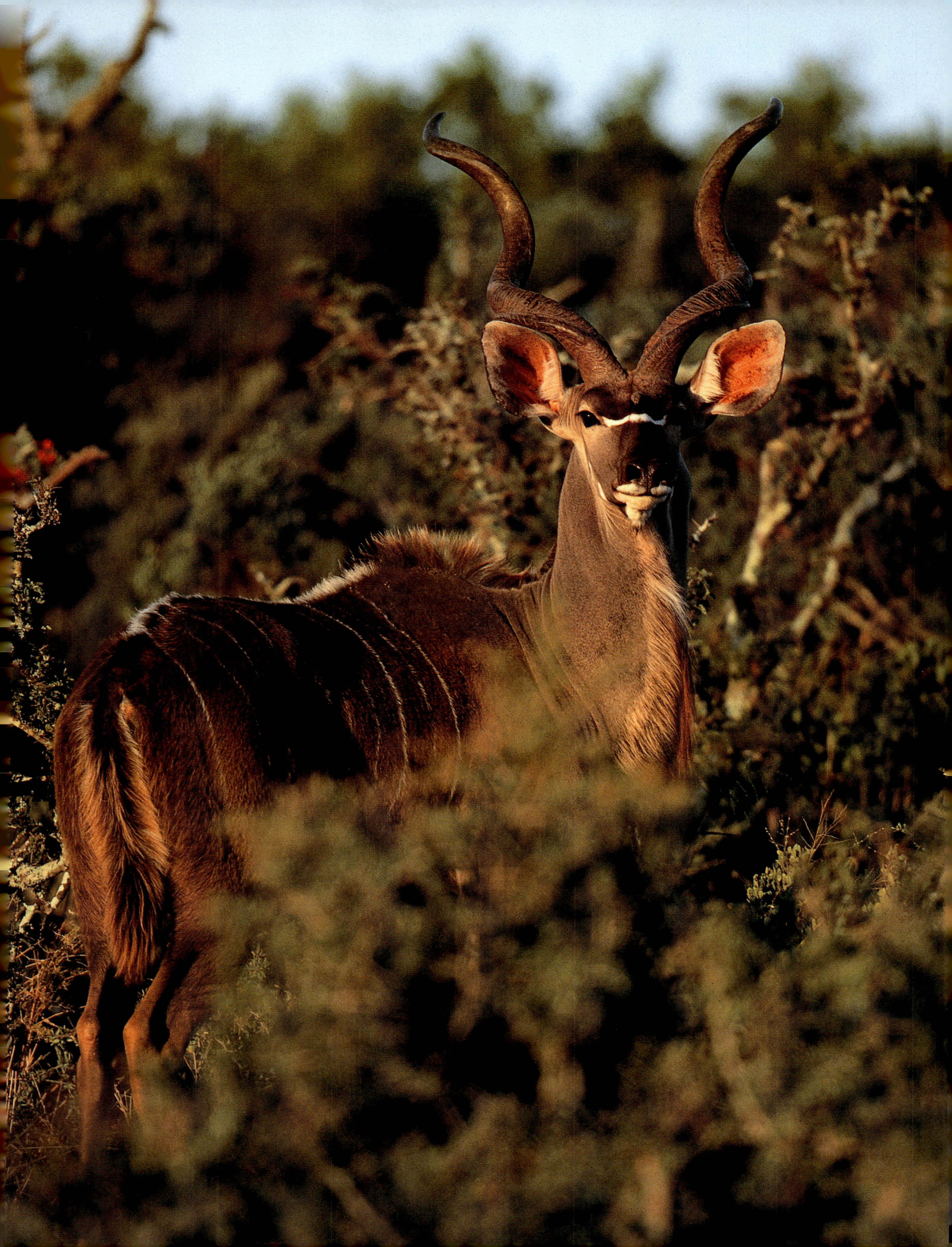

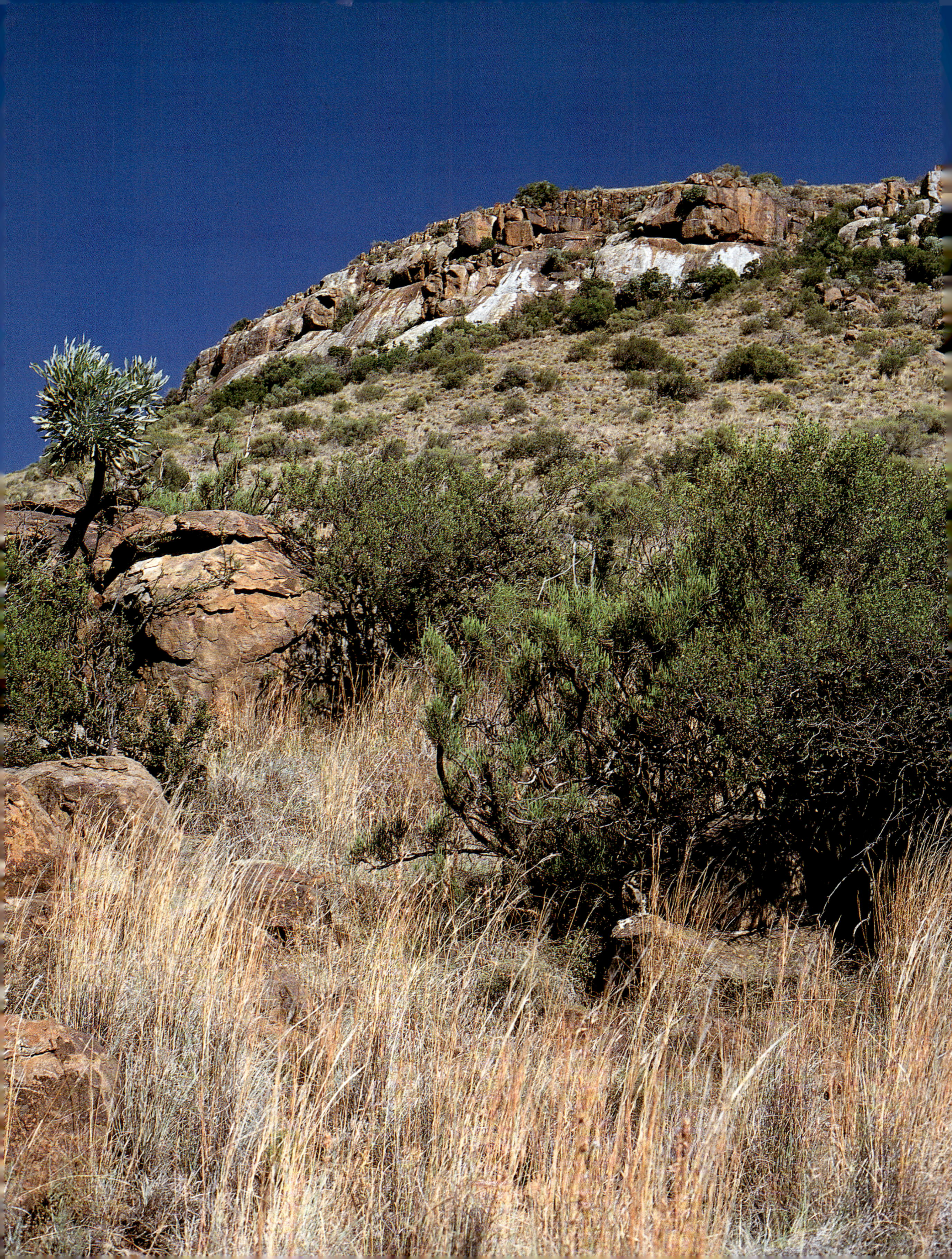

Eastern Cape

Mountain Zebra National Park
Last redoubt of the mountain zebra

There are about 300 Cape mountain zebras in this park – the world's largest herd, and they are among last representatives of a unique species. Through the combined effects of habitat loss and the trophy hunters' passion for their magnificent hides, they were almost wiped out. The few remaining individuals seemed condemned to extinction until one of their last refuges was given park status in 1937. The Mountain Zebra National Park, covering some 6,500 hectares, came into being.

Having climbed up a steep track that weaves through unending hairpin bends, I stop my off-road vehicle on the high plateau which dominates the grandiose landscapes of the park. Down below, the small Wilgerboom River, which has dug its bed in the craggy relief, flows nonchalantly. A few white-tailed gnus, with their prehistoric silhouettes, gambol in the high grasses under the placid gaze of a handful of springbok antelopes. While watching these animals with their oversized horns, I notice, in the distance, three pale specks coming down over the rocks. Mountain zebras! They are there! One of the rangers told me that they often descend to quench their thirst when the heat on the plateau becomes particularly oppressive.

I decide to approach very slowly, letting my vehicle advance at idle. The landscape shelters me; I am able to watch their progress without being seen. After a few minutes they are only around thirty metres away: a male, a female and their foal. I take advantage of the situation, and capture this beautiful image on film. The foal stays behind its parents, while I take a few close-up portraits of the adults, which make the distinctive feature of the species clearly visible – a large fold of skin on the neck. The male appears to have detected my presence. Within a few seconds, and without any sound other than that of their hooves beating the ground, the mountain zebras disappear. They will regain the security offered by the park, their last refuge from the folly of mankind.

Now that this magnificent encounter is at an end, I have to think of getting back, because the sky looks threatening, and I do not want to witness one of the violent storms trapped by the summits. After taking one last photograph of the splendid landscape bathed in storm light, I set off on the return trip, happy to have met some of the last representatives of this beautiful and endangered species.

The absence of predators in the Mountain Zebra National Park explains the rather placid attitude of this hartebeest (above).

I must reach the summit of this rocky ridge covered with dry vegetation in order to approach the last remaining representatives of the mountain zebras in the wild (opposite).

Having climbed up a steep track that weaves through unending hairpin bends, I stop my off-road vehicle on the high plateau which dominates the grandiose landscapes of the Mountain Zebra National Park.

As I watch lying in wait for the mountain zebras, which could arrive at any moment, a stormy atmosphere sweeps across the vast expanse of savannah (above).

After the rains, a myriad of small flowers immediately bloom (opposite, bottom).

The mountain zebra can be distinguished from its plains relative by its smaller size, its lighter coat, stripes which run down to its hooves and, above all, by a flap of skin which hangs under its throat (following pages).

MOUNTAIN ZEBRA NATIONAL PARK | 89

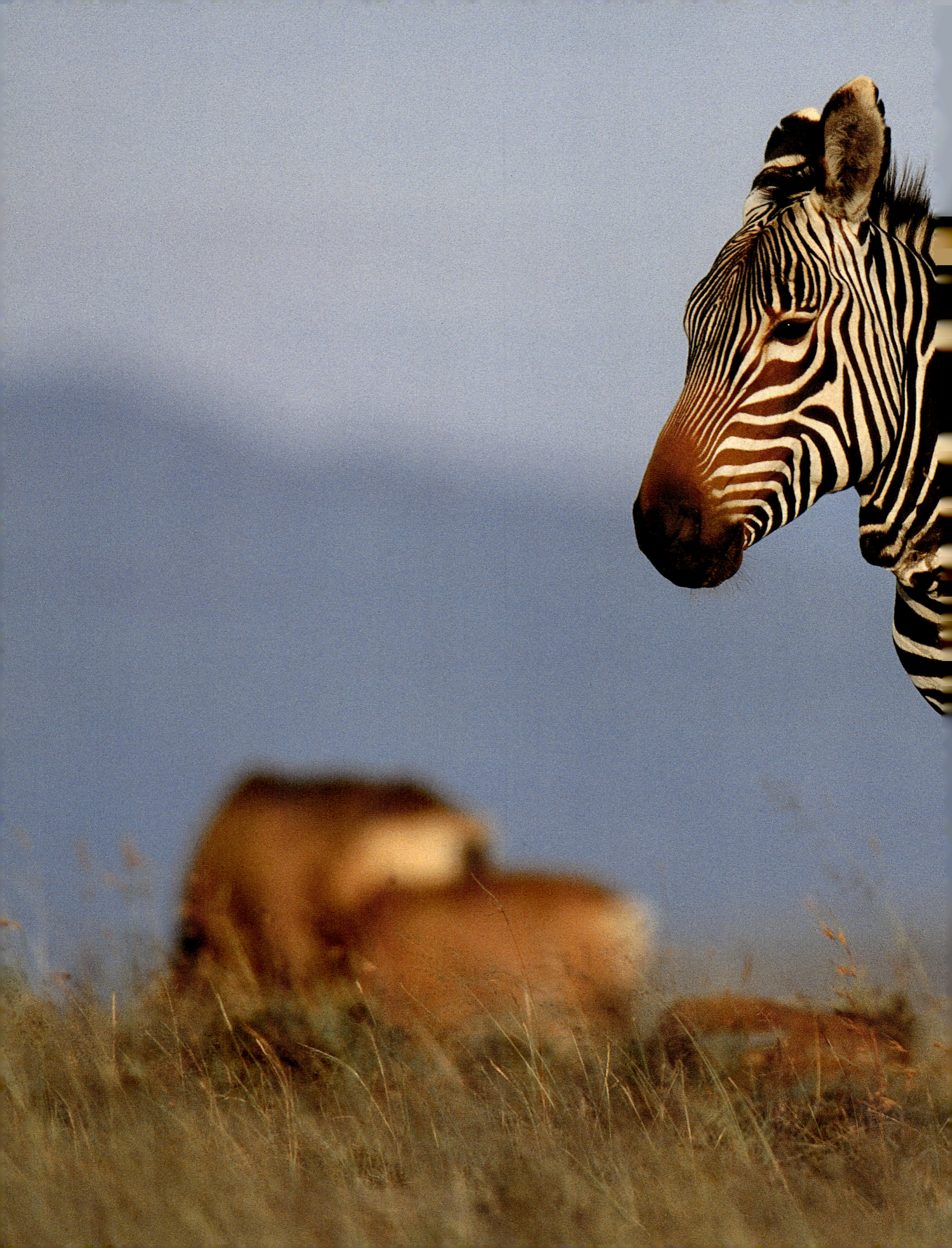

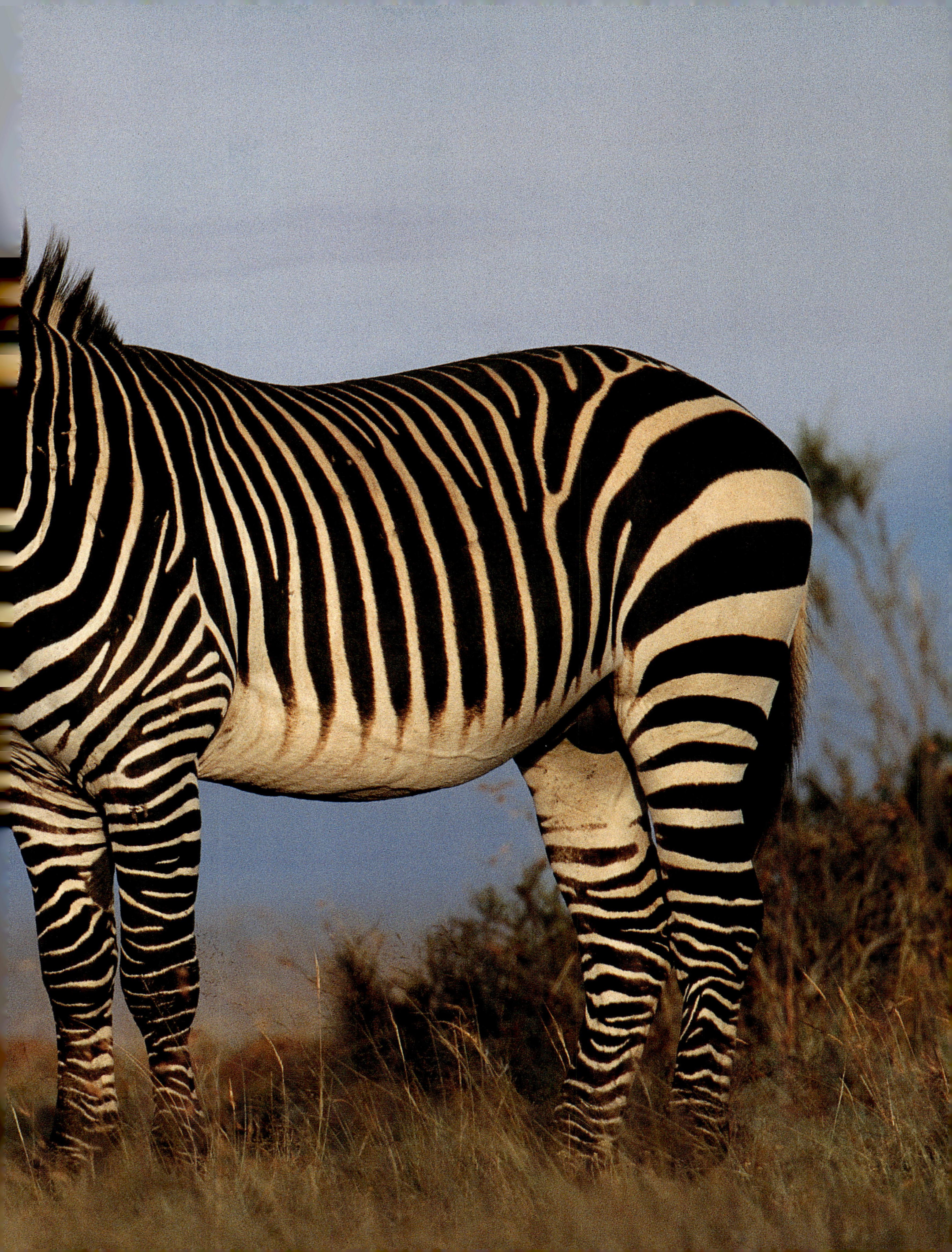

White-tailed gnus, with their prehistoric silhouettes, gambol in the high grasses. While watching these animals with their oversized horns, I notice, in the distance, three pale specks coming down over the rocks. Mountain zebras!

The park's herd of mountain zebra is about 300 strong (below).

Thanks to this area of savannah, which has been set aside for them, the zebras can live in freedom, sheltered from predators (opposite, top).

A white-tailed gnu, a species that is much rarer than the one that famously migrates every year between Kenya and Tanzania (opposite, bottom).

MOUNTAIN ZEBRA NATIONAL PARK | 93

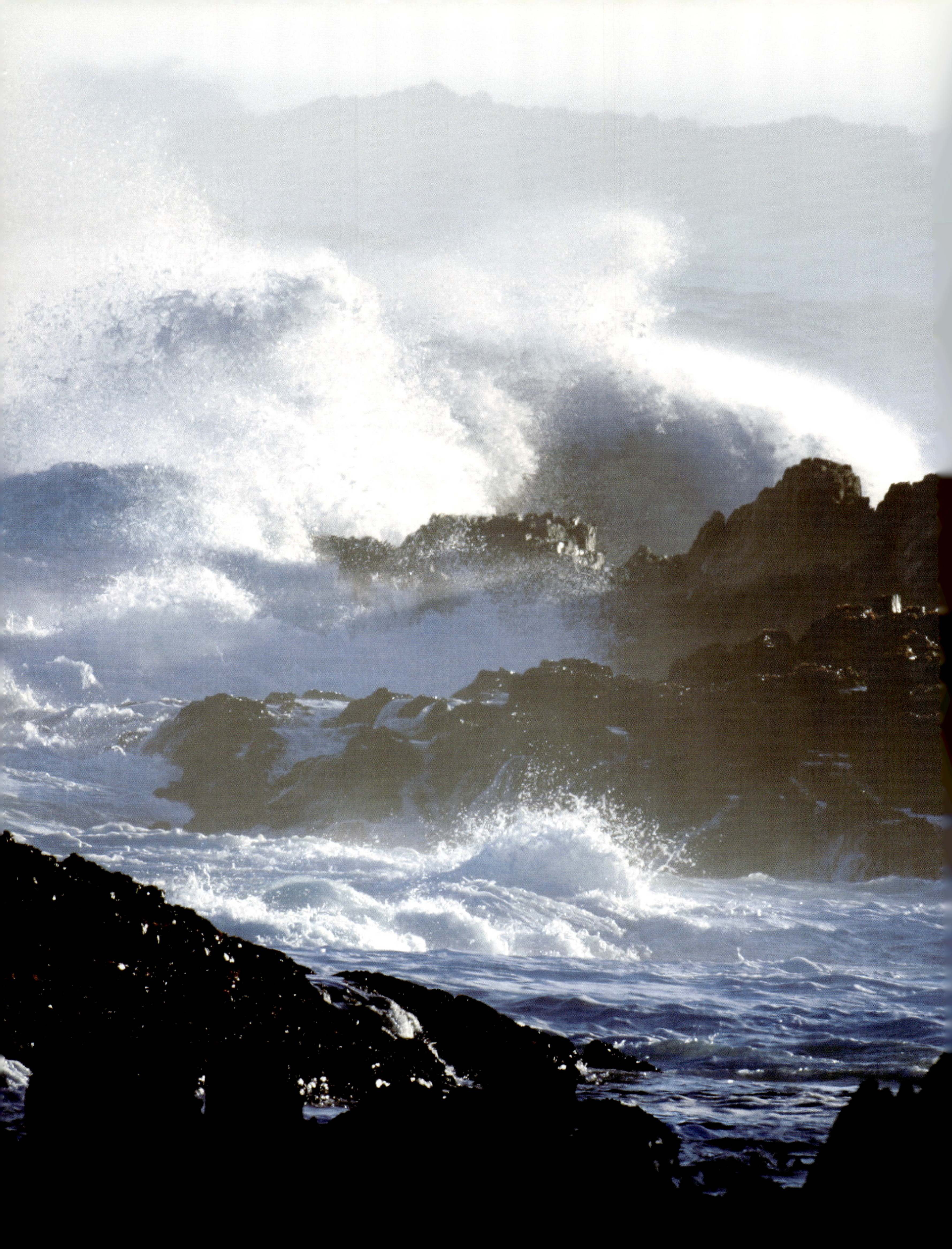

Eastern Cape

Tsitsikamma National Park
Temple of raging waters

The park is situated in the heart of the very touristy Garden Route – a name which remains a mystery to me, as there is not a single garden anywhere on the route – which follows the coast between Mossel Bay and Port Elizabeth, at the foot of Tsitsikamma mountain range. Tsitsikamma was named by the Khois, its original inhabitants, who baptised their land "there where there is much water". It is a name particularly well suited to the National Park, which opened its gates in 1983, because it protects a coastal strip of 80 km of craggy rocks battered by the powerful waves of the Indian Ocean.

As soon as I enter the park, I find myself immediately spellbound by the beauty and power of the scenery: the ocean forms, with the force of wave upon wave, not only the large blocks of rock, but also the fine sandy beaches which fringe a thick carpet of multicoloured vegetation. Water is an omnipresent element in the park, be it sea water or rains cascading from a sky that is often temperamental – the rainfall averages 1,200 mm per year. These rains have managed to erode deep fissures in the mountainous relief of the Tsitsikamma, leading to the ocean: millions of years ago a valley was formed that dumped the brown waters of Storm River into the turquoise waters of the sea.

In order to observe the estuary that links the calm fresh waters of the rivers to those which rage in the sea, an impressive suspension bridge must be crossed – an experience to give you goose bumps, but the reward is a spectacular view. This suspension bridge allows me to take the Otter Trail, the most famous hiking trail in South Africa, which owes its name to the Cape otter. These shy, but mischievous little dark brown-and-white creatures, which spend the greater part of their time in the water looking for crustaceans and frogs, are rarely seen. It must also be noted, that the Cape otter is nocturnal, and will not, except in very special circumstances, emerge from its lair in the daytime. Perhaps I will be lucky enough to meet one on my trip. The Otter Trail allows me to follow the jagged coastline, so much so that this expedition becomes truly athletic. The effort is however rewarded by the scene before my lens; the raw green of the vegetation appears to plunge into the blue of the ocean, the two colours together forming a fragment of rainbow. Before this scene of untouched and violent nature, I feel as if I am the first man to explore this universe of jungle and water, a jewel that must be conserved in its crown of greenery.

The heat and humidity of the sea air favour the growth of luxuriant vegetation, such as these aloes with their magnificent bright red flowers (above).

The tides of the Indian Ocean break on the jagged rocks of the coast, creating a dramatic vista (opposite).

These seabirds have lived on the shores of the Tsitsikamma park forever (above and below).

Over the course of thousands of years, the mighty waves of the ocean have sculpted the rocks of the shoreline, giving them shapes which one could think have sprung straight from human imagination (opposite).

The violent beauty of the Tsitsikamma slopes, which harmoniously blend the blue of the water with the green of the vegetation, has often led nature lovers to become infatuated with this wild park (following pages).

With the force of wave upon wave, the ocean shapes the giant blocks of coastal rock.

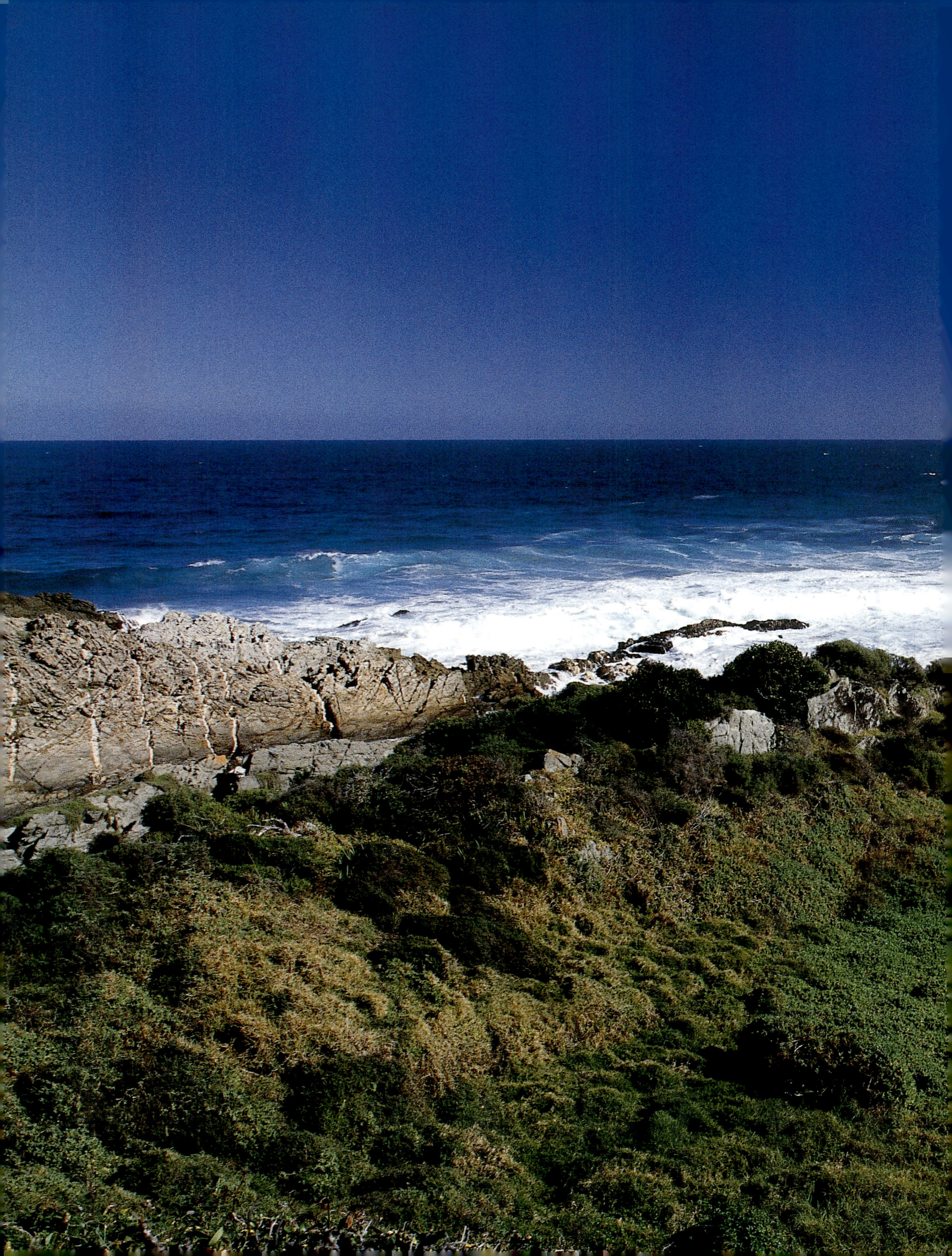

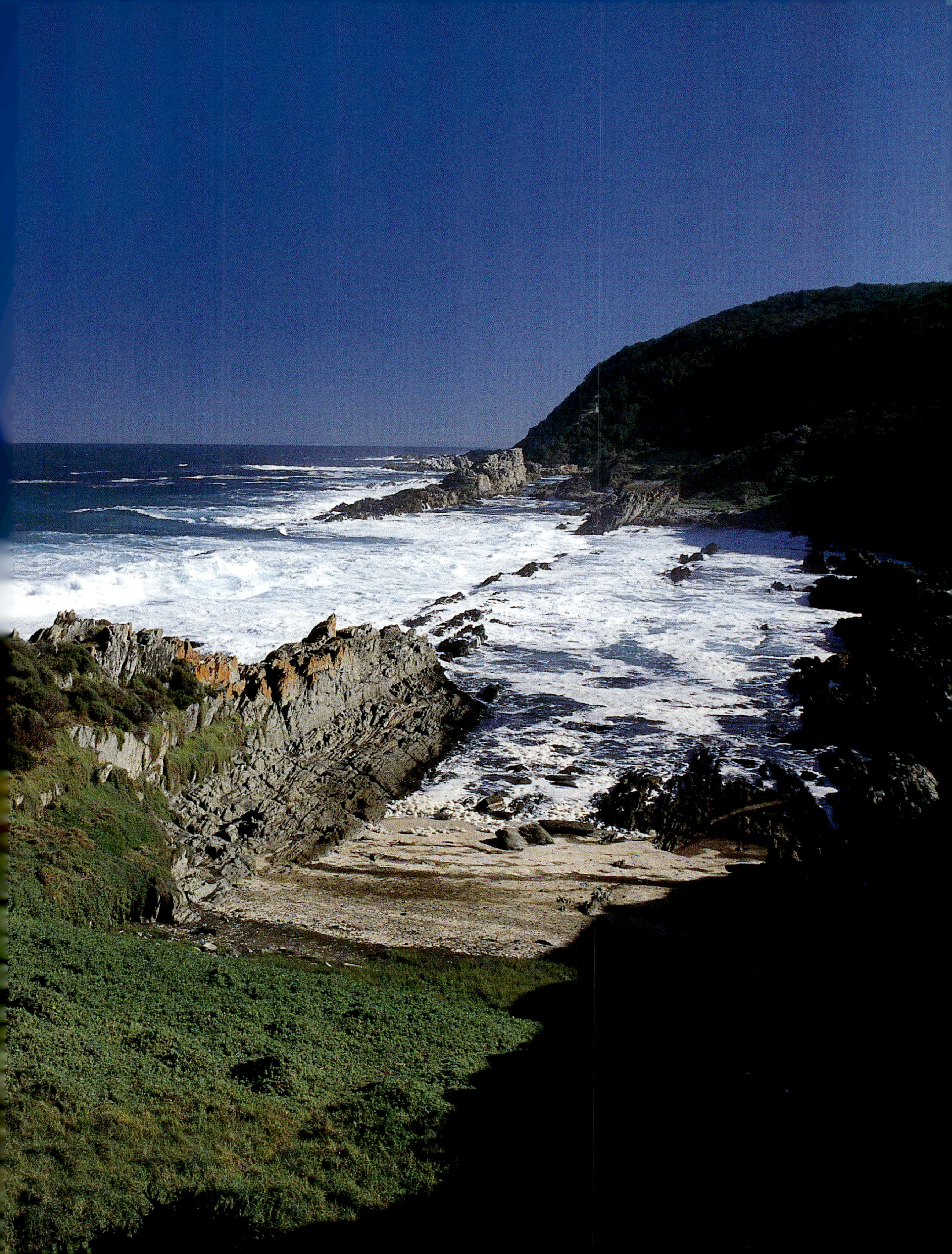

Sea-green

The humid air of the coastal areas of Tsitsikamma Park allows serene vegetation to flourish and face the rough sea (above).

The numerous plant species that grow on the coast are well watered by an ever-changing sky (right).

An impressive suspension bridge spans the calm waters of Storm River, before they are dumped into the turbulent ocean (opposite).

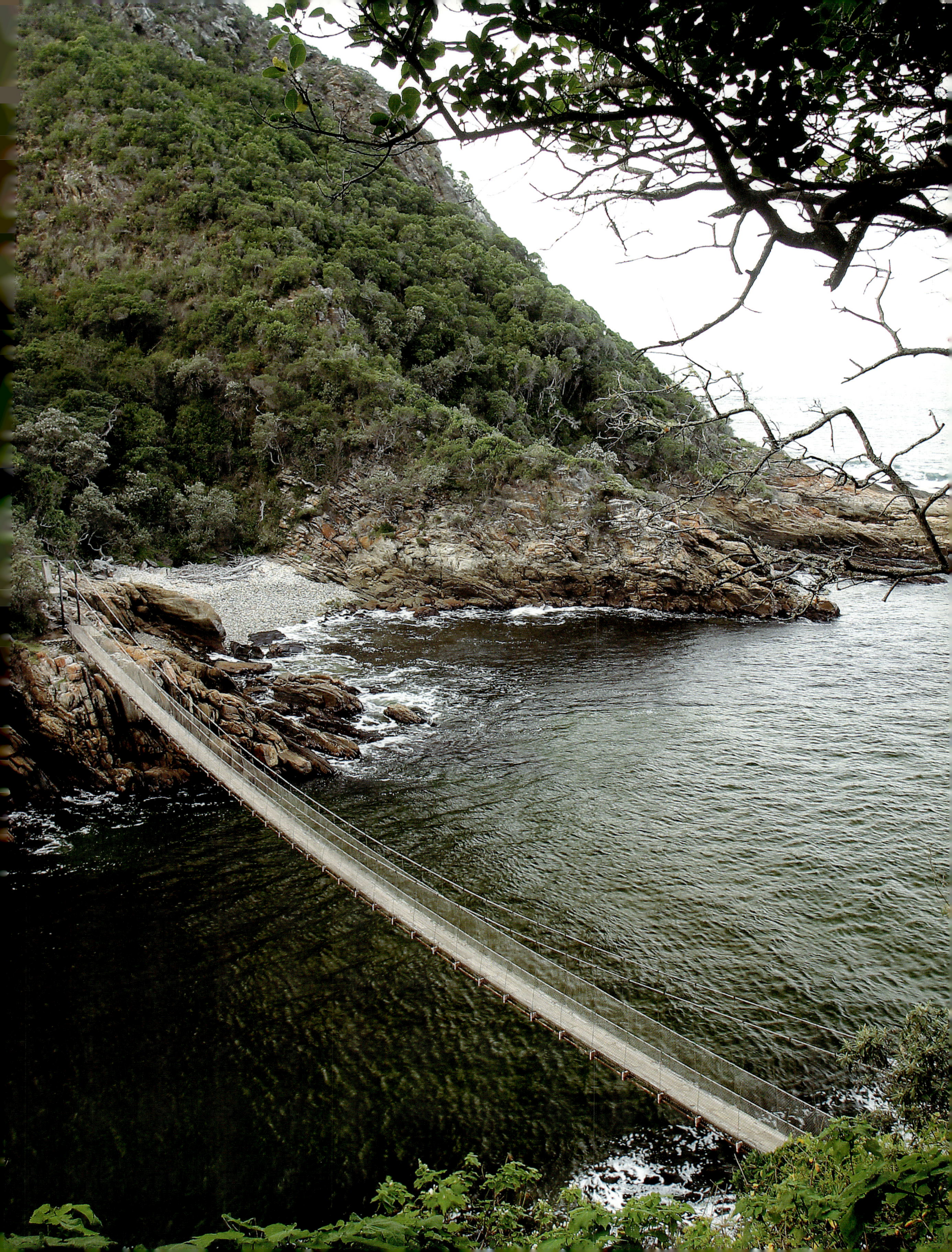

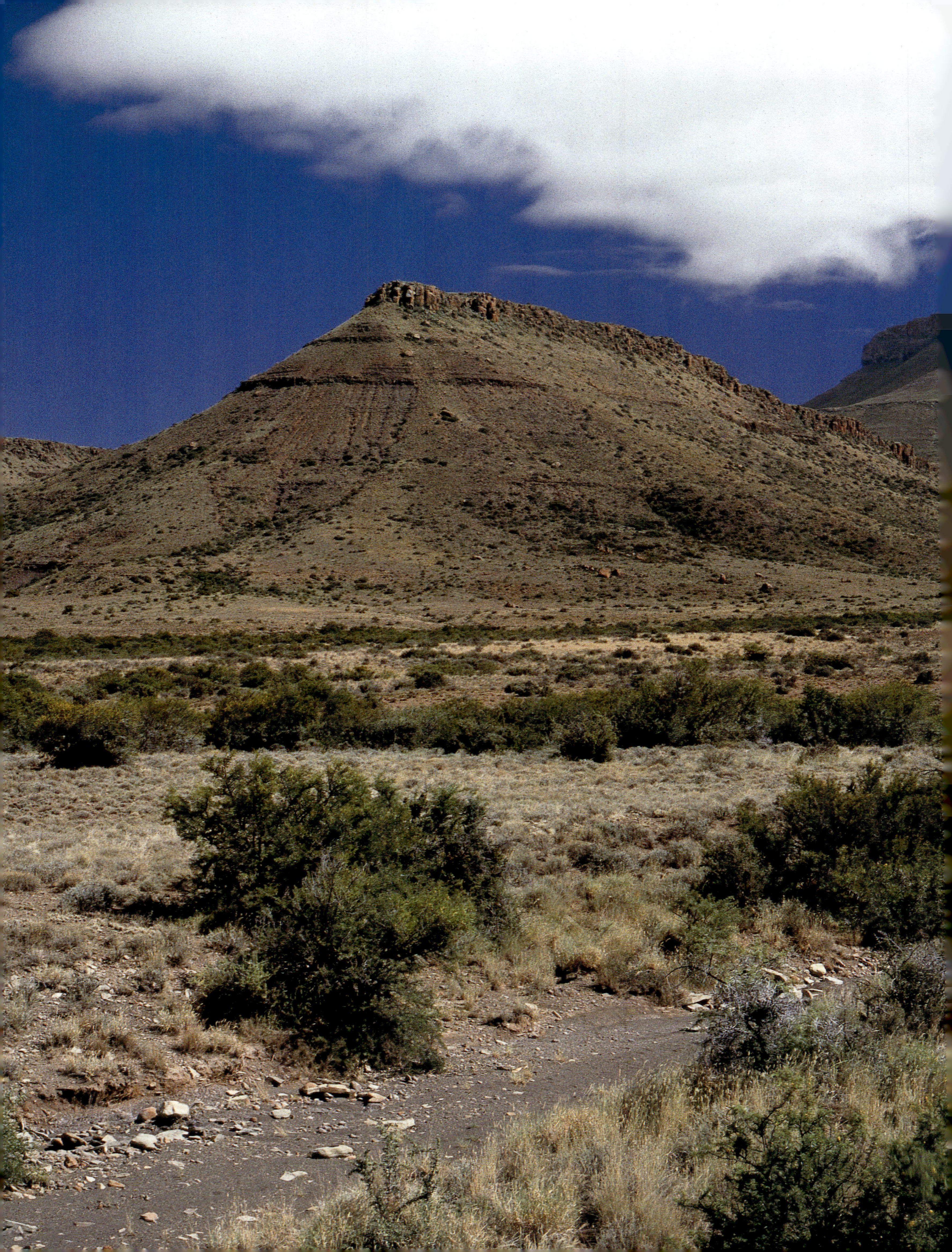

Western Cape Province & Cape Peninsula

Karoo National Park

The heart of prehistory

Around 10 km from Beaufort West, the landscape takes on the rounded shape of a female silhouette. This dominates the schistose terraces and sandstone sparsely covered with vegetation from which a few shrubs struggle to emerge. This arid environment is that of the Nuweveld Mountains, on the Karoo plateau, of which the park of the same name occupies a small part. And yet, despite the fact that the Karoo is the most important South African plateau, its ecosystem was long ignored, probably due to the harshness of its terrain: it was not until 1986 that 80,000 hectares of this scenery were elevated to the status of a protected reserve.

I have barely started searching the rocks of the park, when the air, hot with a breeze, bringing with it large particles of dust, attacks my lungs. I have difficulty distinguishing a large brown mass wandering peacefully a few metres away. I approach: it is a tortoise, a Cape leopard tortoise in fact, which can be found in the wild almost nowhere other than in this rocky region of the world. And, thanks to the efforts of the authorities, the Karoo National Park has permitted plants that had been on the brink of extinction to proliferate; this tortoise has little trouble in finding aloe plants, with a flavour that suits its particular taste.

The slow steps of this animal are joined by the rapid footfalls of an enormous lizard, which in a flash finds shelter in the dry branches, before I have even had the time to photograph it. The presence of these incredible reptiles, which appear to have emerged straight from a science-fiction film, give the park a prehistoric flavour, as if these vast open spaces were an open-air theatre demonstrating Darwin's theory of evolution. This strange feeling makes me regard the animals of Karoo in a different way, especially as I follow a footpath created for fossil hunters, which allows me to walk in the footsteps of the dinosaurs that roamed the earth millions of years ago.

Large prehistoric predators may no longer haunt these arid areas, but here one can nevertheless imagine how it could have been in the past: the monitor, which I watch in its search of food, resembles it distant relatives, *Scymnosaurus* and *Hipposaurus*; and even the weaver bird, quietly occupied with the construction of its nest, reminds me of its winged ancestors, which were formidable predators. Today wildlife is at peace in Karoo. In fact, the only predator with real menace in this park, are me and my kind!

Among the numerous species of reptiles present in the park, there are no less than five species of tortoise, among them the Cape leopard tortoise (above).

The nights get extremely cold, but in the daytime temperatures can rise to 40°C. These extreme climatic conditions, together with the scarcity of water, define the arid land of the park (opposite).

I follow a footpath created for fossil hunters; it allows me to walk in the footsteps of the dinosaurs that populated the earth millions of years ago.

In bygone days, dinosaurs lived at the foot of the rocky outcrops that dominate the park (above).

In addition to rare reptile species, the Karoo National Park accommodates many other animals, including the common zebra (opposite).

Always on their guard, the female ostriches gaze into the distance (right hand page).

The landscape of the Karoo appears not to have changed since the dawn of time (following double page).

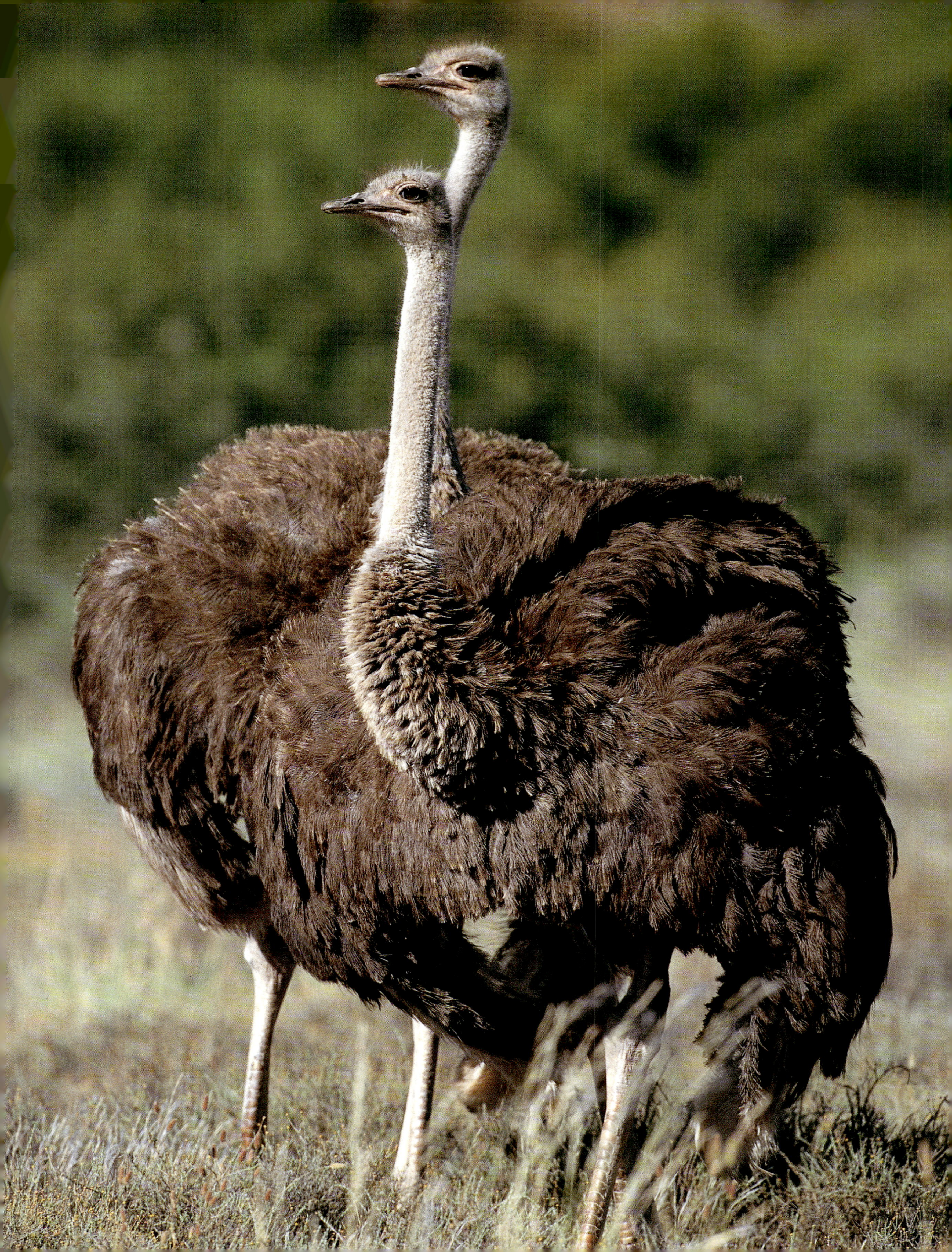

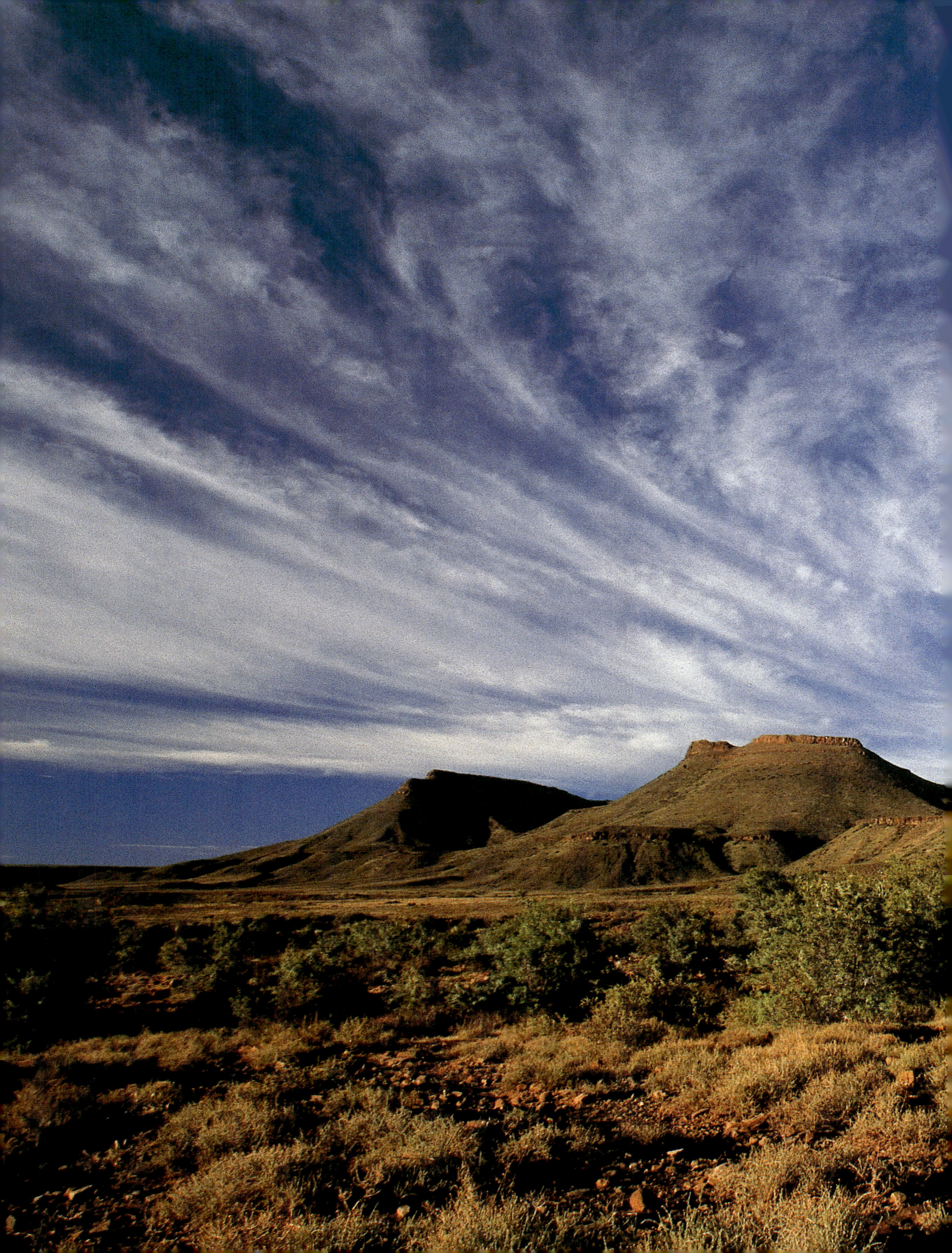

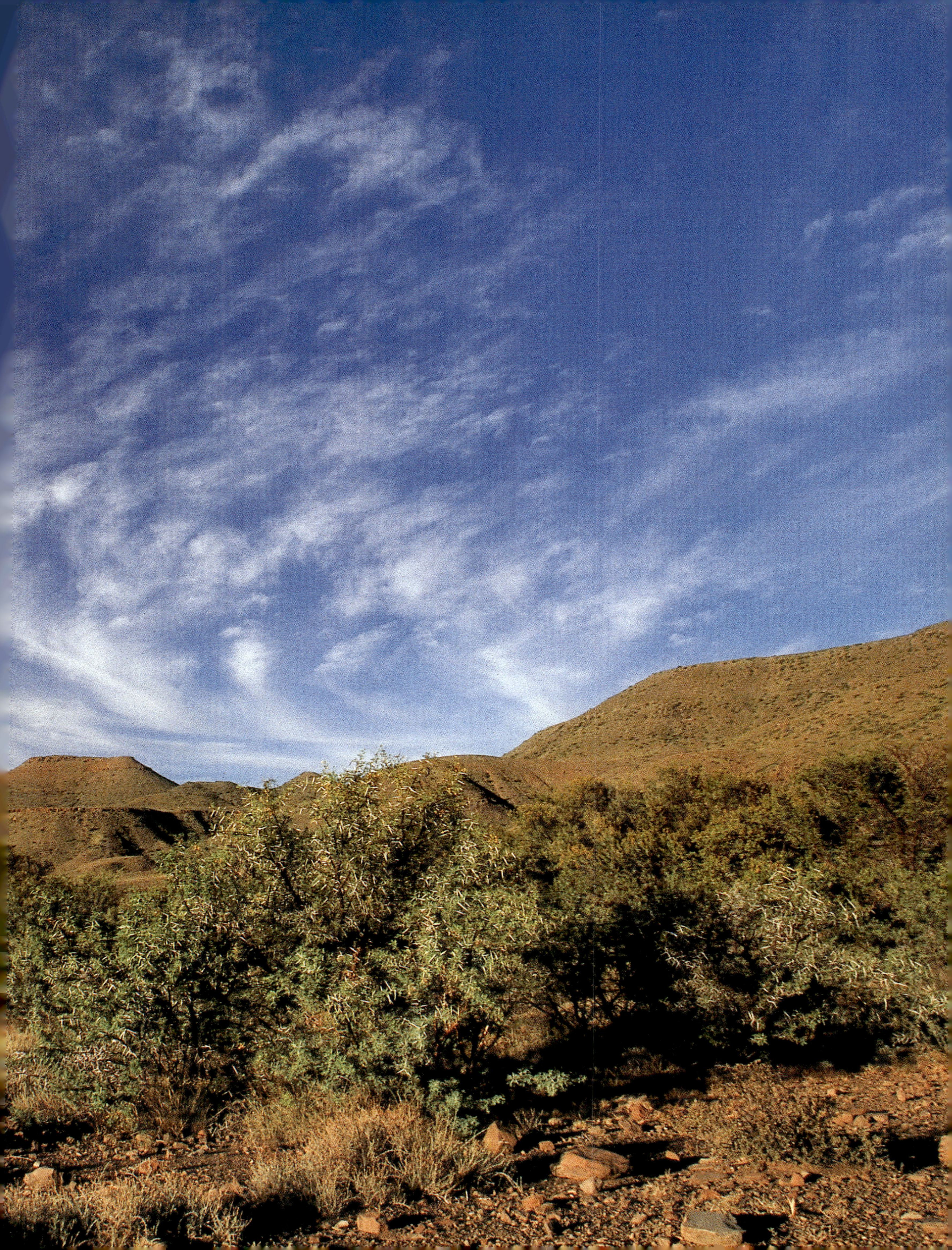

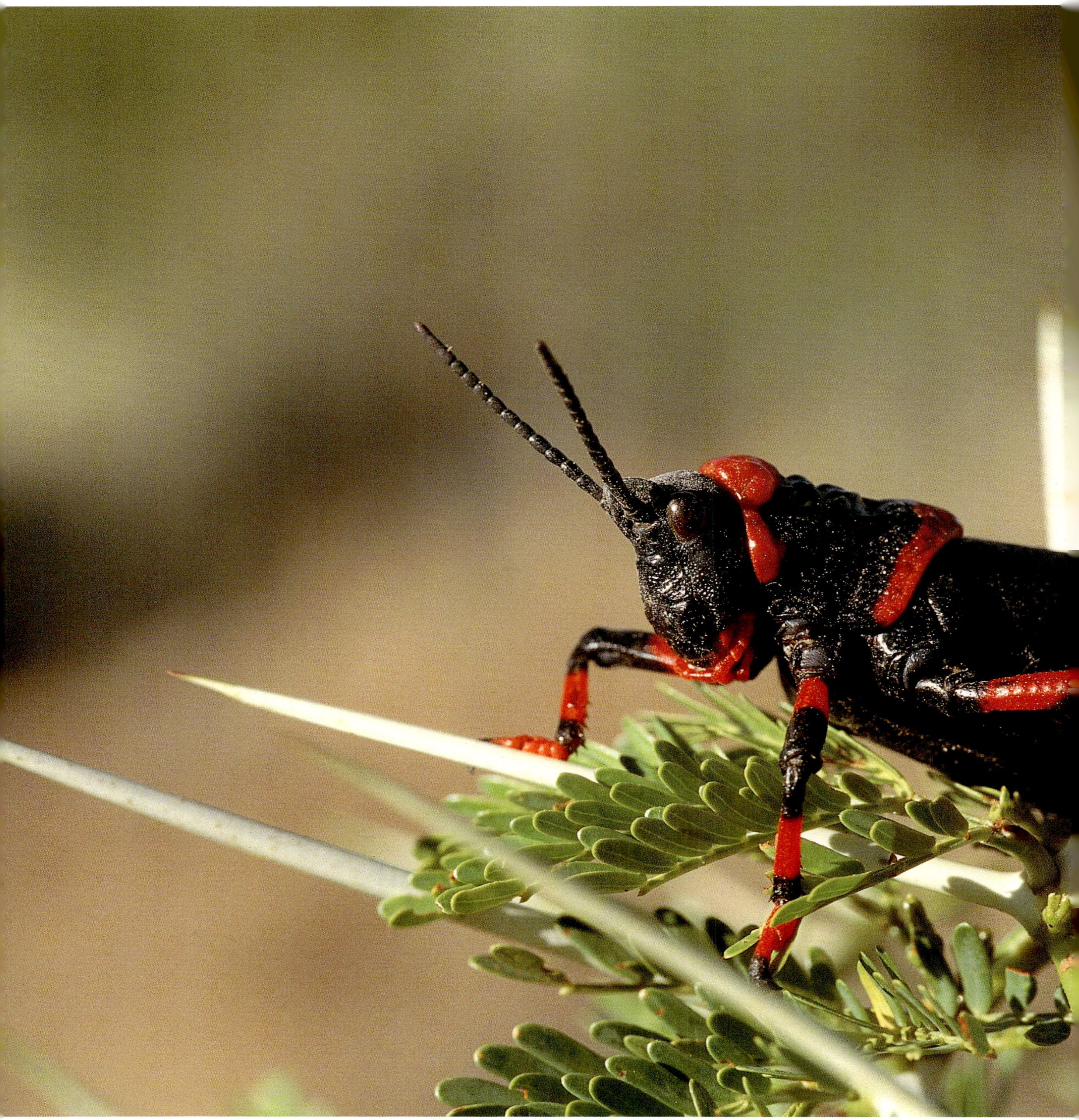

An orthopteran finds refuge between the thorns of an acacia (left).

The klipspringer is the king of climbing. It seems to defy gravity thanks to its hooves, which give good grip on rocky surfaces (above, top).

The monitor lizard is one of the rightful heirs of the dinosaurs that populated the Karoo millions of years ago. It uses its forked tongue to pinpoint and capture its prey (above).

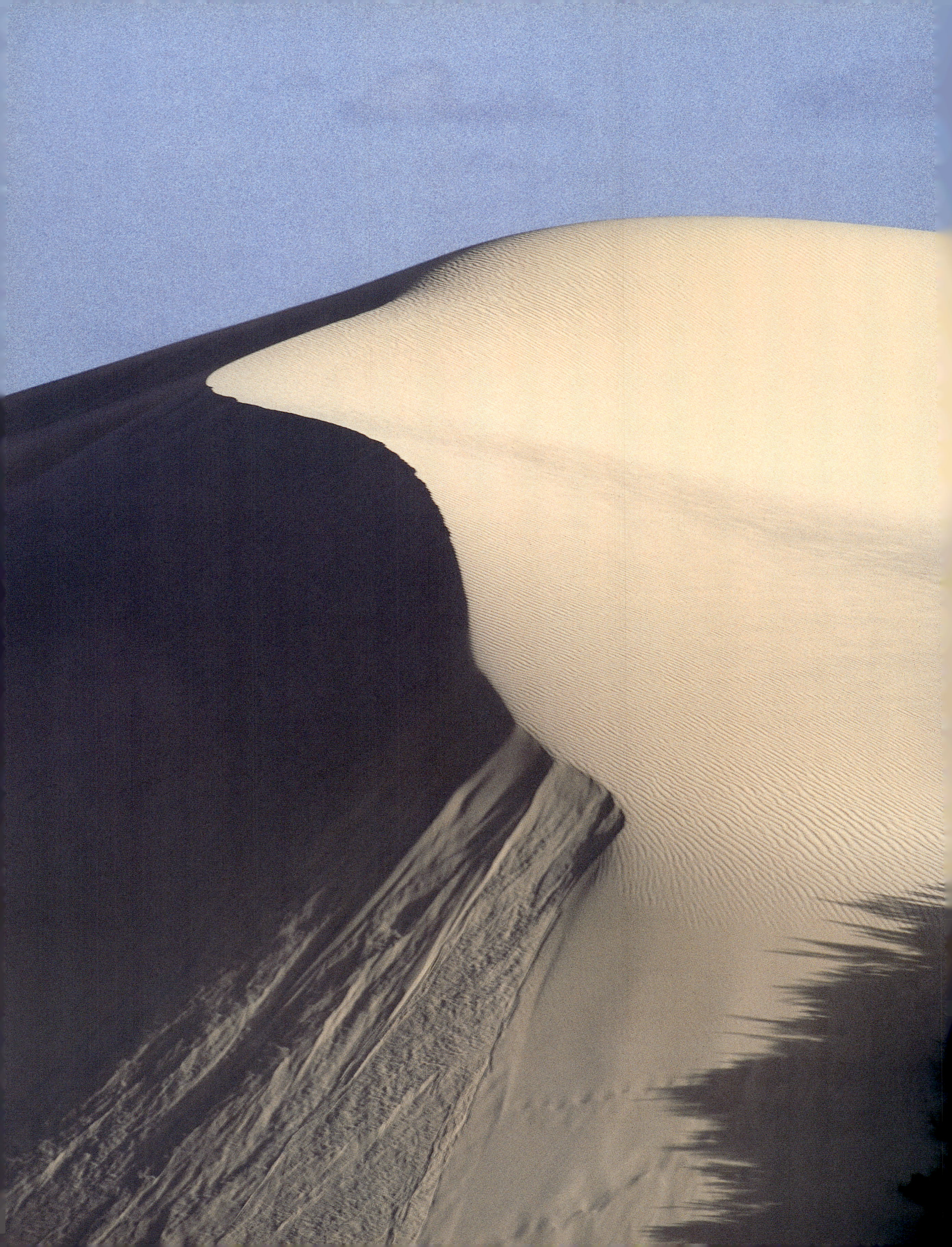

Western Cape Province & Cape Peninsula

De Hoop Nature Reserve

The African oystercatcher

To create a reserve for the purpose of protecting a bird might appear to be a considerable challenge. Unfortunately animals tend not to achieve protected status unless they have some symbolic significance or their future is in danger.

The authorities of the Western Cape Province took this gamble in order to protect some tiny birds – the last African oystercatchers. By allocating the status of nature reserve to a small area situated on the coast, not far from the famous Cape Agulhas – the most meridian geographic point of the African continent, where the troubled waters of the Atlantic and Indian oceans meet – the authorities set out to save the last members of this endangered species. The De Hoop Nature Reserve came into being.

The African oystercatcher, also called the black oystercatcher, has found its sanctuary in the magnificent surroundings of the De Hoop. The long coastlines of this small reserve, lined with deserted beaches, dunes and rocky cliffs, give this small, bright, red-beaked bird what it needs to survive. Changing tides regularly expose large quantities of shellfish attached to the rocks and the oystercatcher is spoilt for choice of food, which it accesses with taps of a beak capable of breaking even the hardest shells. The fine sandy beaches allow it to hunt for small crabs shifted by the currents, and the cliffs are an ideal sheltered nesting spot.

Yet the interest of the De Hoop reserve does not stop with its small protégé; the reserve hosts a very particular ecosystem. The large sand dunes of immaculate white sand rise in the middle of vast plains covered with fynbo bushes, amongst which grows the South African emblem: the protea flower. The De Hoop reserve, due to the richness of its plant life, is part of the Cape Floral Kingdom, and harbours a large part the kingdom's 9,000 identified species, of which two-thirds are not to be found elsewhere in the world.

The small reserve also possesses a lake, 16 km long, pushed up against the high dunes that separate it from the salt water of the Indian Ocean, and with varying salinity. The perimeter was classified by Unesco as one of the protected Ramsar sites (see page 23) due to its ecological interest. The ecological value of a site is not always in proportion to its size.

The reserve was created in order to protect a tiny bird whose survival was in danger: the African oystercatcher (above).

These dunes of white sand, situated on the coast not far from the Cape Agulhas, protect the De Hoop reserve's territory (opposite).

The boulders along the waterfront host large quantities of shellfish that provide the oystercatcher with a rich and varied diet (following pages).

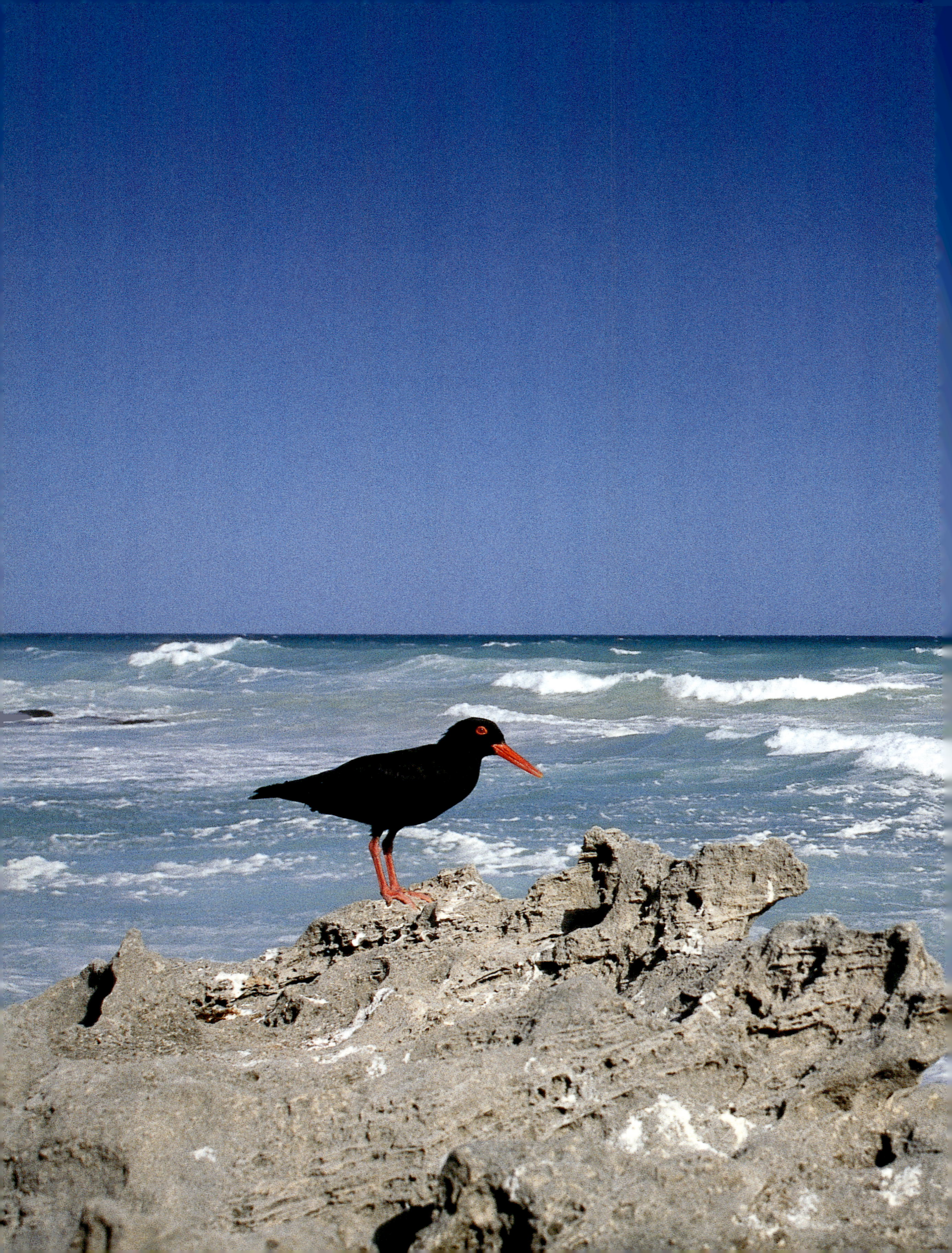

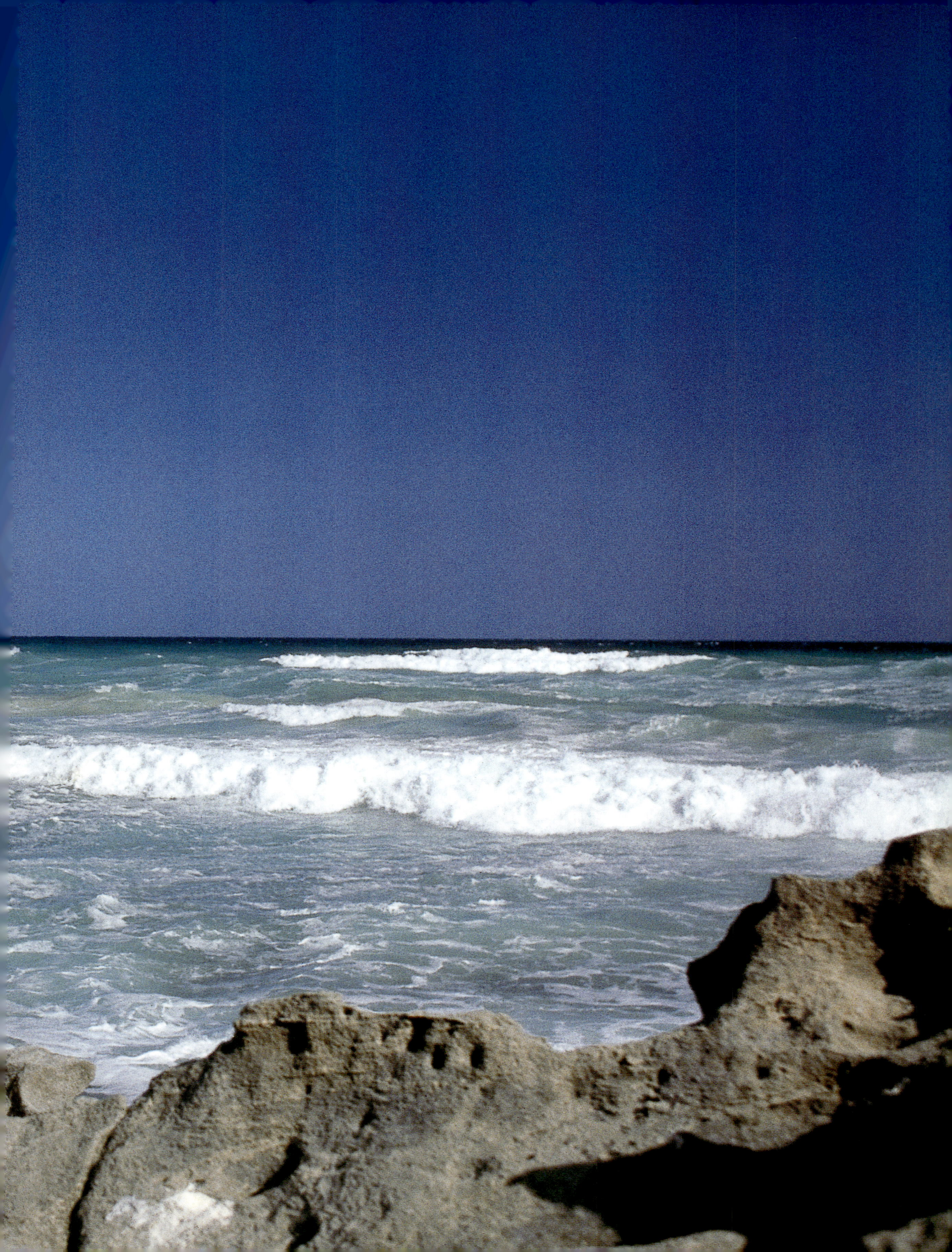

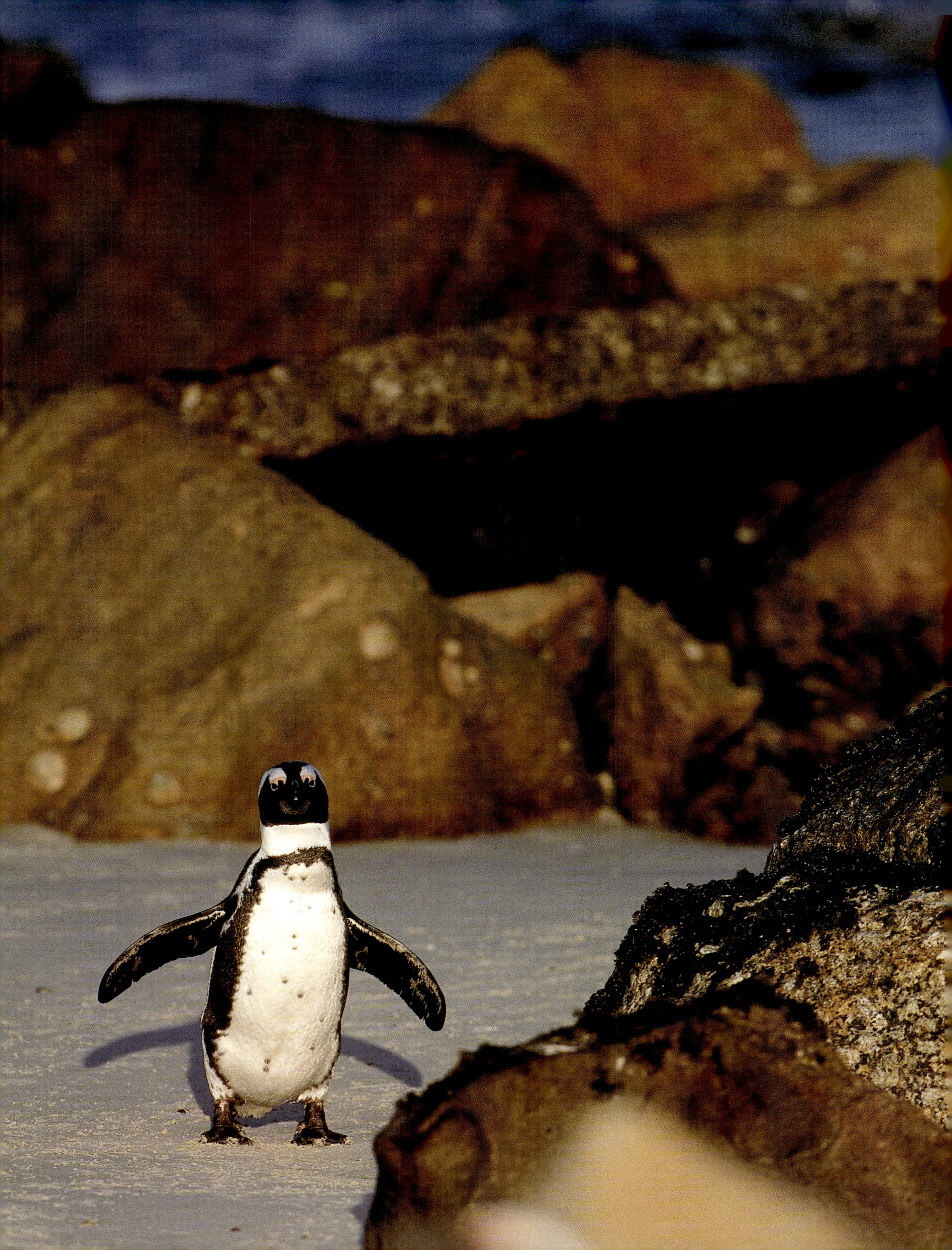

Western Cape Province & Cape Peninsula

Cape Peninsula Nature Reserve

Rare African penguins

It is a quiet morning at the end of July. It is mild, almost cool, on Foxy Beach, which is sheltered by large blocks of granite – probably fallen rocks from the Twelve Apostle Mountain Range nearby.

I have to get up early in order to be alone with the site's popular natural hosts, the famous African penguins. People flock to admire these insolent birds that, paradoxically, have found refuge near to man – up until recently humans threatened their very survival. Today, the species that has colonised Boulders Beach and Foxy Beach – among the few places left on earth where African penguins can still be seen – finds itself on the World Conservation Union's red data list, listing all endangered species. Judging them to be not very fierce, I move a little closer to these amusing and animated hosts, and accompany them to the water. They are remarkable divers, able to stay under water for over twenty minutes and reach depths of many hundreds of metres. I keep a respectful distance, as I imagine being pecked could be an unpleasant experience.

Such scenes are possible thanks to the work of the local authorities that protect the bay, allowing these clipped-winged birds to live in tranquillity. Maintaining the precious ecosystem has been helped by a reduction in quotas for fishing sardines and anchovies, which form the base of the penguins' diet. The colony of African penguins has grown to over 3,000 individuals, fruit of the labours of two pairs of birds that established themselves on Boulders Beach in 1982.

The sun begins to fade. The adult penguins return from a successful fishing trip with food for their young. They cross the sands in their hundreds, doing their funny walk and, despite their small size, making a considerable amount of noise. Their cry is reminiscent of the bray of a donkey, which probably earned them the nickname "jackass penguins". This chorus is even more formidable in spring, during the mating season. The males, preoccupied with seducing their mates with strident calls, are imperturbable, unless a Cape seal, their principal predator, is prowling around. The beach blackens: the colony is almost complete. There is a flurry of activity on all sides. In July the colony has just accommodated some new mouths to feed on the beach, turning it into a kindergarten.

A young African penguin, proof of the impressive success of the protection of this species (above).

Despite its clumsy walk, the adult penguin does not lack elegance: his black-and-white coat resembles a dinner jacket (opposite).

African penguins are not timid, so are easy to approach, but beware of pecks (following pages).

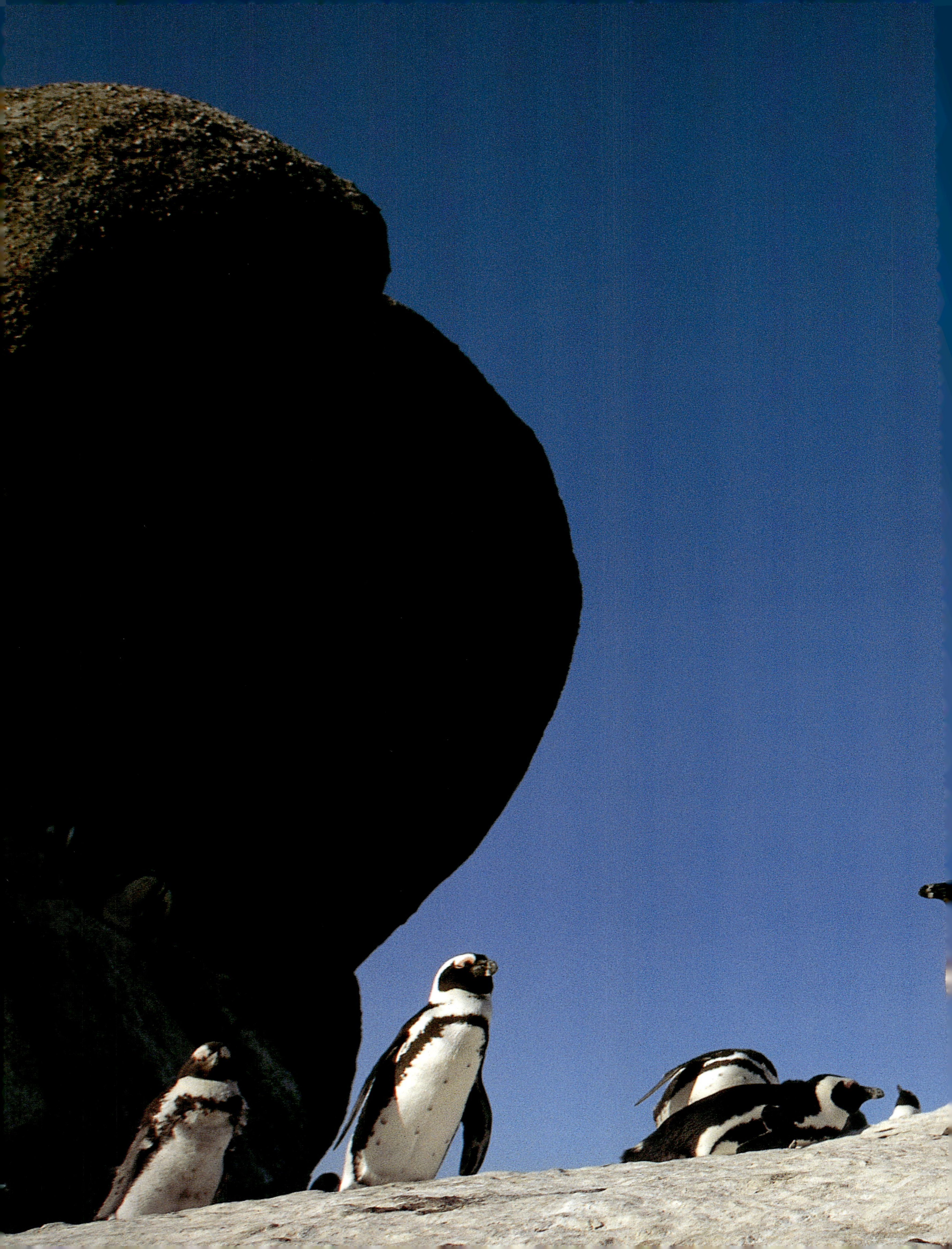

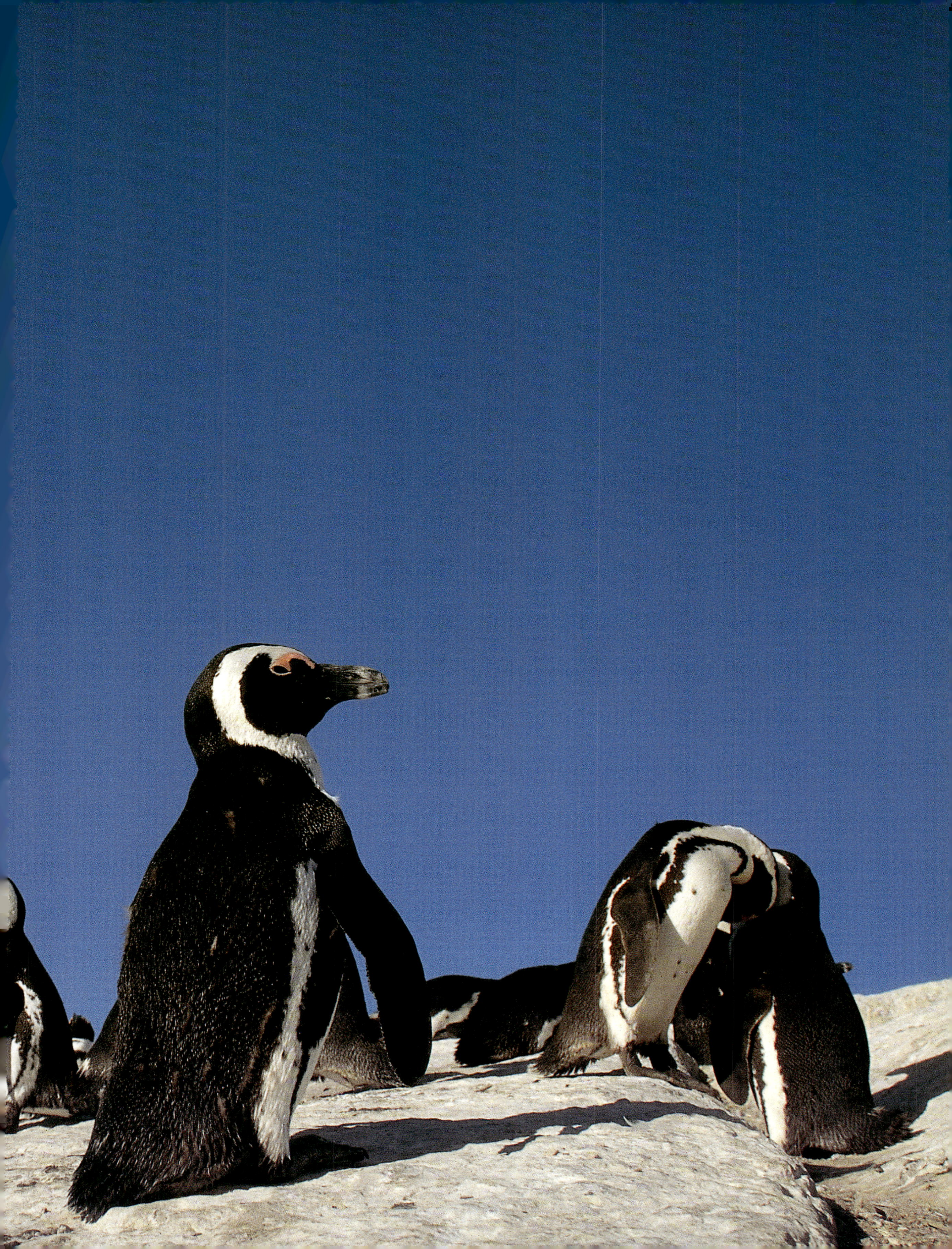

African penguins are incredibly noisy. Yet when in a crowd, one has to make oneself heard! They are not nicknamed jackass penguins for nothing (above).

The males return from fishing. They must hurry to fill the stomachs of the colony's new arrivals (right).

CAPE PENINSULA NATURE RESERVE | 119

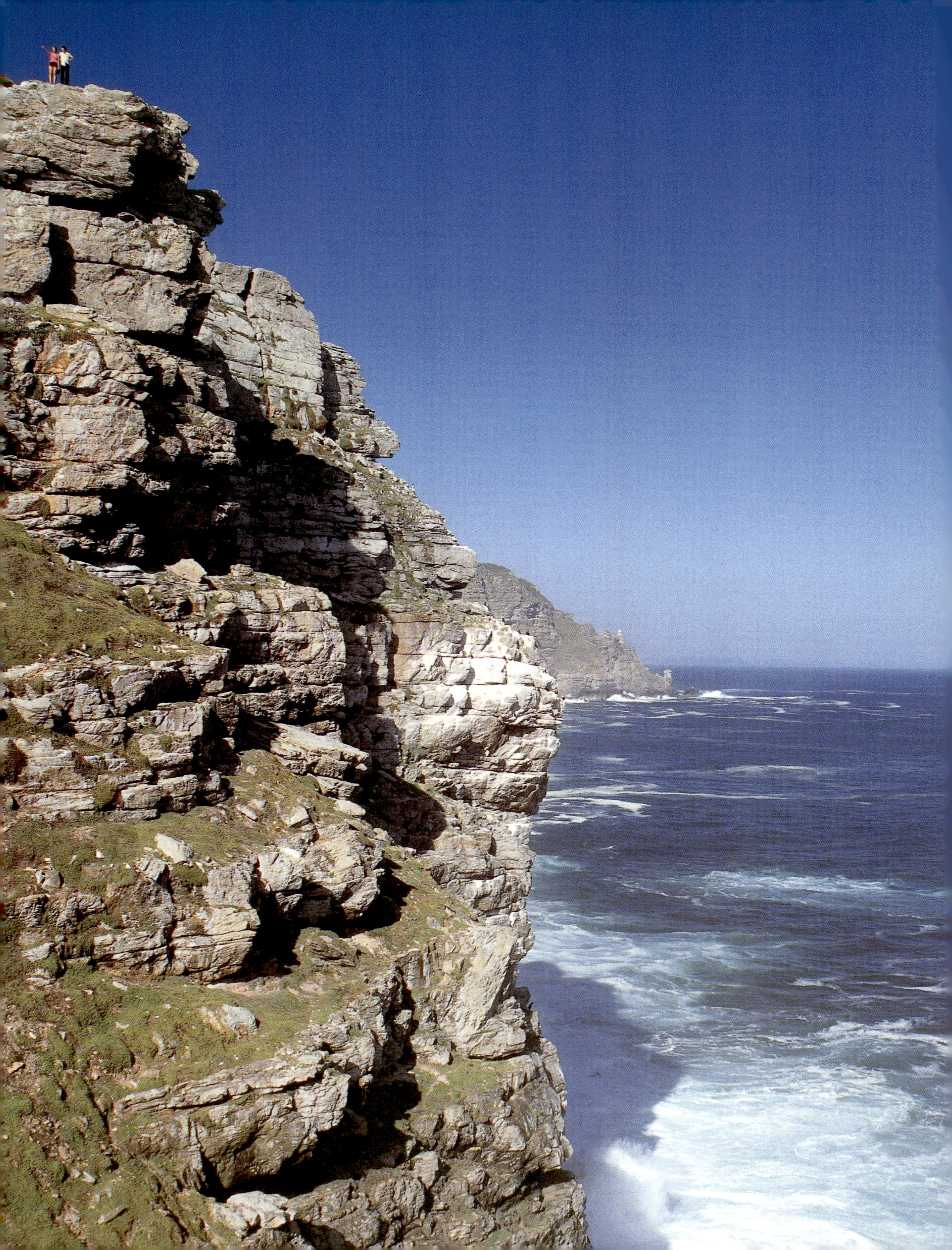

Western Cape Province & Cape Peninsula

Cape of Good Hope Nature Reserve
Forces of nature

In the Cape of Good Hope Nature Reserve, now part of the Cape Peninsula National Park, maritime history and the forces of nature combine to create one of the most spectacular landscapes that I had the chance to view in South Africa. Having left Cape Town in sunshine, I begin with my customary reconnaissance trip, before returning the next day to take my photographs. Travelling at night is not permitted within the park.

Faced with the prodigious open expanses of the Cape, on a coastline caressed by the rays of the sun, I am able to translate French poet Victor Ségalen's phrase "distant extremes" into images. A strange feeling comes over me: before this huge natural vista, with its seemingly limitless horizon, I feel very small.

Suddenly, a few hundred metres away from this place of legendary significance for the world's navigators, a thick mist falls. Within a few moments, I lose all visibility. The mist becomes fog, helping to reinforce the tragic and desolate aspect of the windswept landscape. I understand better why the Portuguese sailors Bartholomeo Dias who discovered the Cape in 1488 and Vasco de Gama called it the "Cape of Storms". I can well imagine the apprehension of the sailors, centuries ago, as they approached these towering blocks of stone, at night or in heavy fog, with no navigation aids other than reckoning, trying to catch the Benguela and Agulas currents, which would allow them to reach their destination. Many lost their lives, as the many wrecks, washed up on the beaches to the north of this terrible reef, bear witness.

Having lashed the coast violently, the wind dies down and the sky clears again, slowly regaining its azure blue tone. The display of nature in metamorphosis is beautiful enough to take your breath away: the shattered landscape, sculpted by the elements, contrasts with the immense beaches of fine sand where a few boats have come to die. Animal life seems almost absent: the ground is too poor, too sandy to provide food. Only the occasional antelope, birds and reptiles have succeeded in colonising this silent park where an atmosphere of mystery, enchantment and history reigns.

At the end of the 16th century, the famous navigator, Sir Francis Drake, declared that the Cape of Good Hope "…is the most stately thing and the fairest Cape we saw in the whole circumference of the earth". I can only agree with him.

The white-breasted cormorant is one of the rare birds willing to nest on the weather-beaten cliffs of the Cape (above).

This boundless space and the brutal and savage nature of the Cape of Good Hope instil a sense of humility (opposite).

Faced with its prodigious open expanses on a coastline caressed by the sun's rays,
I am able to translate French poet Victor Ségalen's phrase "distant extremes" into images.

In the evening, as the sun sets, the sea's humidity rises and the mists begin to enfold the land (above).

The Cape of Good Hope, a place filled with history, has fascinated and frightened many a sailor (opposite).

In calm weather, the landscape of the Cape is very peaceful. Then it becomes suddenly dangerous as the elements awaken (following pages).

CAPE OF GOOD HOPE NATURE RESERVE | 123

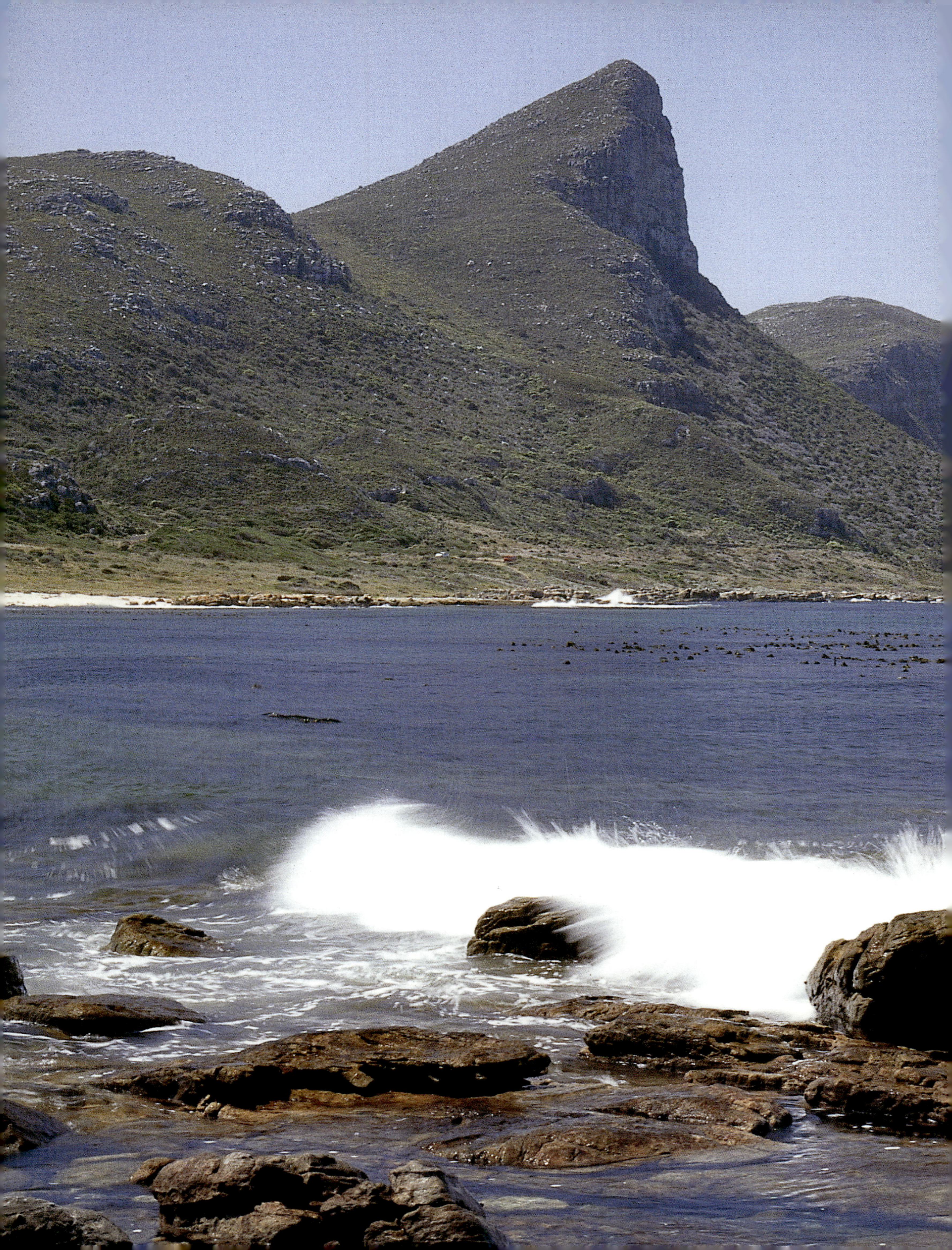

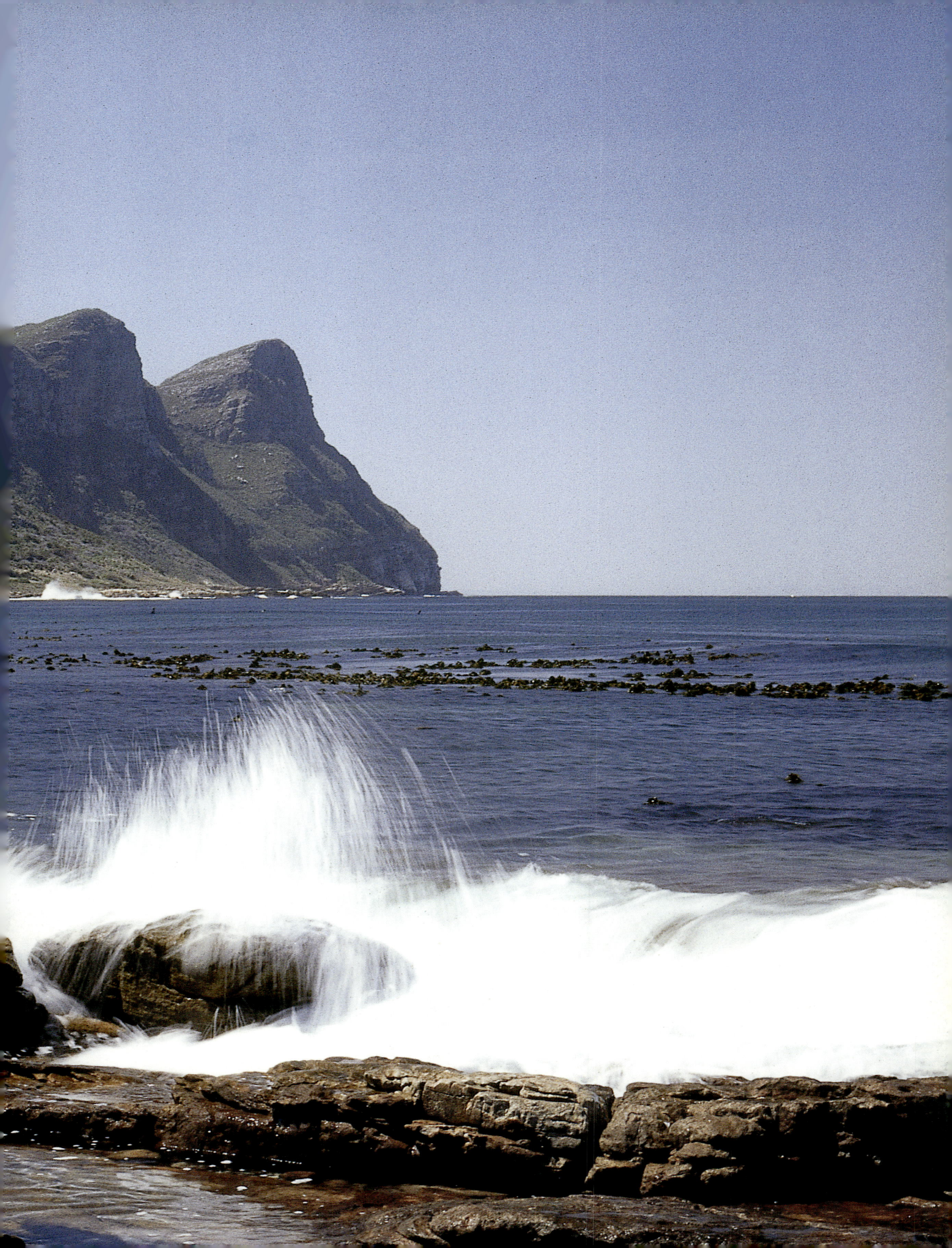

Only the occasional antelope, birds and reptiles have succeeded in colonising this silent park, where an atmosphere of mystery, enchantment and history reigns.

A South African fur seal benefits from the warmth of the sun's last rays before returning to the cold currents that sweep the Cape (above).

Cape gulls, as everywhere on the south african coast, are present here, always watchful for a shoal of fish (right).

A colony of cormorants has installed itself on the side of the rocks, ideal for taking off and from where they have a commanding view of the nourishing tides (opposite).

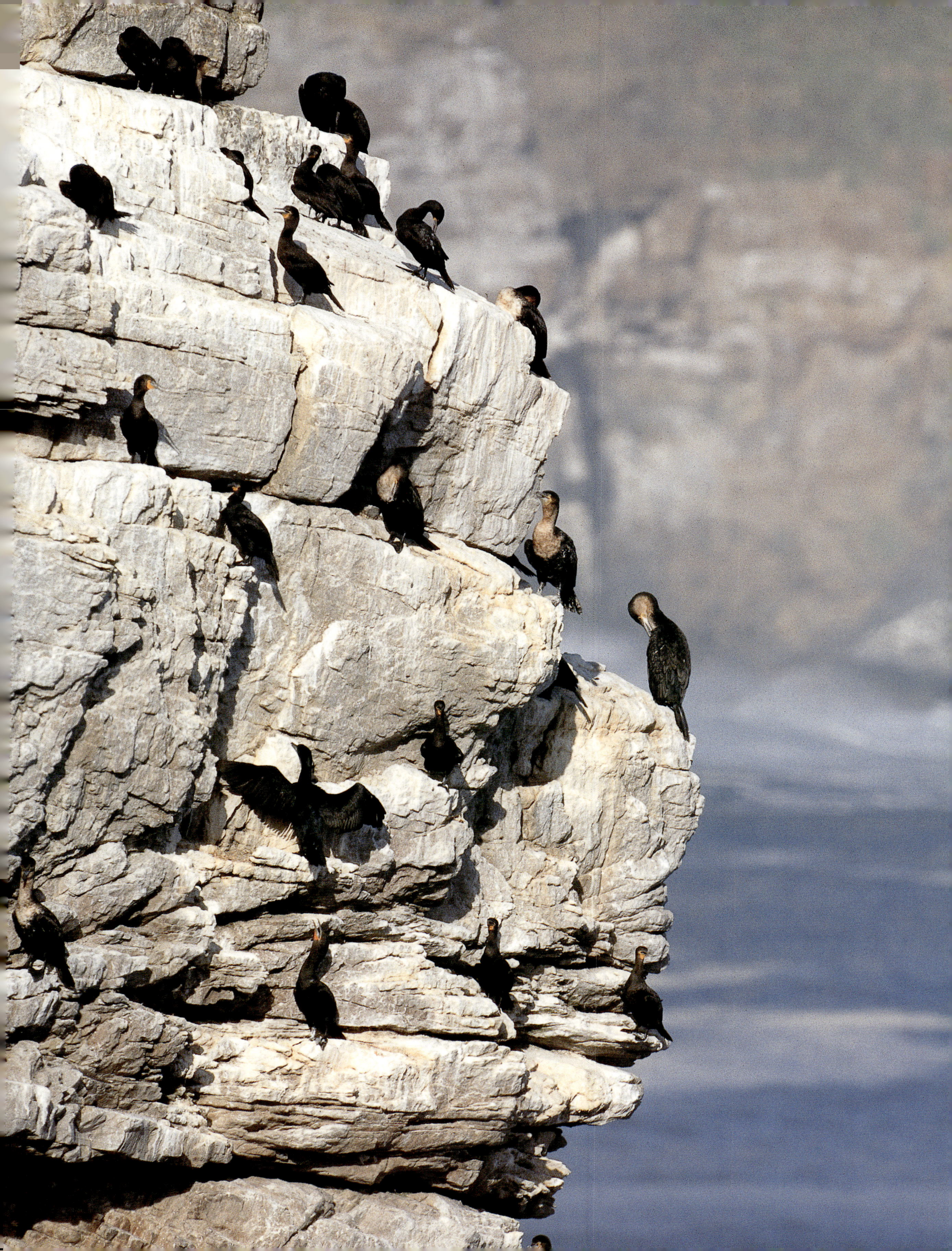

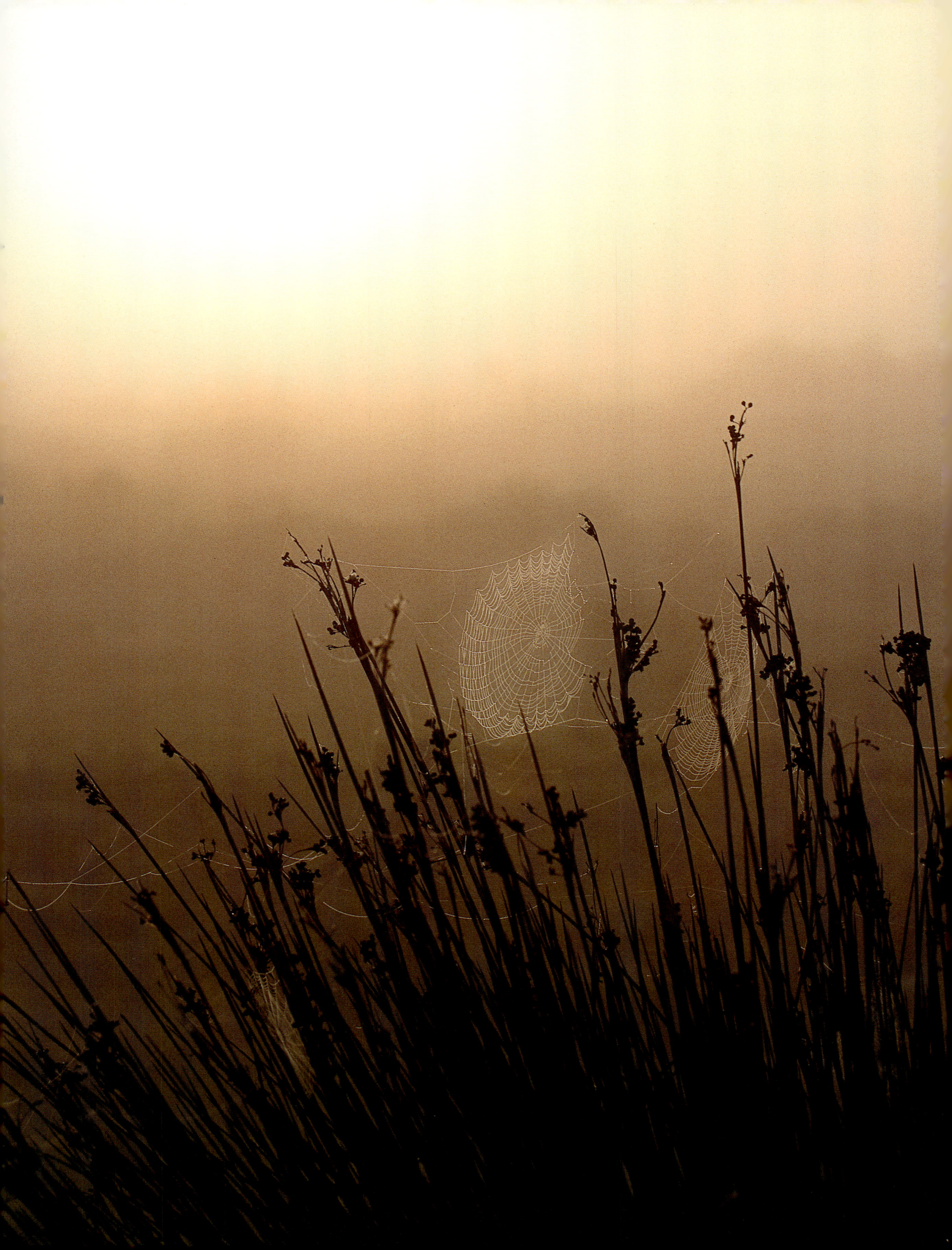

Western Cape Province & Cape Peninsula

West Coast National Park
A little corner of paradise

South Africa is probably one of only few countries of the world to offer such a diversity of ecosystems. With its numerous wetlands, the West Coast National Park situated in the north of the Cape, on the Atlantic coast it shares with Namibia, is a perfect example.

Having crossed the high sand dunes, which were formed over 20,000 years ago, I reach the sharp rock reef. A landscape of unequalled beauty, yet one which is responsible for numerous shipwrecks. Wrecks of vessels, victims of the tempestuous ocean, are unveiled at low tide, upon the immense expanses of fine sand. In this maritime cemetery, Cape gannets come to fetch crabs, bloodworms and small fish, food they are sometimes obliged to share with the gulls, the cormorants and the other sea birds who live in the 27,000-hectare park.

I continue, crossing a thick mass of plants and fynbo bushes. Further on I surprise some mongooses and springboks in their search for food. Suddenly, I see a movement, a caracal hides, then leaps into view: it has spotted a group of springboks. A few seconds suffice for these small antelopes to disappear from their predators' view and their haste causes the mongooses to retreat to their strategically placed burrow. The caracal gives chase, following its prey as they disappear into the vegetation. Within moments, I find myself alone in this wild expanse, and I continue my expedition towards the immense salt-water wetlands, the largest in South Africa, stretching out of sight. They remain unexploited, other than by the few inhabitants who have the privilege of living in this secluded spot, in a hamlet of houses with walls whitewashed with lime and dominated by a tiny church sweltering in the sun. I sit on a bench by its door. One of the most sublime panoramas ever to have been revealed to me unfolds: a lagoon of turquoise water. This extraordinary viewpoint, this islet of humanity in an ocean of nature, is aptly named: Church Heaven. I savour the calm and plenitude that emanates from this scene, and share with the few other visitors to this corner of paradise my feeling that you do not leave Church Heaven quite the same person.

A tree with a contorted trunk, rocks sculpted by an often turbulent sea punctuate the prodigious landscape of the park (above).

In the early hours of the morning, a thick mist covers the West Coast National Park (opposite).

Undoubtedly exhausted by
the harshness of the elements,
a Cape gull yawns (above).

Numerous ship carcasses,
abandoned to rust and to
the turbulence of the waves,
bear witness to the violence of
the Atlantic Ocean (opposite).

When the tide drops, it reveals
immense deserted beaches
(following pages).

WEST COAST NATIONAL PARK | 131

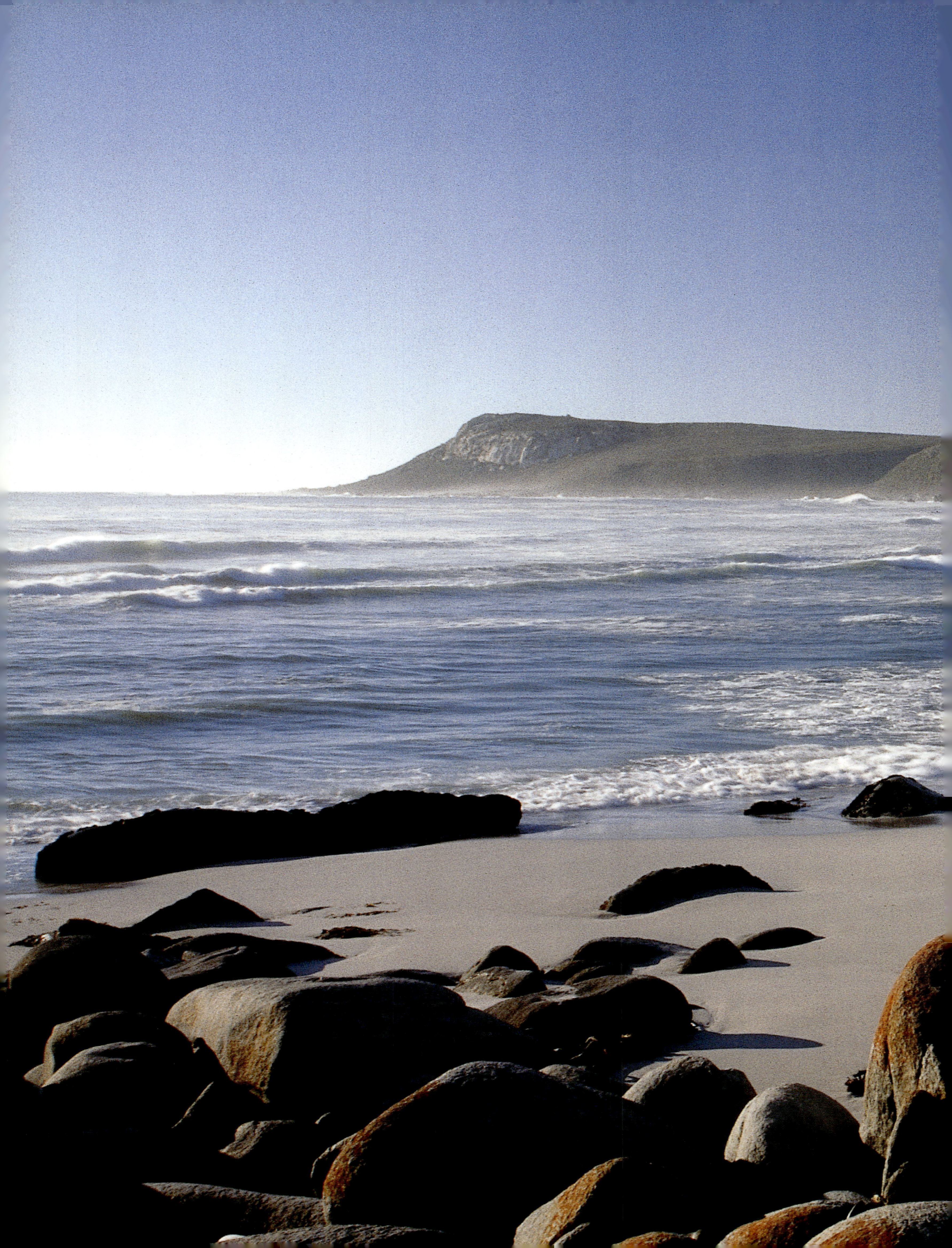

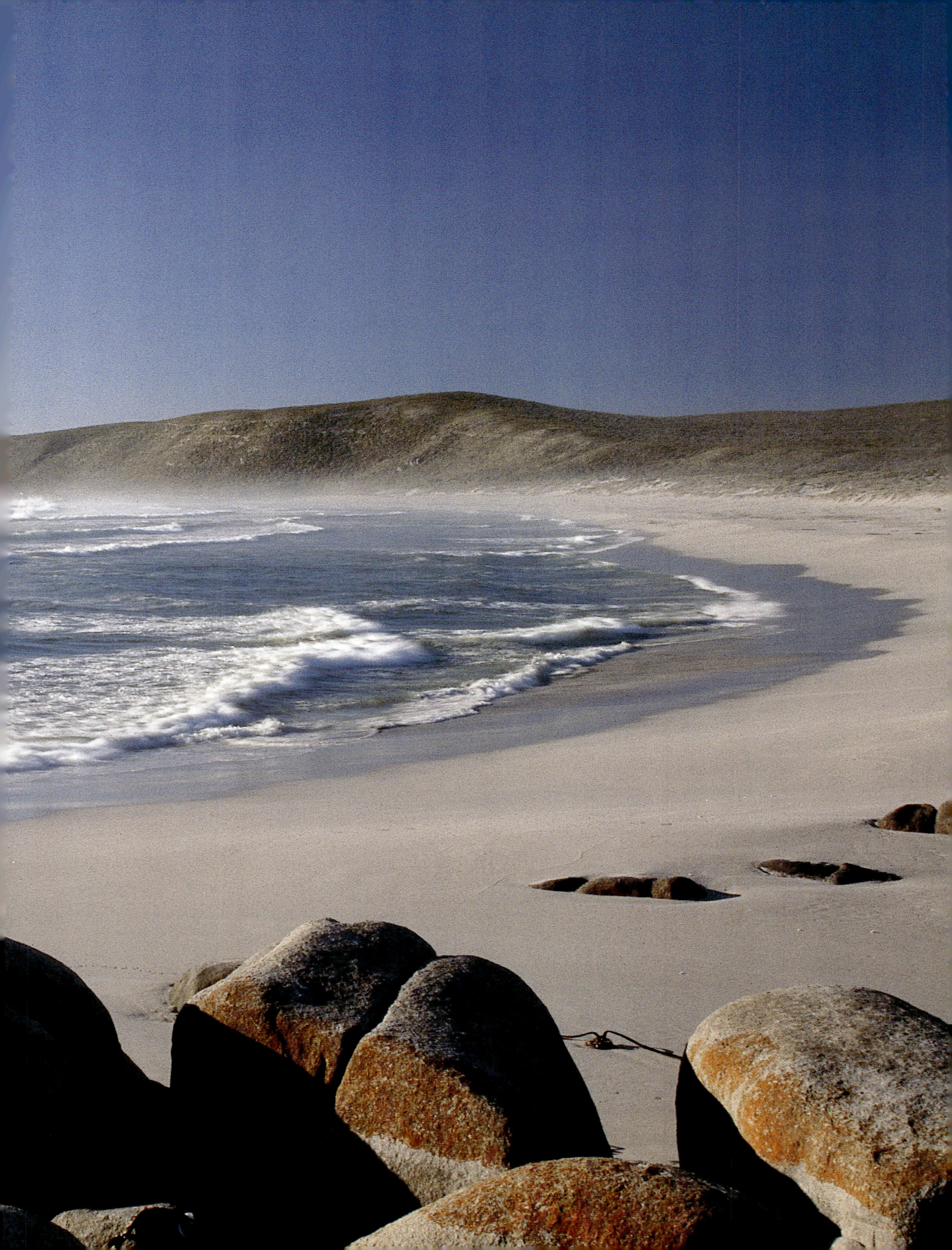

I continue my expedition towards the immense salt-water wetlands, the largest in South Africa, stretching out of sight.

There are lagoons of salt water in the dense vegetation, transforming the land into a veritable patchwork of rounded forms (below).

A multitude of lush plants and flowers illuminate this coastal setting (opposite, top).

The small suni antelope rarely ventures far from a watering hole. When surprised, it freezes and then takes flight, bounding away and emitting small high-pitched cries (opposite, bottom).

WEST COAST NATIONAL PARK | 135

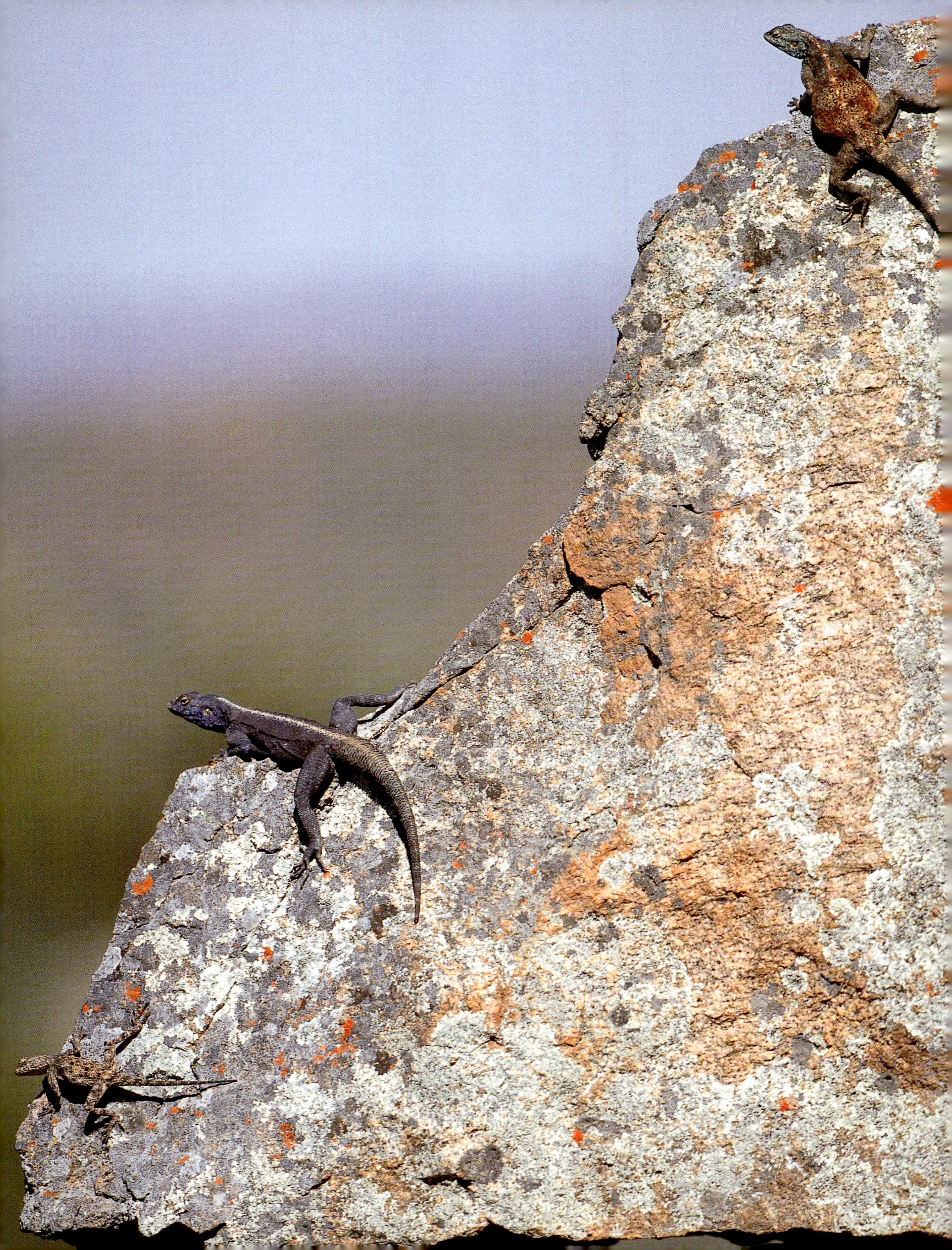

Northern Cape Province

Namaqua National Park
Pearl of the Northern Cape

In a region squeezed in between the Atlantic coast and the desert outskirts of the small town of Pofadder, the flat landscape of the Namaqua park is covered with bleached and chapped vegetation, struggling against drought for most of the year. Less than 200 ml of rain falls here annually. This sparse land serves as pasture for a few antelopes and African hares, as well as their predators, the caracals and other jackals, which rule this territory. One asks oneself why the South African government would create a 300-hectare floral park in this inhospitable environment, as they did in 1999, and refer to it as "the pearl of the Northern Cape".

However, between July and September, one of nature's miracles happens. Clouds filled to bursting with water are carried from the Atlantic Ocean to Namaqua by the winds and, within days of the first southern winter rains falling on this barren and scorched land, it is covered with an immense carpet of flowers. A gigantic open-air tapestry stretches into the furthest corners of the plains, illuminating the landscape with a splash of colour. The atmosphere is filled with the scent emanating from Gumbleton African daisies (*Arctotis gumbletonii*), with their little red and orange petals, Cape marigolds (*Dimorphotheca sinuata*) and bunches of geraniums (*Pelargonium incrassatum*), representing only a few of the countless species that reveal themselves during this short period.

I am lucky enough to be present at this rare and dazzling spectacle. I could not have imagined that the arid land that I discovered upon entering the park, could be transformed into a Garden of Eden. Yet this blossoming is as fleeting as it is enchanting. In a few days, the explosion of plantlife will disappear, leaving only the multitude of perfectly formed and coloured petals as a reminder. The Namaqua National Park will become dormant; it will be many long months before other rains allow the new seeds to germinate and clothe the desert again in its technicolor coat.

The southern winter rains allow millions of flowers to burst into a palette of colours. A brief blossoming that lasts only a few days (above and following pages).

The lizards, well suited to the dryness of the Namaqua Park, camouflage themselves in the grey colour of the desert's characteristic rock (opposite).

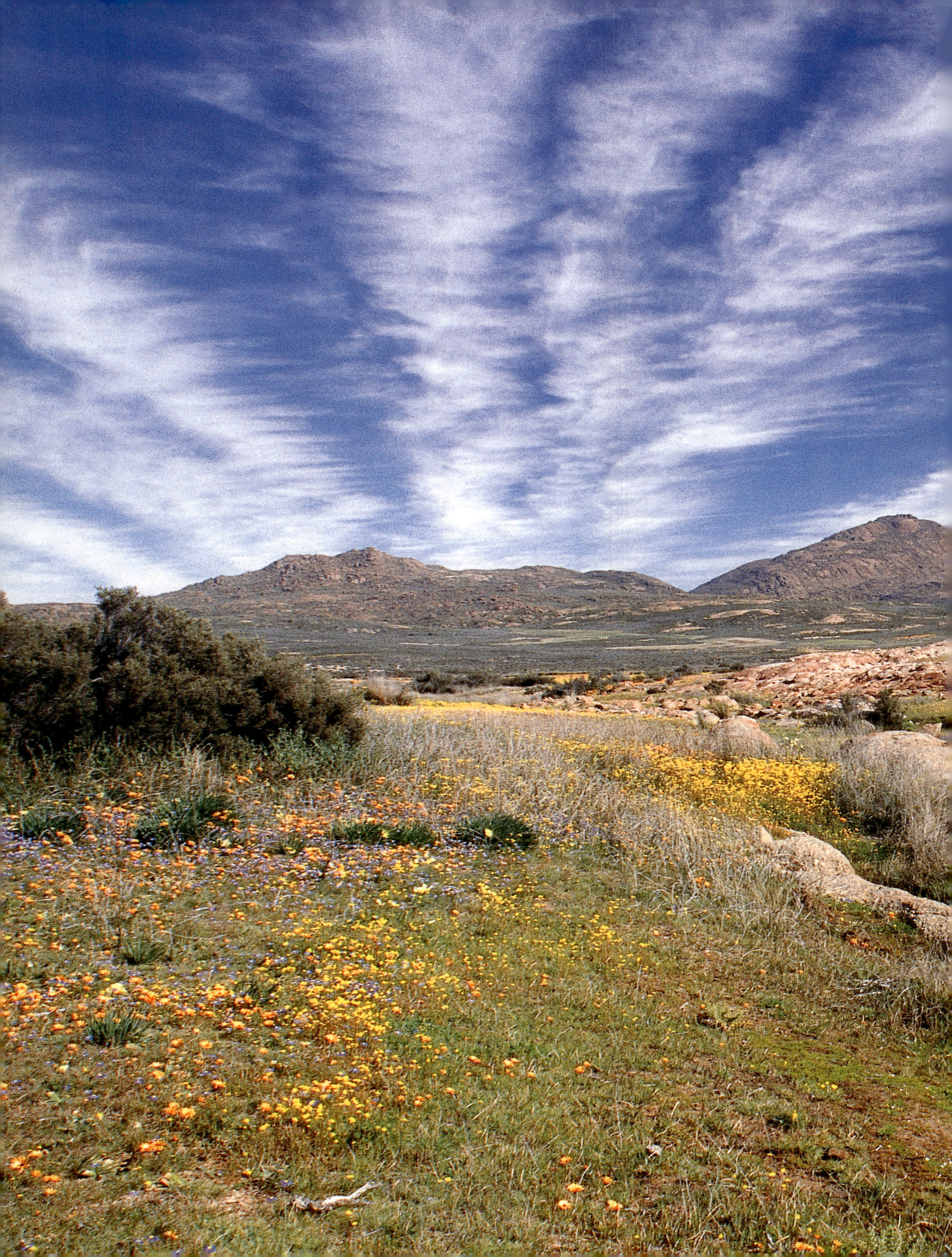

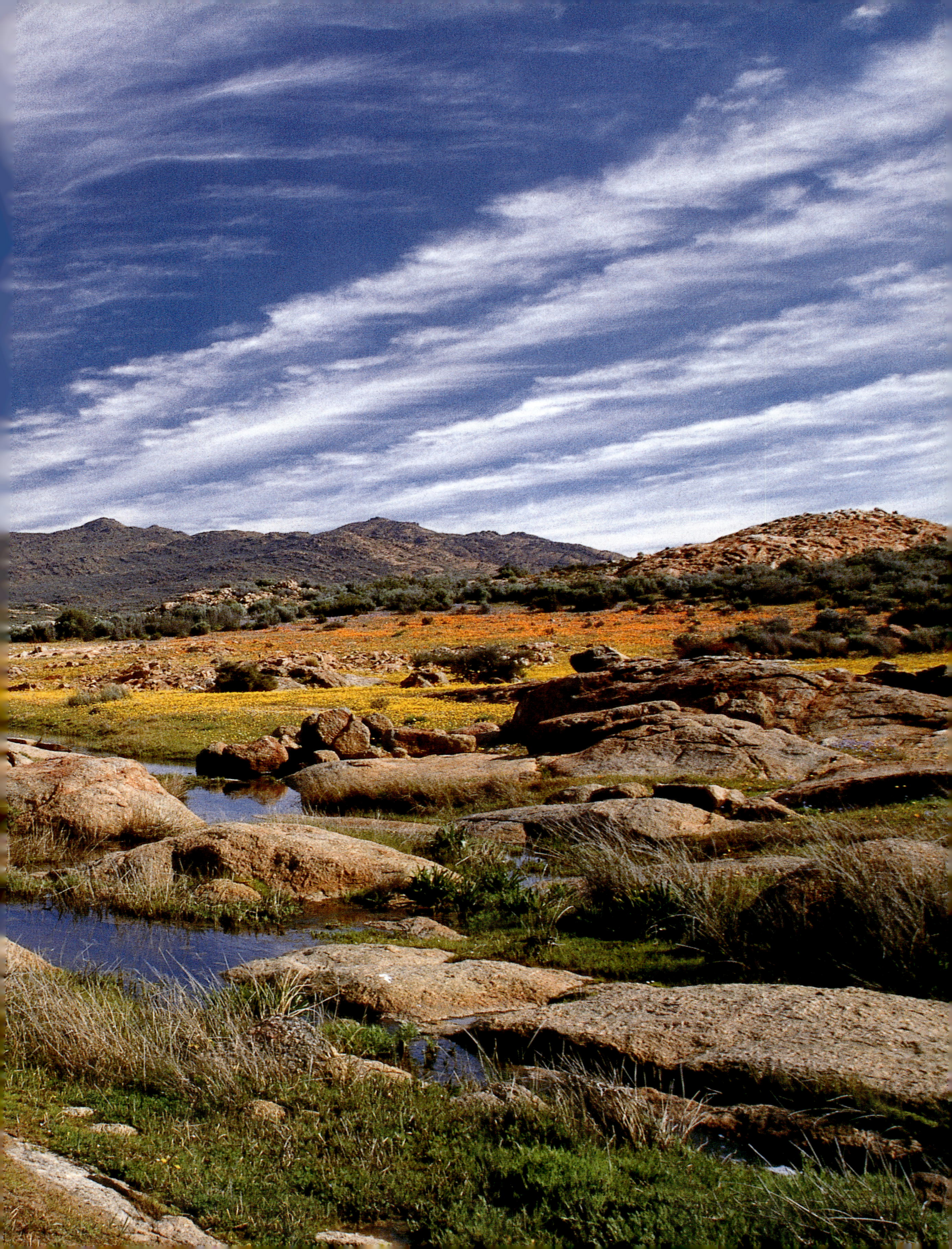

Between July and September, in the space of a few hours, the Namaqua landscape becomes covered with an immense carpet of flowers, composing an enormous open-air tapestry. It seems inconceivable that the soil of the Namaqua, so arid for most of the year, can produce such a well-orchestrated display of colourful flowers and one almost asks oneself where the mad gardener, capable of producing such a miracle, is hiding (above, below and right).

An explosion of colour...

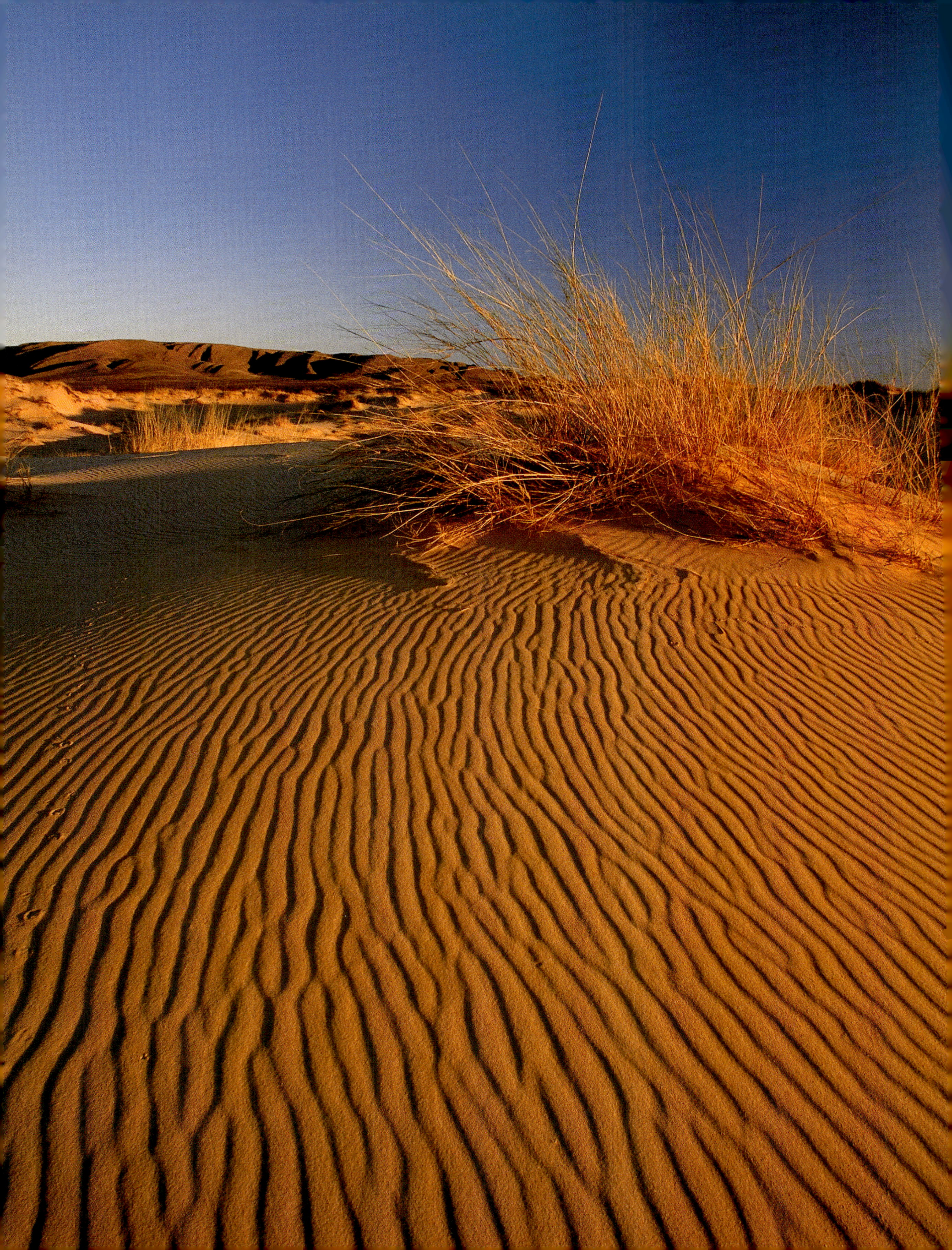

Northern Cape Province

The Witsand Nature Reserve
The roaring sands

In the Witsand Nature Reserve, a wild area of land nestling at the foot of the Langberg mountain range, well away from the road that links Kimberly to Upington, I am able to observe one of South Africa's most remarkable natural curiosities: a ribbon of dunes, nine kilometres long, rises out of a vast semi-arid plain scattered with shrubs, while the red sand dunes of the Kalahari desert stretch away to the horizon. Less well known than their illustrious neighbours, the dunes of Witsand have no reason to be outclassed by larger deserts – some of the dunes reach heights of 60 metres.

I launch myself into the dunes, which form a scene both of ethereal and captivating beauty. The immaculate white sand is so light and fine that it manages to get into the smallest folds in my clothes. I climb slowly, the more so as the heat is oppressive, almost deafening. A curious phenomenon adds itself to the savage atmosphere: each of my footsteps is accompanied by a dull sound, which does not appear to be made by my shoes. It is far too deep, like a muffled rumble, almost alive. I have the feeling that I am waking a monster, as if in a fairytale. In fact this strange noise is made by the sand itself! On these dunes, which have formed above underground waters, the rain has washed away the iron oxide with which the sand was covered – hence its white colour – and, under the weight of my footsteps, the hot air trapped between the grains escapes, making this strange rumbling noise.

However, the roaring sands, a phenomenon robbed of its magic by a scientific explanation, are far from being the only treasure of Witsand. The park possesses a rare richness of ornithological fauna, attracting bird enthusiasts from around the world. The birds are particularly numerous around the park's unique watering hole, as it represents their only chance of survival in this desert environment. The authorities keep an eye on it at all times to prevent it from drying up, as this would mean the death of many species. I take advantage of the hide built near the little pool to admire the birds' multicoloured plumage. Between a flock of weavers or a family of mousebirds, who come to bathe and drink, some small mammals approach in order to share the element so essential to their survival.

As incredible as it may seem, animal life reigns in this arid universe. And it remains discrete; as I leave the watering hole, all that remains are a few tracks of the inhabitants of the desert of roaring sands.

The curators of Witsand judiciously built an artificial watering hole to allow the animals to drink in this arid environment, to the great pleasure of the ornithologists (above).

Caressed by the winds, the dunes of Witsand are covered with the light tracks of a few animals, which will be erased by the next breeze (opposite).

In the reserve, a scent of desert and of solitude reigns (following pages).

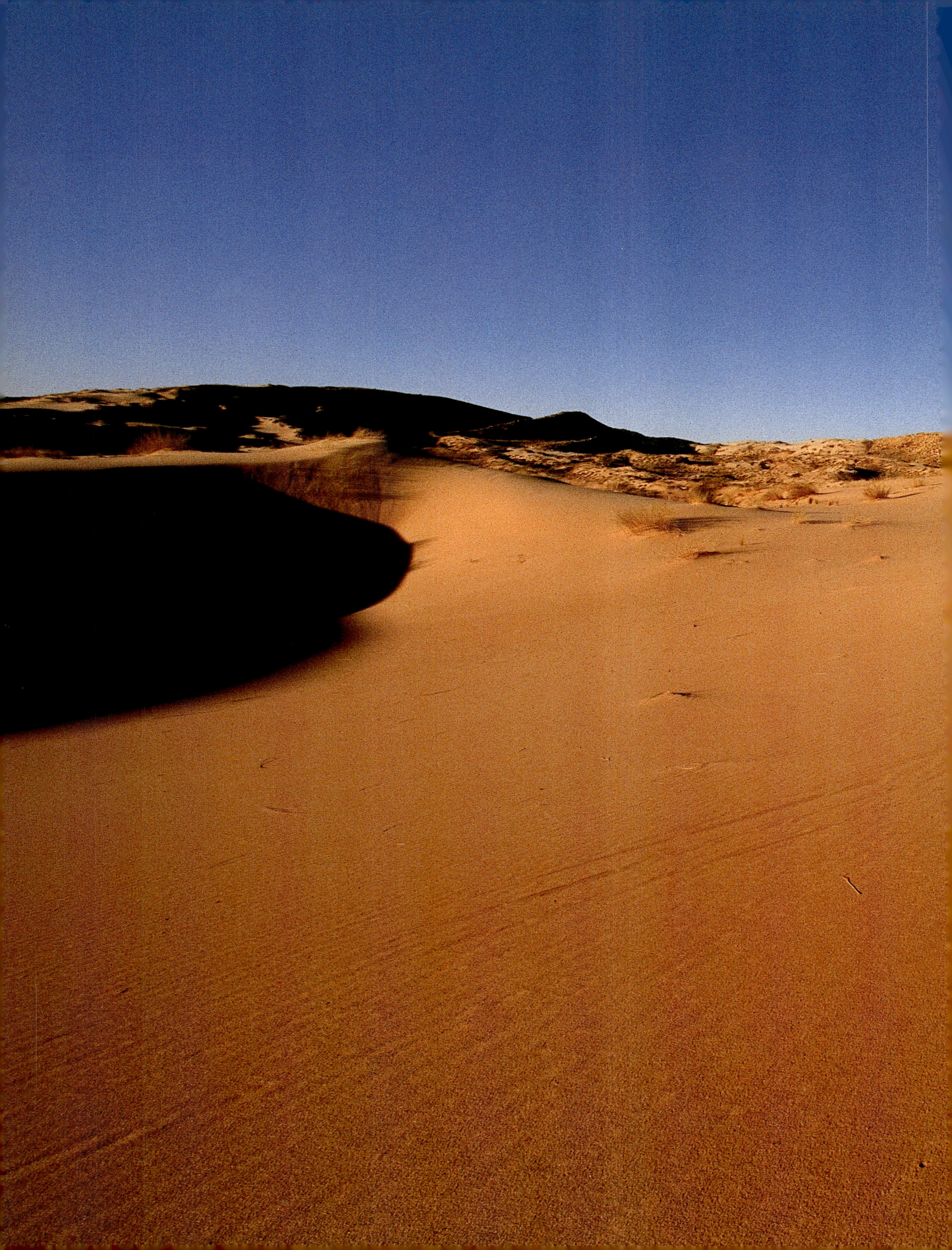

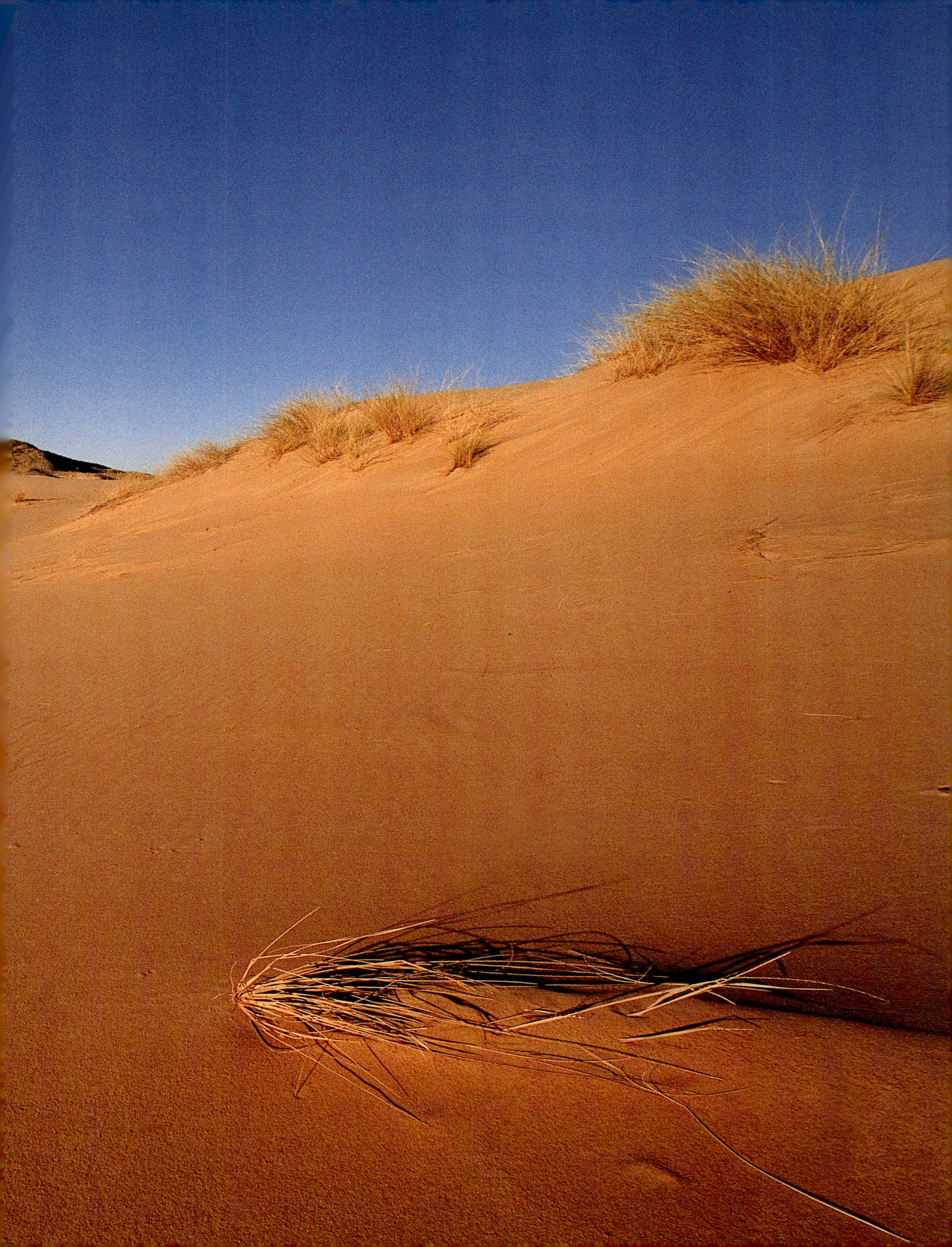

Even in a universe as arid as that of the Witsand reserve, animal life manages to establish itself (above and below).

The wind draws graphic lines upon the light sands of Witsand, creating an abstract yet fleeting work of art… (opposite).

Sands…

The sand is so light and fine that it manages to get into the smallest folds in my clothes.
I climb slowly, the more so as the heat is oppressive, almost deafening.

Drawn up on its hind legs, the Mangoose gazes inquisitively into the distance. It has just discovered my lens and within seconds disappears from view (left).

The relics of a storm: lightening struck and, through the violence of the heat produced, the sand melted forming this curious glass sculpture (below).

Mousebirds arrange to meet near the watering hole. The insects that have come to refresh themselves will pay the price (opposite).

I take advantage of the shelter near the little pond to admire the enchanting display of wings of thousands of colours. Between a flock of weavers or a family of mousebirds, some small mammals approach in order to share the element so essential to their survival.

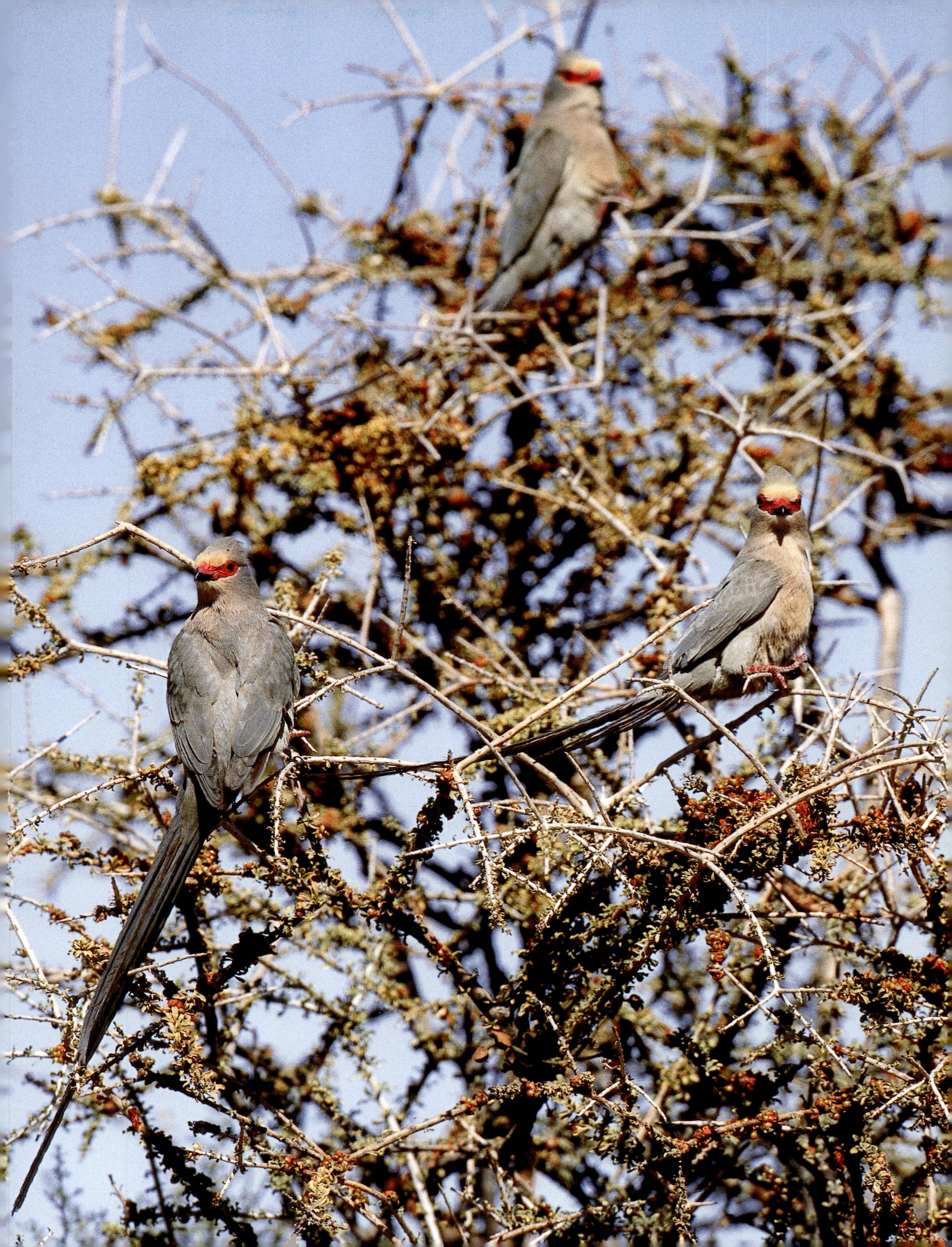

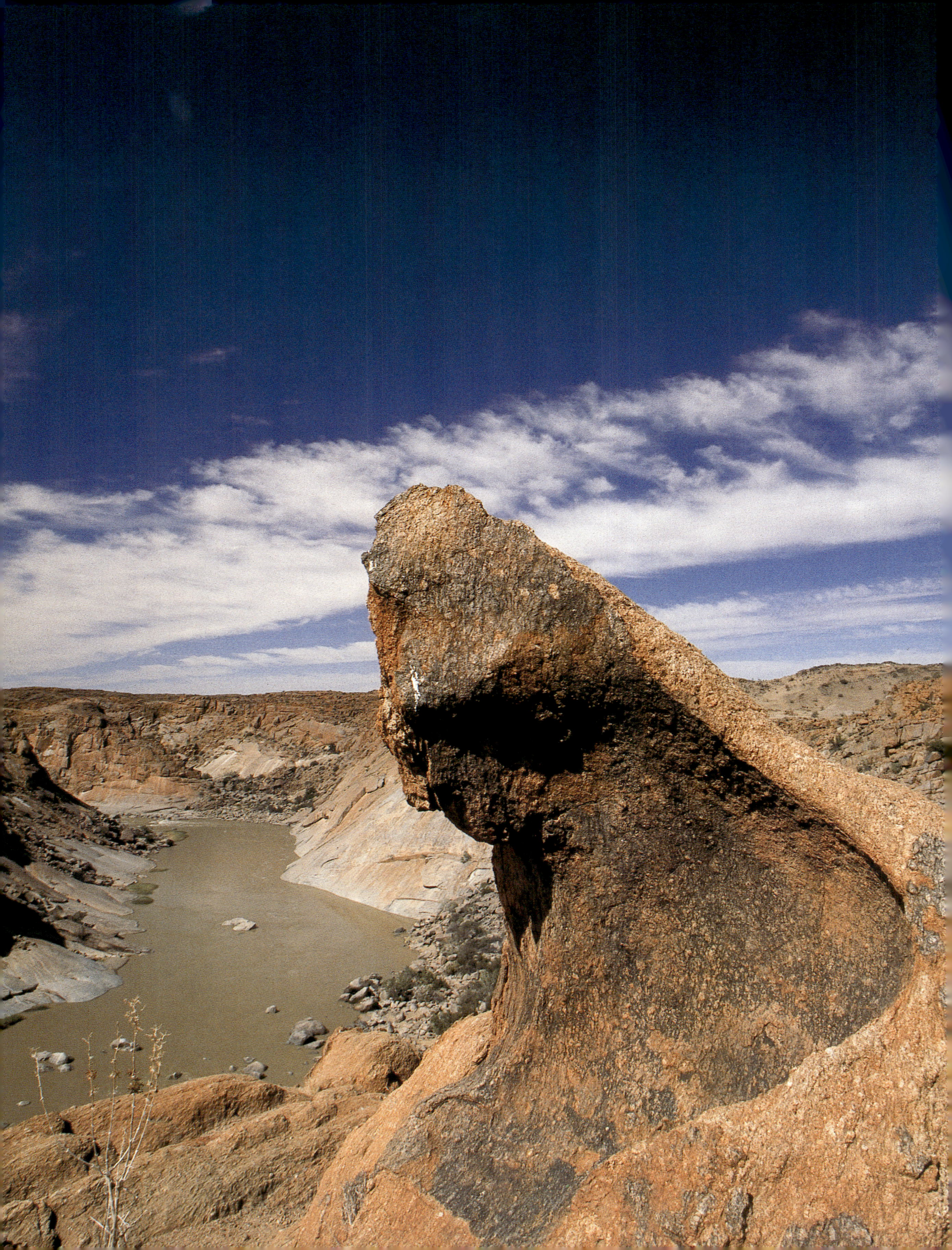

Northern Cape Province

Augrabies Falls National Park
"A river runs through it..."

The sun has just come up, yet the first rays are already burning as I enter the Augrabies Falls National Park, which adjoins the Namibian border. It is worth noting that it is not far from Upington, the town that every year holds the record for being the hottest place in South Africa. In a giant setting of pebbles and enormous blocks of granite – the park spreads over around 50,000 hectares – only the occasional bush or clump of grass are visible, as if as a reminder of the fact that life can still exist in this arid universe where the temperature of the rocks can sometimes reach 70 degrees.

The Augrabies Park is not a place one would at first glance classify as hospitable. The more so because the silence that normally reigns over stony desert is here disturbed by a distant muted rumble. A rumble, which, as I approach the canyon dividing the park, becomes a terrible roar. Evidently, Augrabies lives up to its name, inherited from the term khoi aukoerebis ("the land of great noise"). This din is that of the waters of the Orange River – the largest river in South Africa – which, at first calm and peaceful, dramatically drops 191 metres as a veritable wall of water. In bygone days, the Khoi did not dare approach the waterfall because it was said to shelter a terrible monster. It is true that the millions of cubic metres of water which crash heavily onto the granite below produce a dreadful racket.

It is easy to imagine how Hendrik Wikar, the Swedish deserter, having followed the Orange River, discovered this natural wonder in 1778. Nothing appears to have changed since, in this spectacular setting where, despite the hostility of the arid and rocky environment, many animals thrive. The star of this spot is the klipspringer, a graceful and vigorous small antelope, which has found its promised land in this craggy environment. I come across a family after a few hours' hike on the rocky slopes of the reserve. The klipspringer often shares this rugged land with rock hyraxes, which have colonised the terrain of the park, and especially the amazing "Moon Rock".

The climb up this gigantic dome of granite, which appears to have fallen from the sky, demands a colossal effort in such heat. I do not regret it: the highest point of the park, at a height of over 150 metres, this immense rounded block reveals an incredible panorama. In the distance the cloud of vapour released by the waterfall is visible; farther still the prominent Ararat rocks rise above the gorges they dominate. The spectacle is grandiose, almost excessive. From here, I look upon the waters of Orange River, which have regained their peaceful flow.

In this almost lunar scenery, only giraffes can look down (above).

After the fury of the falls, the waters of Orange River regain their calm. They flow peacefully at the bottom of the immense canyon of tortured landscapes (opposite).

The branches of a quiver tree, symbol of the region, were chosen by weavers as a site for their large, heavy nest (left).

In the rocky faces of the Augrabies, rock hyraxes have found a terrain in keeping with their agility (above).

A klipspringer has left its slope to nibble the young buds of a bush (opposite).

The waters of the Orange River make an incredible descent: hundreds of cubic metres of water per second are dropped into the valley of the canyon, 191 metres below (following pages).

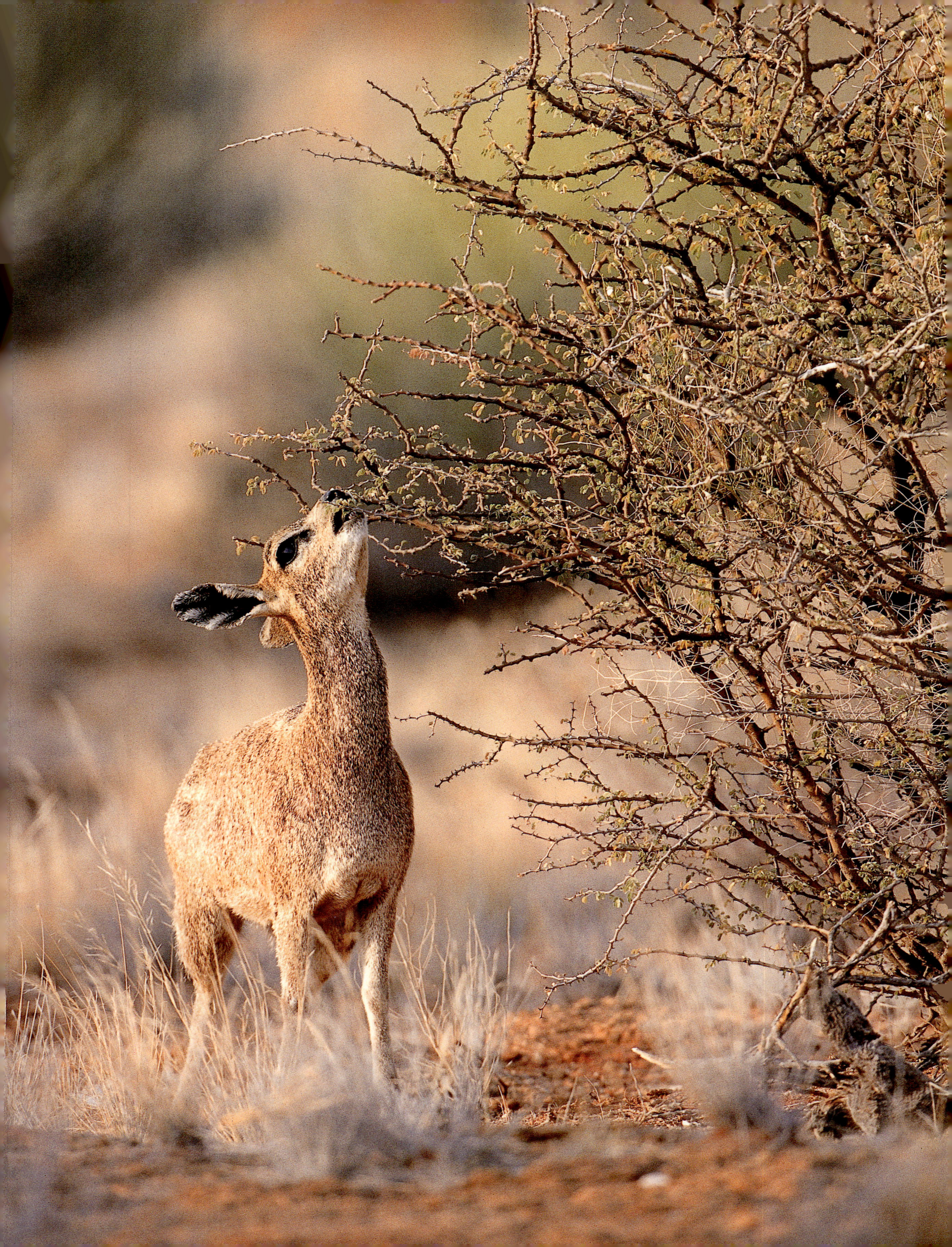

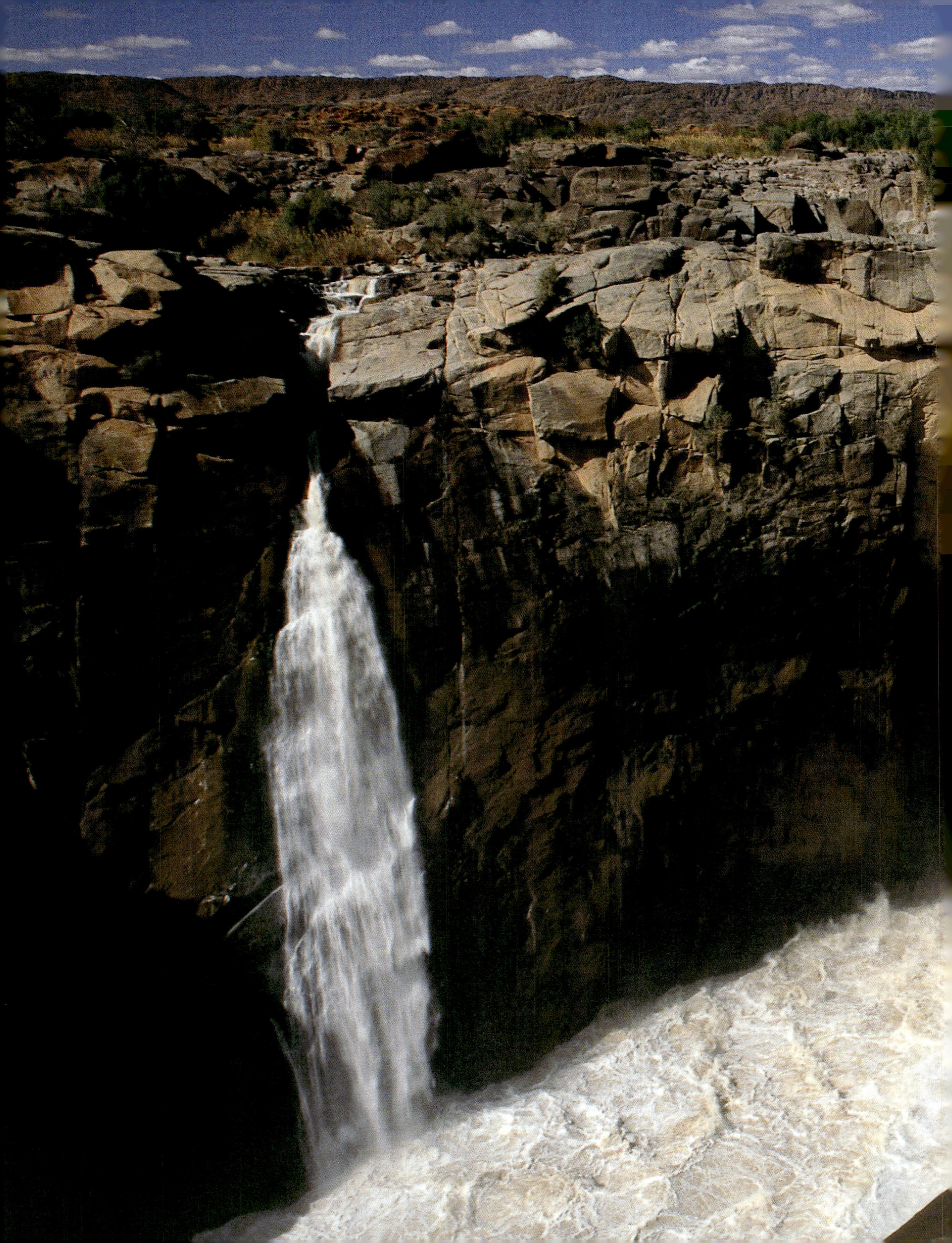

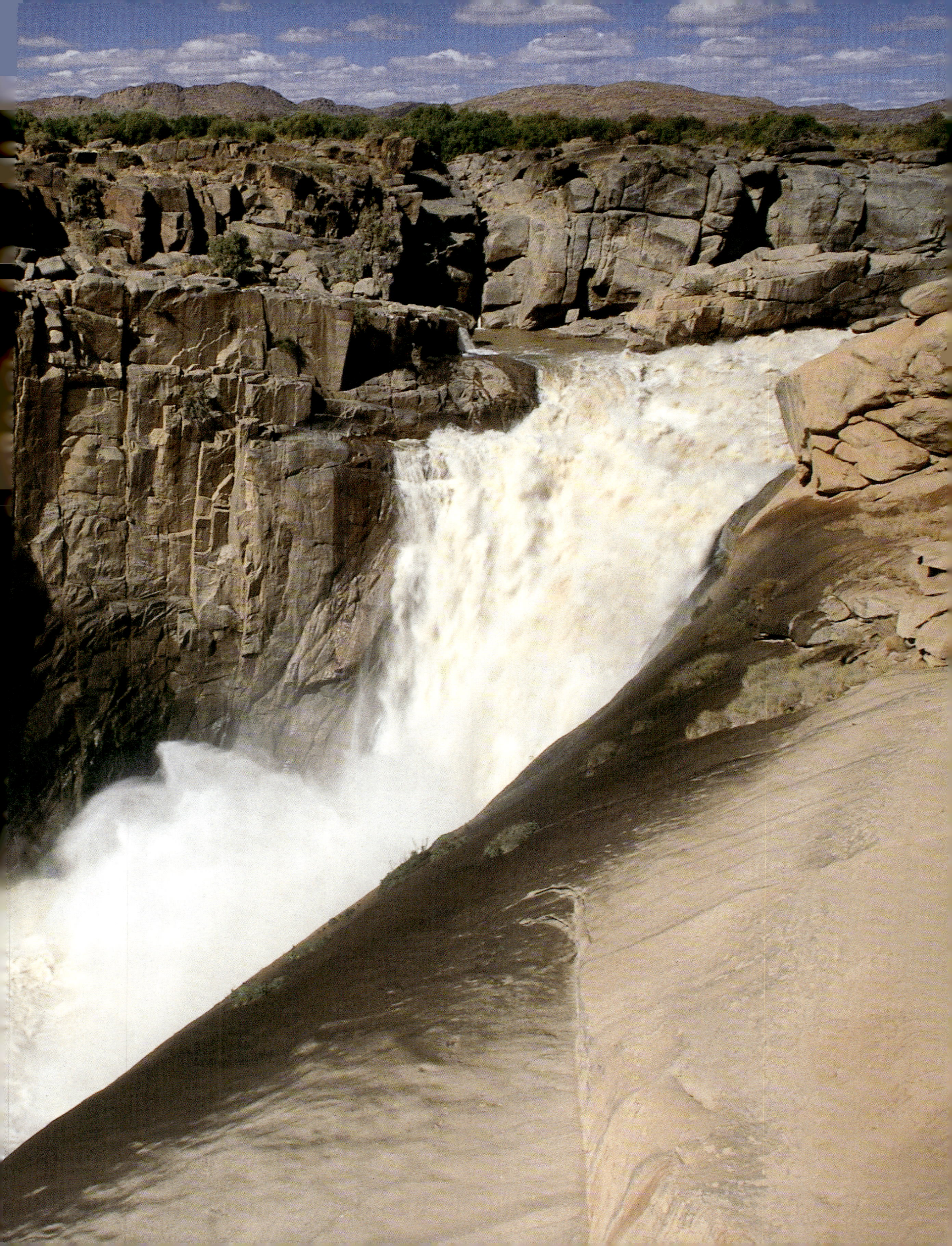

In a vast backdrop of pebbles and enormous blocks of granite, only the occasional bush or clump of grass is visible, as if a reminder of the fact that life can still exist in this arid universe.

The powerful waters of the Orange River have carved their bed into an arid landscape (above and right).

The quiver tree thrives in the dry, rocky ground of the Augrabies, and manages to develop on the steepest land (opposite).

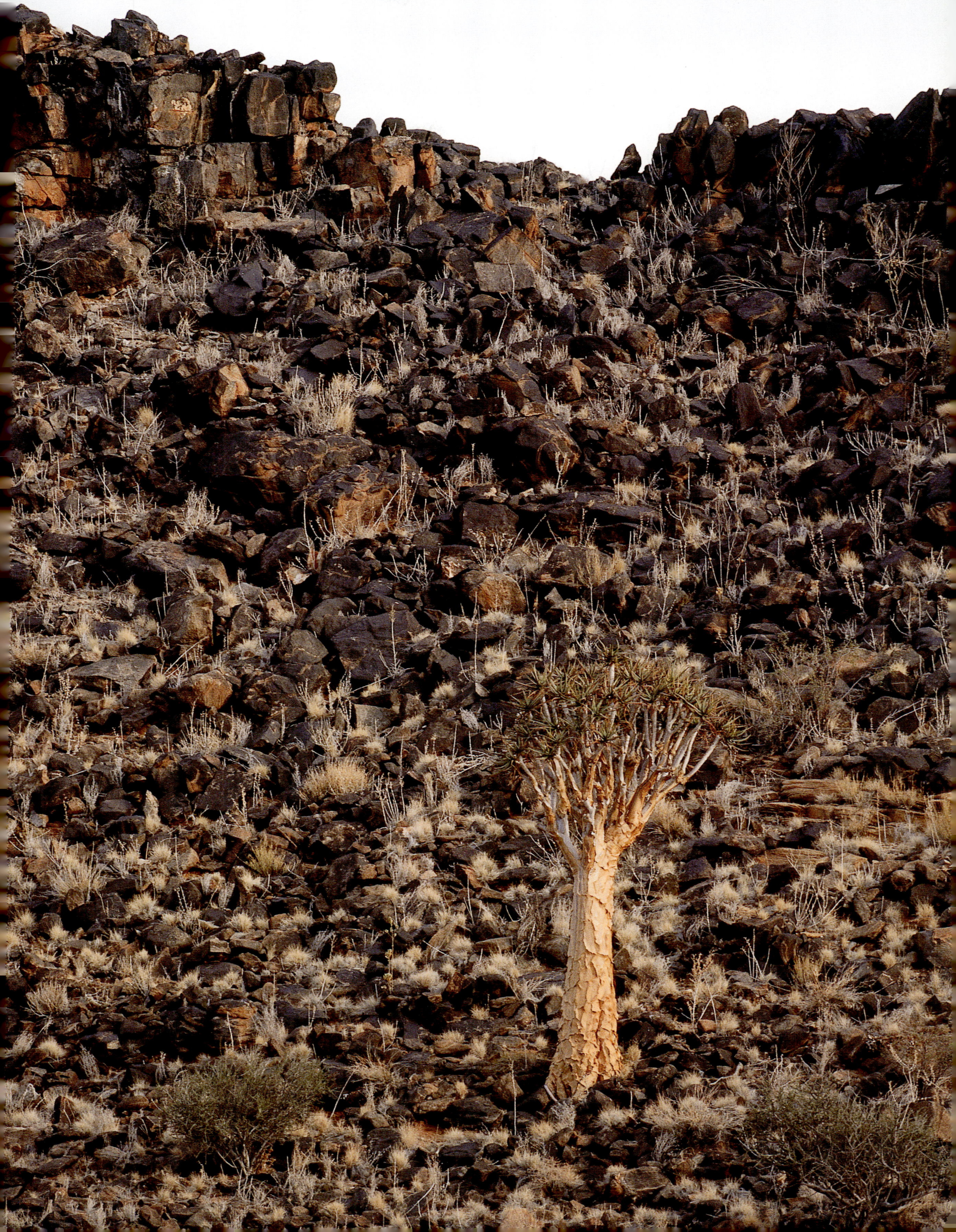

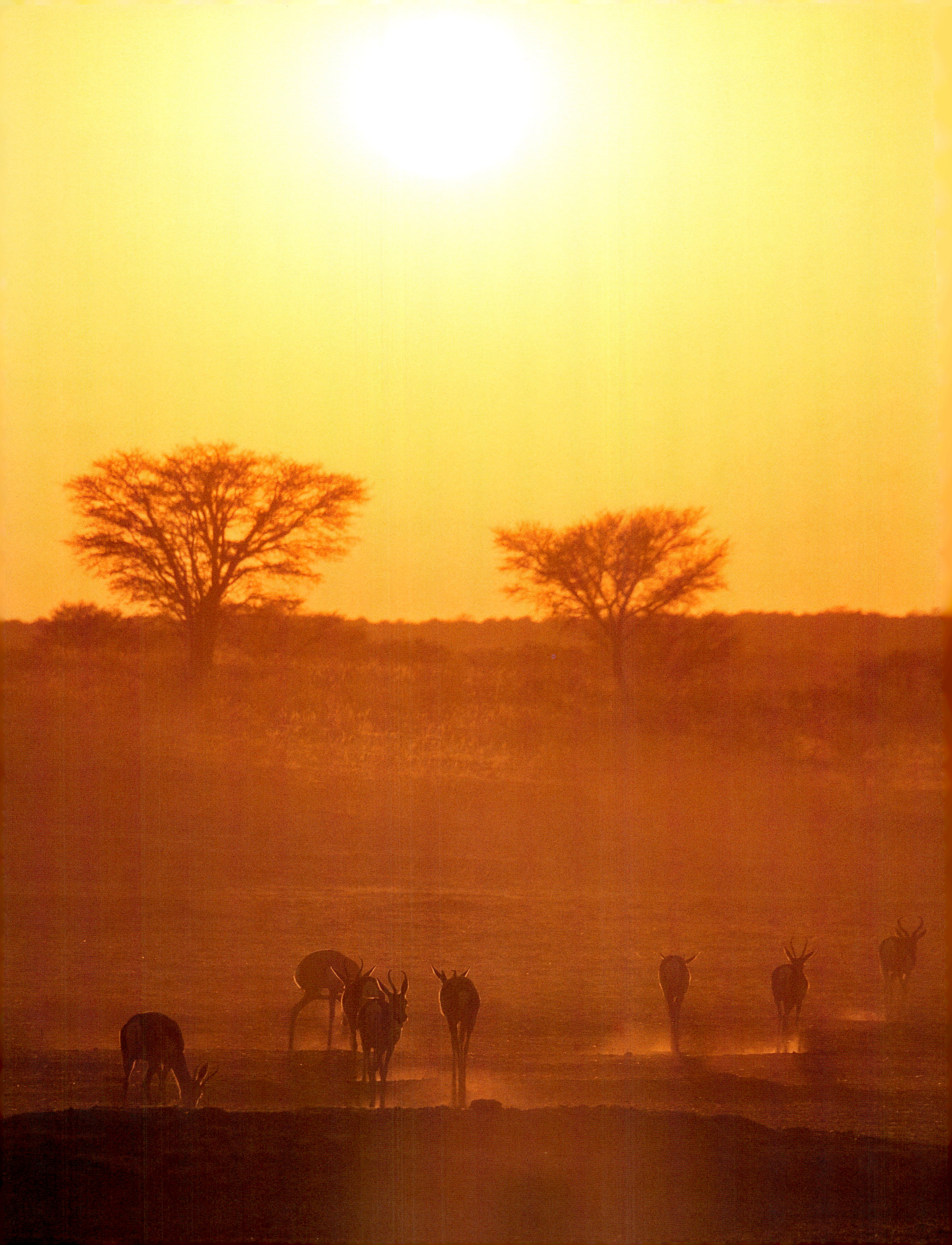

Northern Cape Province

Kgalagadi Transfrontier Park

As hot as hell

I have barely begun my day and already the thermometer reads almost 30 degrees in the Kalahari desert. How high will it climb? Up to 40 or 50? On the other hand, the nights are glacial, the mercury easily drops below zero, and I have difficulty coping with temperature changes as extreme as this. These difficult climatic conditions, which govern the desert, make the exploration of Kgalagadi Park a veritable act of courage, but also a true paradise for nature enthusiasts like me. No infrastructure, no roads have been created in this transfrontier park, which was renamed Kgalagadi Park in 1999, after its reunion with the Botswanian part of the Kalahari.

I leave Camp Nossob – one of the park's most sought-after observation points due to its central location – to travel north. I take a potholed track that runs alongside the watering holes built by the park authorities, the only way to ensure the survival of the herds of zebra, gnus and gemsbok, not to mention their predators. In fact, the lions have decided to rest near the Kwang watering hole. They hardly stir in the intense heat. These lions, renowned as being Africa's most impressive, are all the more imposing in that they are alone in occupying the watering hole, where plants hardly grow. The constraints of the climate have forced them to become better hunters than their cousins in neighbouring regions. Here, there is no question of letting any prey escape; expending that energy in this heat would put its survival and that of the pack at risk. Last night's hunt must have been meagre as the stomachs of the big cats appear to be empty. They seem to be looking for a spot of shade around the watering hole, where they will have to wait for an error of judgement by a thirsty antelope to provide them with a good feed.

Later I catch sight of another feline: the African wildcat, which only Kgalagadi, thanks to its isolation, can protect from breeding with domesticated cats. The large male, perched upon a branch that offers both shade and an ideal look-out point, waits for nightfall to hunt for prey. Perhaps it will be the burrowing squirrel whose lair is near by. As I approach the north of the park, I am witness to an act of rebellion: a honey badger rushes towards the gemsbok at the watering hole, before finally attacking… a signpost! It is true that the sign spoils this untouched universe, but this creature seems to have developed an almost obsessive dislike for it. Once again the rule of law prevails: after a good hour of effort, the badger capitulates and returns to whence he came.

These magical visions of wildlife make the Kalahari a legendary place, yet the harsh climate keeps visitors away. A trip into the desert is well worthwhile, and the privileged few, who – like me – have had the possibility to watch a supernatural sunset over this vast savannah, will not contradict me.

Crossing the desert, a kori bustard is searching for food (above).

The springbok, constantly hunted by the most determined predators, owe their salvation to a quick escape at a speed that can reach up to 95 km per hour (opposite and following pages).

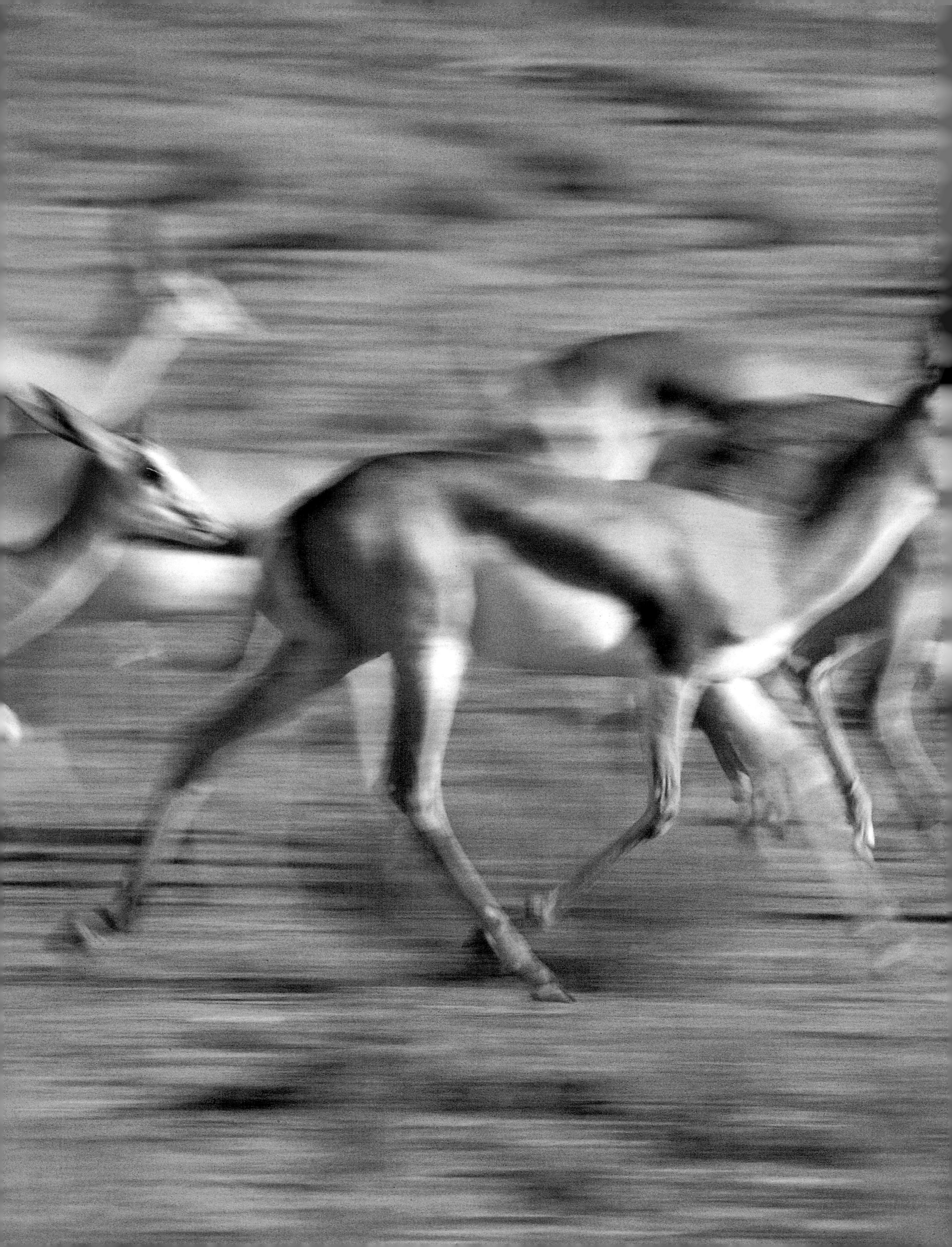

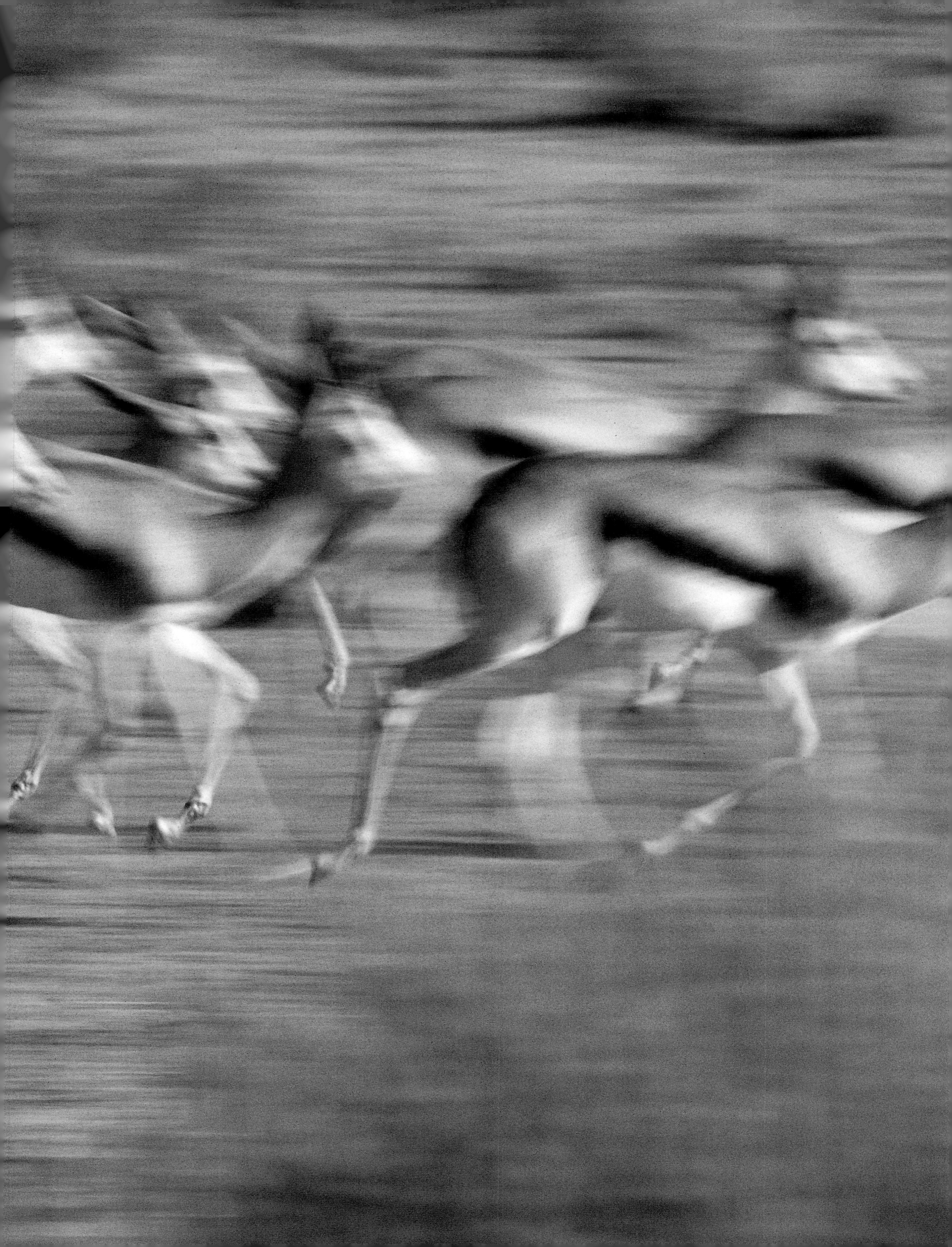

The gemsbok is an antelope that is particularly well adapted to the extreme conditions of the Kgalagadi Park. It can go without water for several days (left).

An ostrich protects its eggs. Male and female take it in turns to shade the eggs with their feathers; otherwise they would cook in the sweltering sun (below).

In order to protect itself from the sun, the Cape burrowing squirrel uses its bushy tail as a sunshade (opposite).

I take a potholed track that runs alongside the watering holes built by the park authorities to ensure the survival of the herds of zebra, gnus and gemsbok, not to mention their predators.

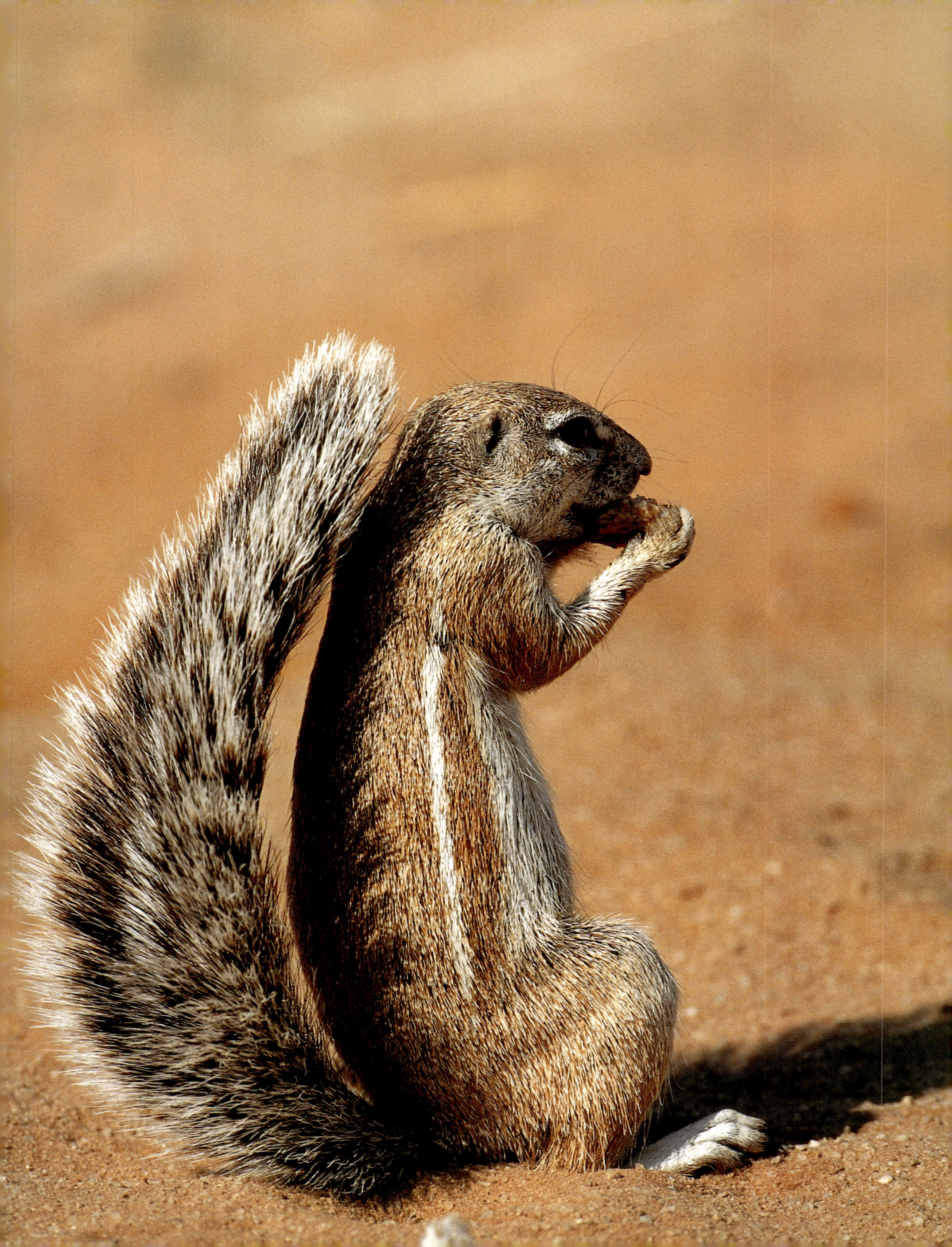

The Kalahari lion has a fearsome reputation because the harshness of the living conditions of the desert allows it no margin of error in the hunt (below).

Comfortably installed on a branch, an African wildcat waits for a rat, a mouse or a bird to pass within reach of its claws. This is a rare species of cat, whose last survivors are only to be found in the Kgalagadi (opposite, top).

The brown hyena acts as the cleaner of the desert. Even though it does hunt, it prefers festering leftovers from other predators. It is capable of grinding and digesting the largest bones, something no other animal can do (opposite, bottom).

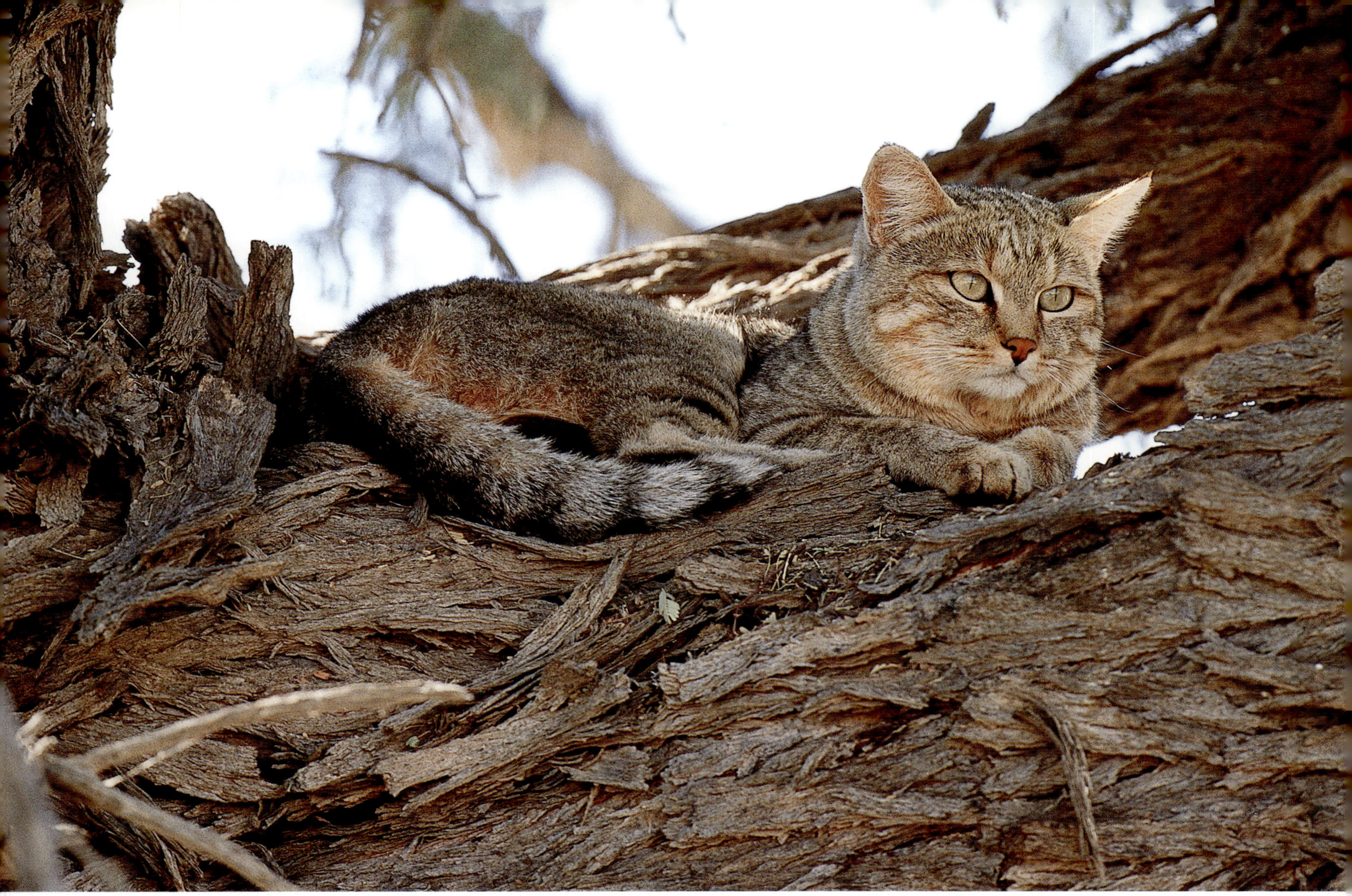

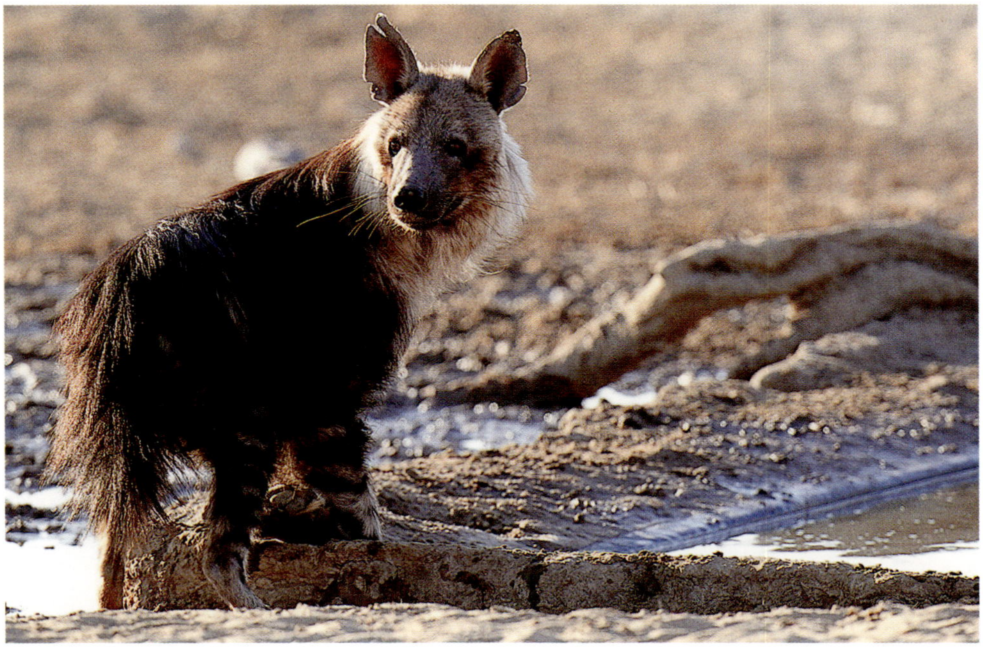

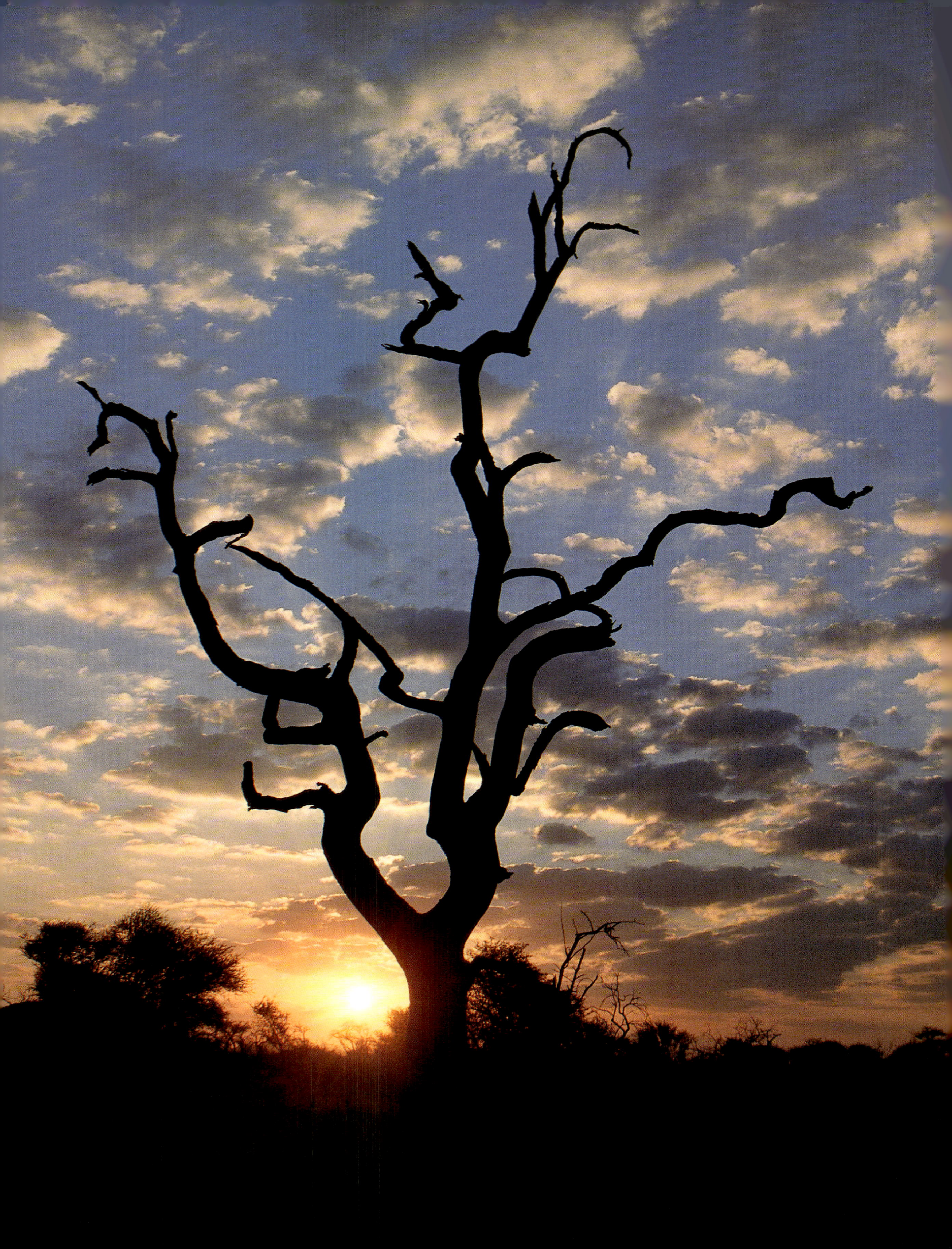

North West Province

Madikwe Game Reserve
A savage Eden

It is five in the morning; the incessant birdsong rouses me from sleep. I get up quickly because I do not want to miss the awakening of the wildlife and leave the base camp where I had chosen to stay, in the immense Madikwe Reserve. Outside, I witness an enchanting and incredible display of birds. They have come to drink at one of the watering holes built for the observation of the numerous animals that populate the vast spaces of this savannah.

Created almost 15 years ago, the Madikwe Reserve covers 61,000 hectares and contains countless treasures. When it opened its gates in 1989, on the initiative of the North West Province authorities, its mission was to save a weakened ecosystem and to ensure the protection of fauna reintroduced into its natural habitat, while working closely with the inhabitants. The vast territory, which borders Botswana, offers little more than poor pastureland to the herds, and is barely able to feed the native population. Today, thanks to the opening of the Madikwe Reserve, visitors from around the world flock to this exceptionally beautiful wilderness area, and the reserve has become a source of employment and income for the local population.

It is daybreak in Madikwe and a dazzling light reigns over the vast plains of bush savannah, dominated by a gentle volcanic relief. The observation point I have chosen is near a watering hole and it becomes, as the hours pass, the scene of a continuous procession of gnus, zebras, giraffes, antelopes and rhinos that stroll slowly and solemnly before my eyes. Suddenly a quick, lively movement disturbs the tranquillity of the herds; in the distance I catch sight of a strange little animal with a pointed nose, and black, white and ochre speckled fur. It has enormous ears. From a distance, its silhouette resembles as much that of a dog as that of a hyena. I approach slowly, gently, without a sound and a few metres farther on, I discover a pack of African wild dogs. These canines are in fact lycaons, and the reserve houses some of the last survivors in the wild.

Tonight I may have the chance to meet, among the park's important population of felines dominated by the lions, the extremely rare caracal. Here, this rather discreet nocturnal predator has found a territory in keeping with its hunting abilities. The small rodents and guinea-fowl offer plenty of possibilities for food. Yet the spectacle has started again, and I leave my shelter to observe the arrival of a family of elephants.

The southern yellow-billed hornbill is one of the reserve's most common feathered inhabitants (above).

The Madikwe Reserve contains a large number of dead trees, which extend their branches to the sky as if to implore the sun to stay a little longer over this savage Eden (opposite).

A few minutes more, and the sun will have totally disappeared behind the hills that surround the watering hole (following pages).

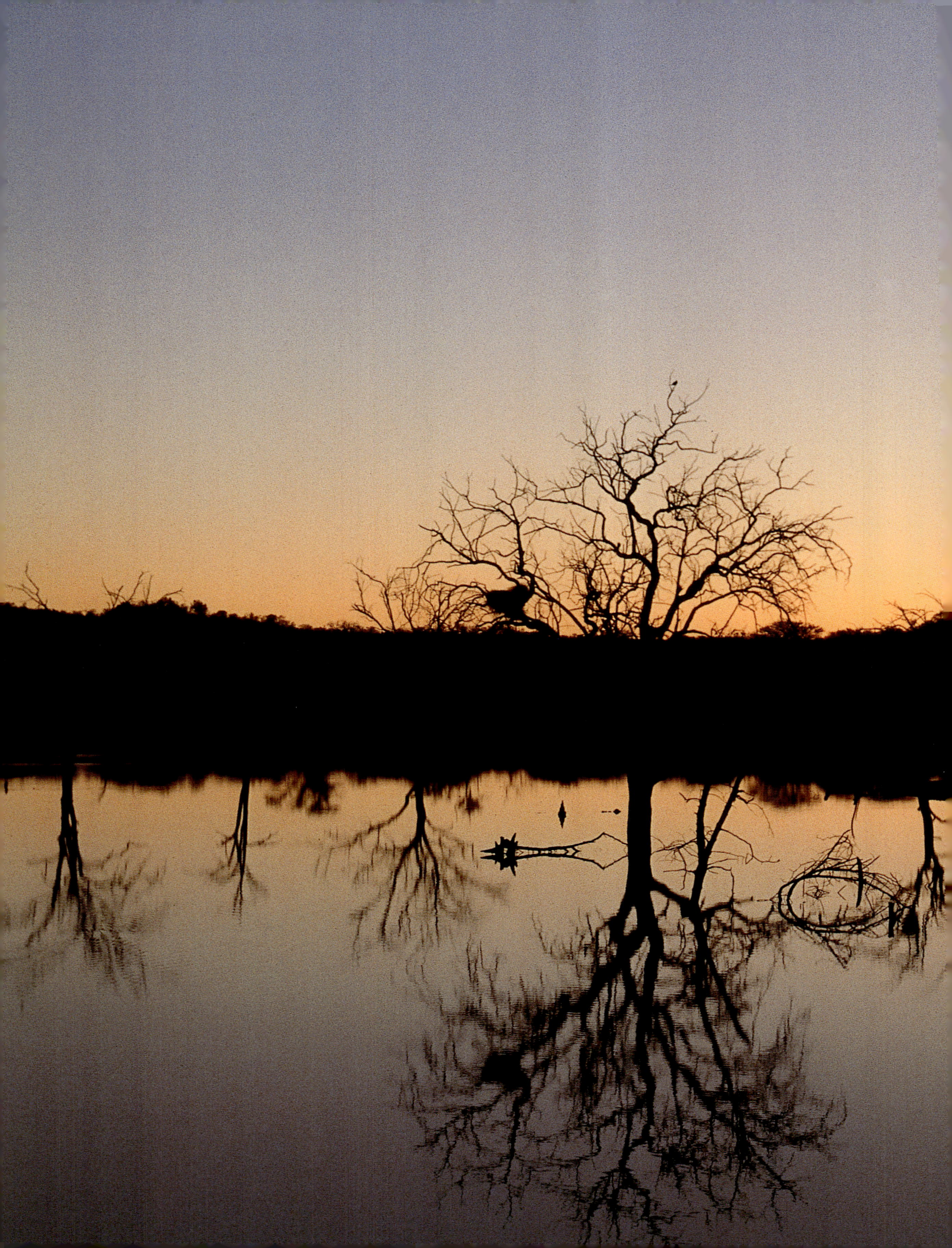

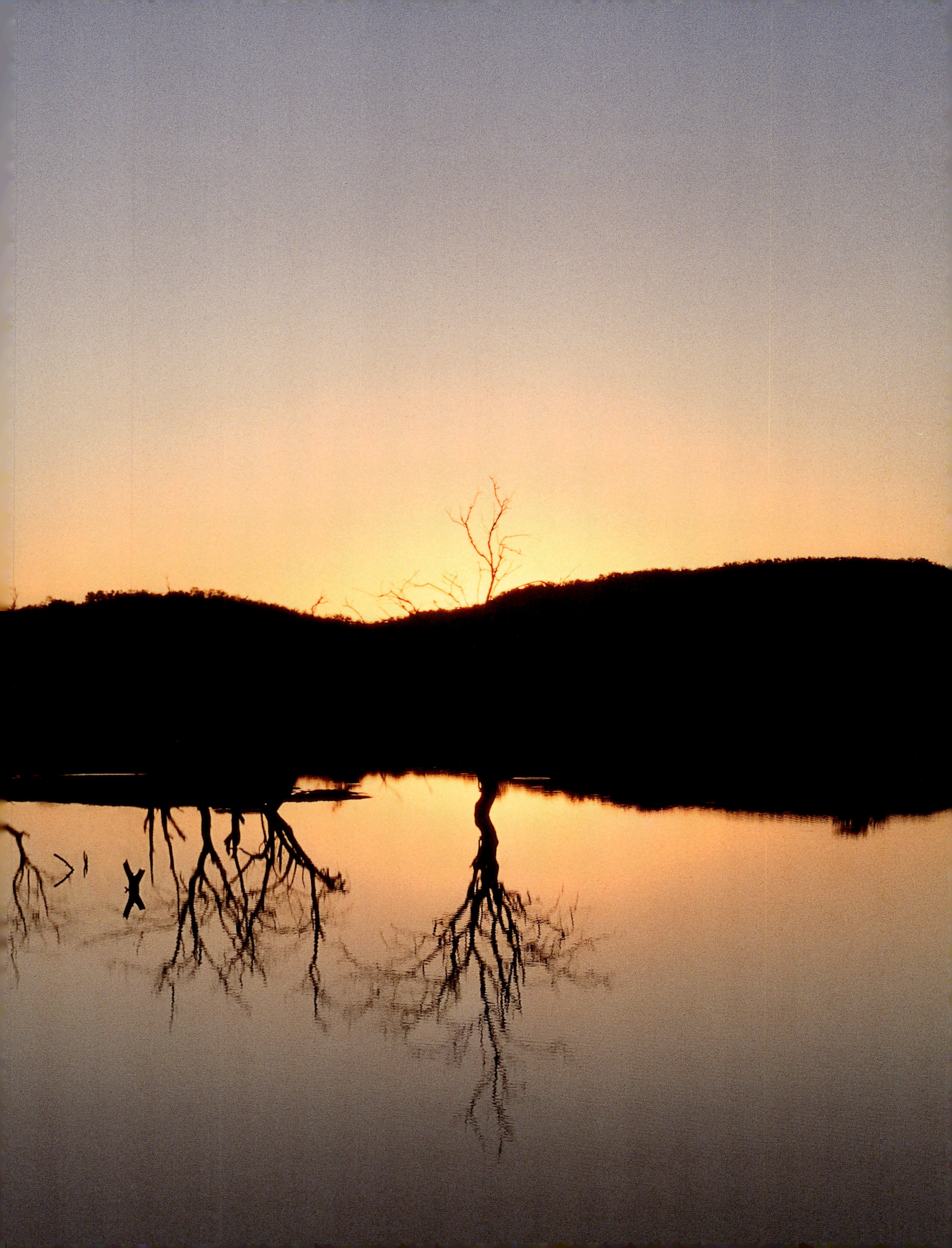

There are many lions in the Madikwe Reserve, despite the fact that they do not live in large families as in other natural parks. Here it is common to meet isolated individuals like this lioness, who rests having hunted a warthog (above).

The white rhino is one of the heavy-weight residents of the reserve. Even if it appears docile, beware of its horn (right)!

In the plains of the reserve, a giraffe comes to water, profiting from the late afternoon calm (opposite).

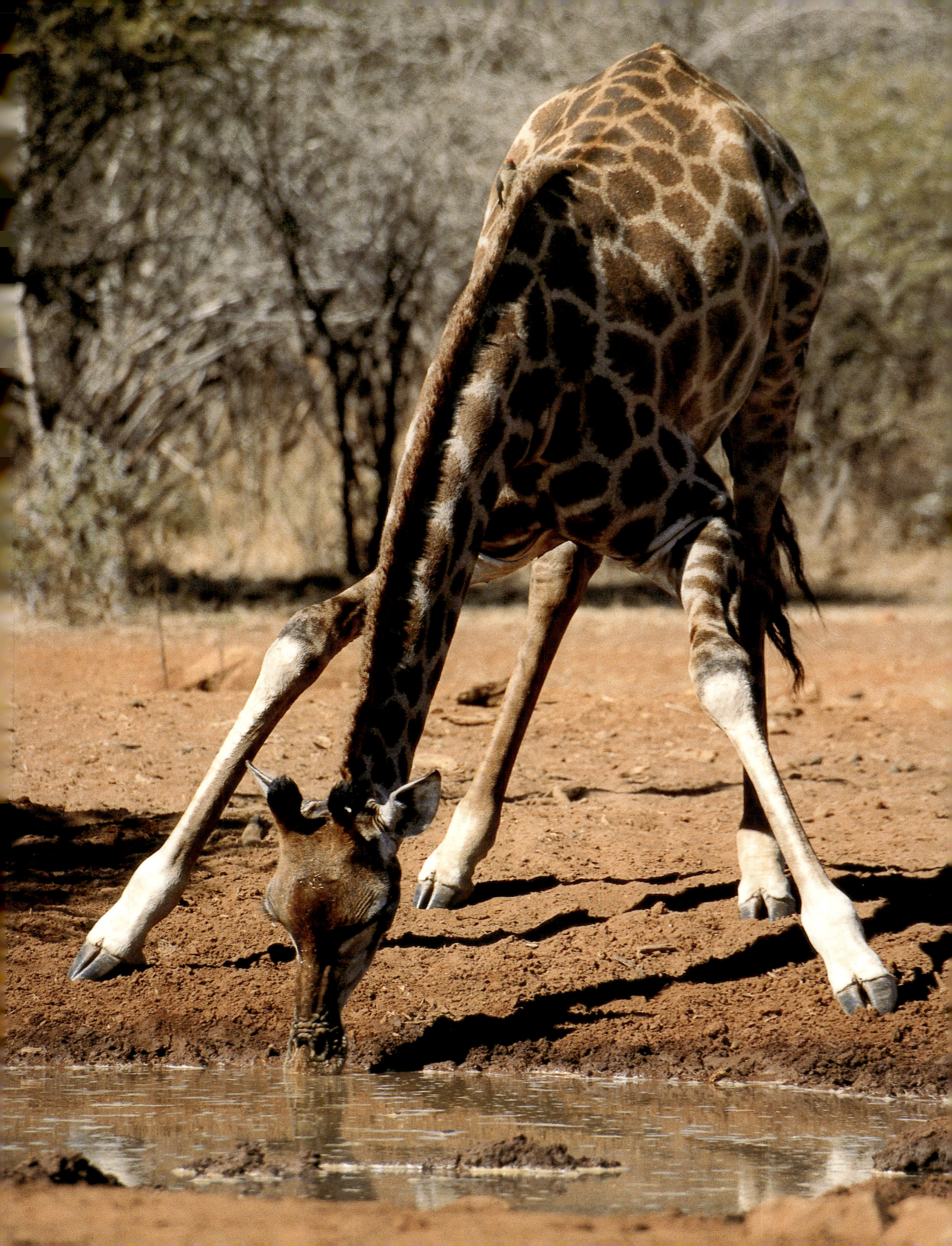

The eagle and the cobra

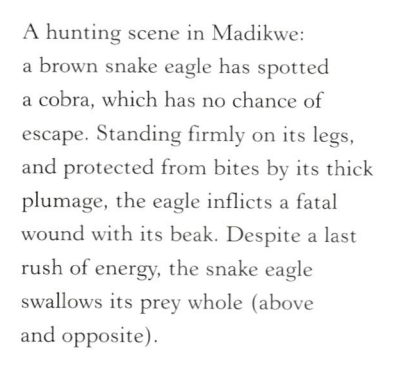

A hunting scene in Madikwe:
a brown snake eagle has spotted
a cobra, which has no chance of
escape. Standing firmly on its legs,
and protected from bites by its thick
plumage, the eagle inflicts a fatal
wound with its beak. Despite a last
rush of energy, the snake eagle
swallows its prey whole (above
and opposite).

Gemsbok often travel in small groups.
The vigilance of each individual –
indispensable when one is aware
of the number of predators –
is necessary for the survival
of the group (following pages).

THE MADIKWE GAME RESERVE | 173

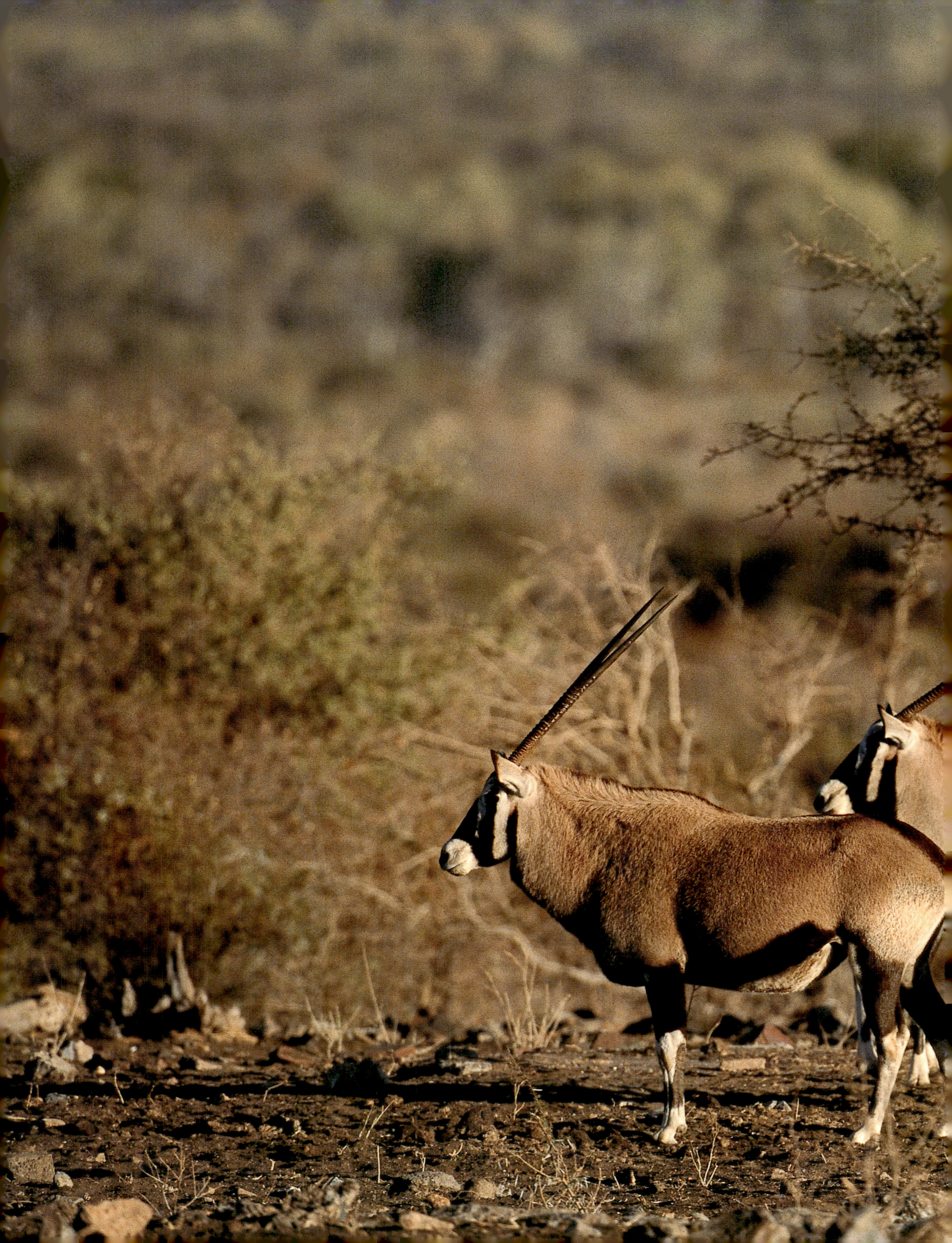

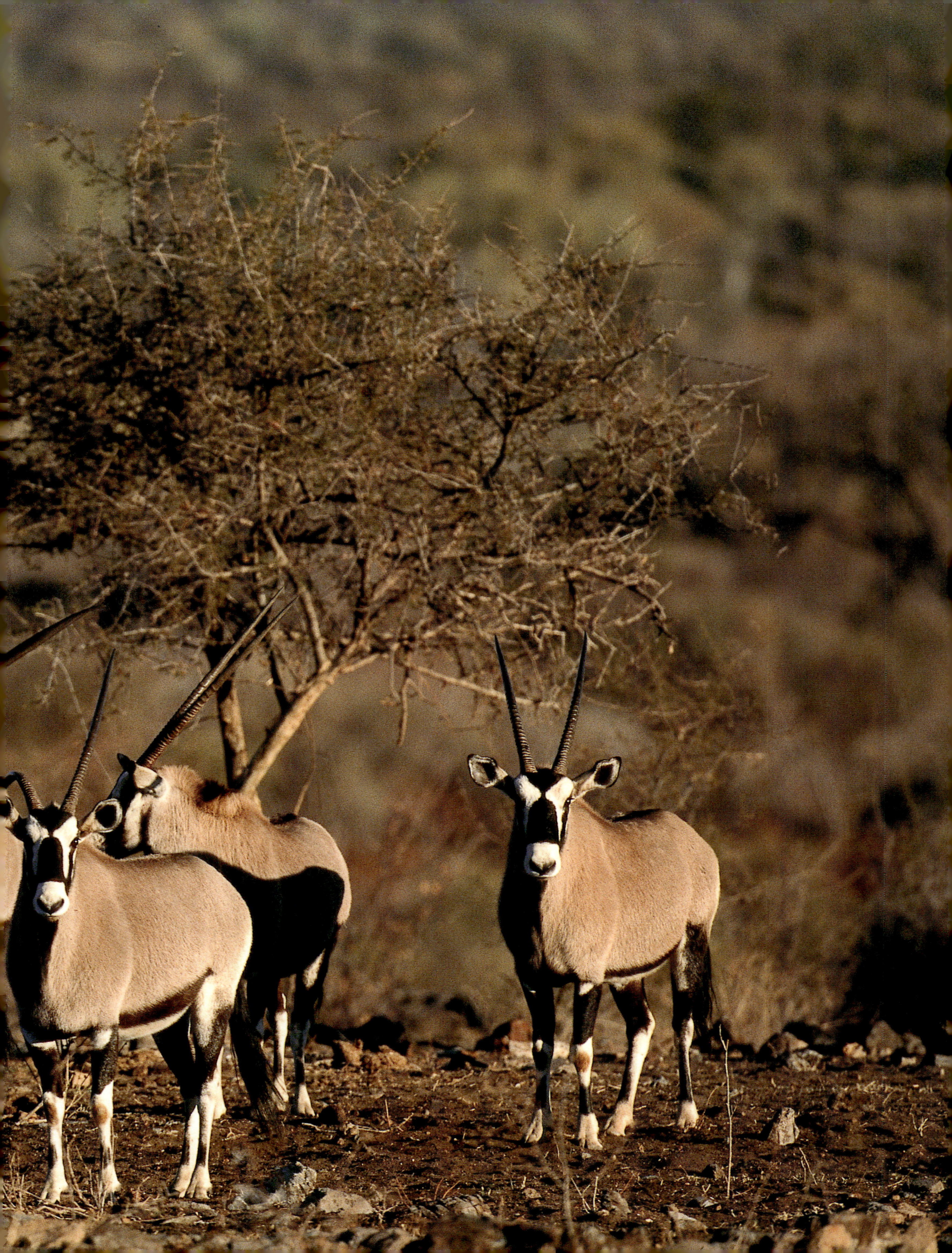

The Madikwe Reserve shelters the last populations of lycaons, a strange little animal with a pointed nose, and black, white and ochre speckled fur.

The lycaon is an emblematic figure for the reserve, which assured its reintroduction, and provides an exciting wildlife spectacle for visitors. Families of these hunting dogs, which were threatened with extinction, have begun to produce young, a sure sign that they have found ideal conditions for their survival (above, right and opposite).

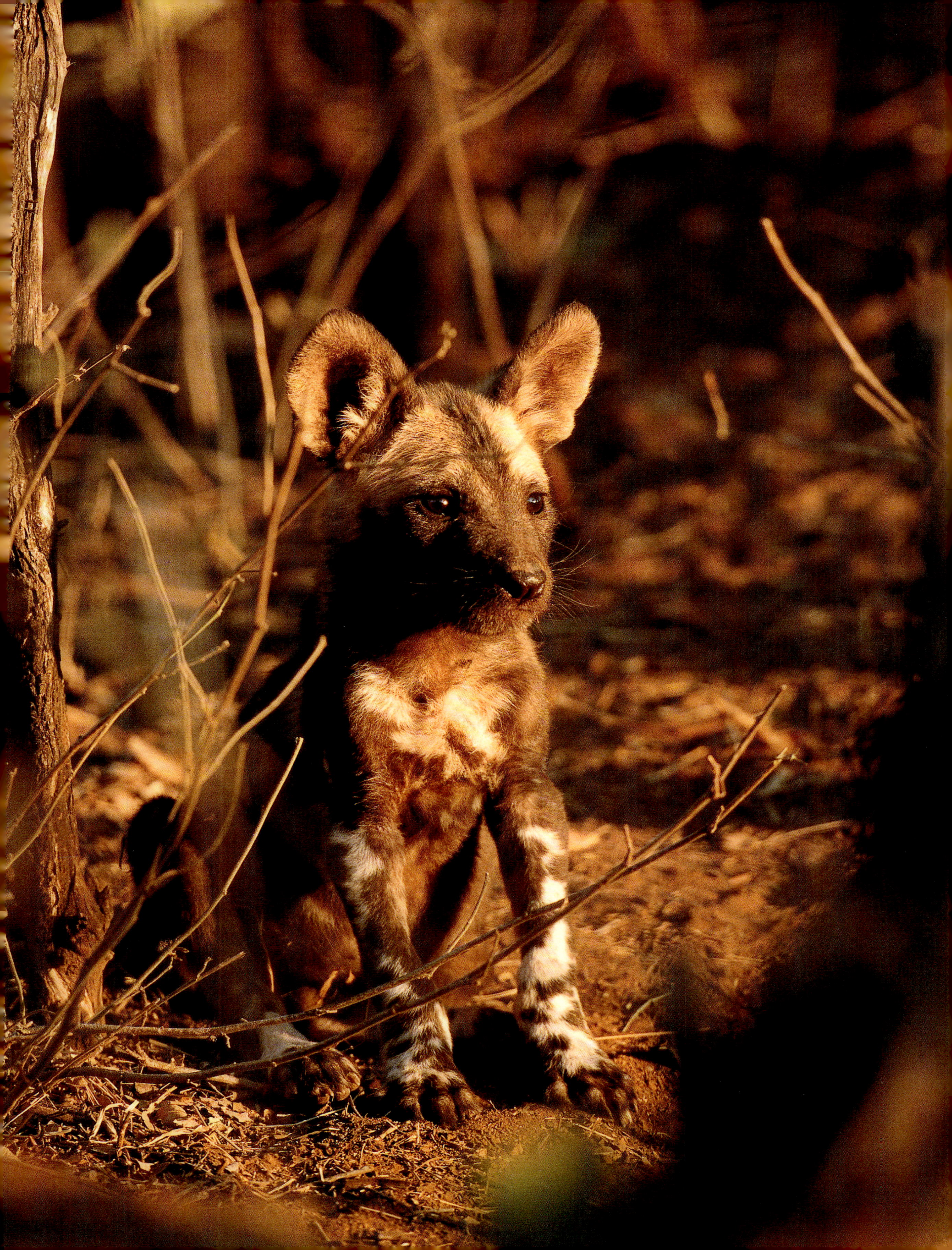

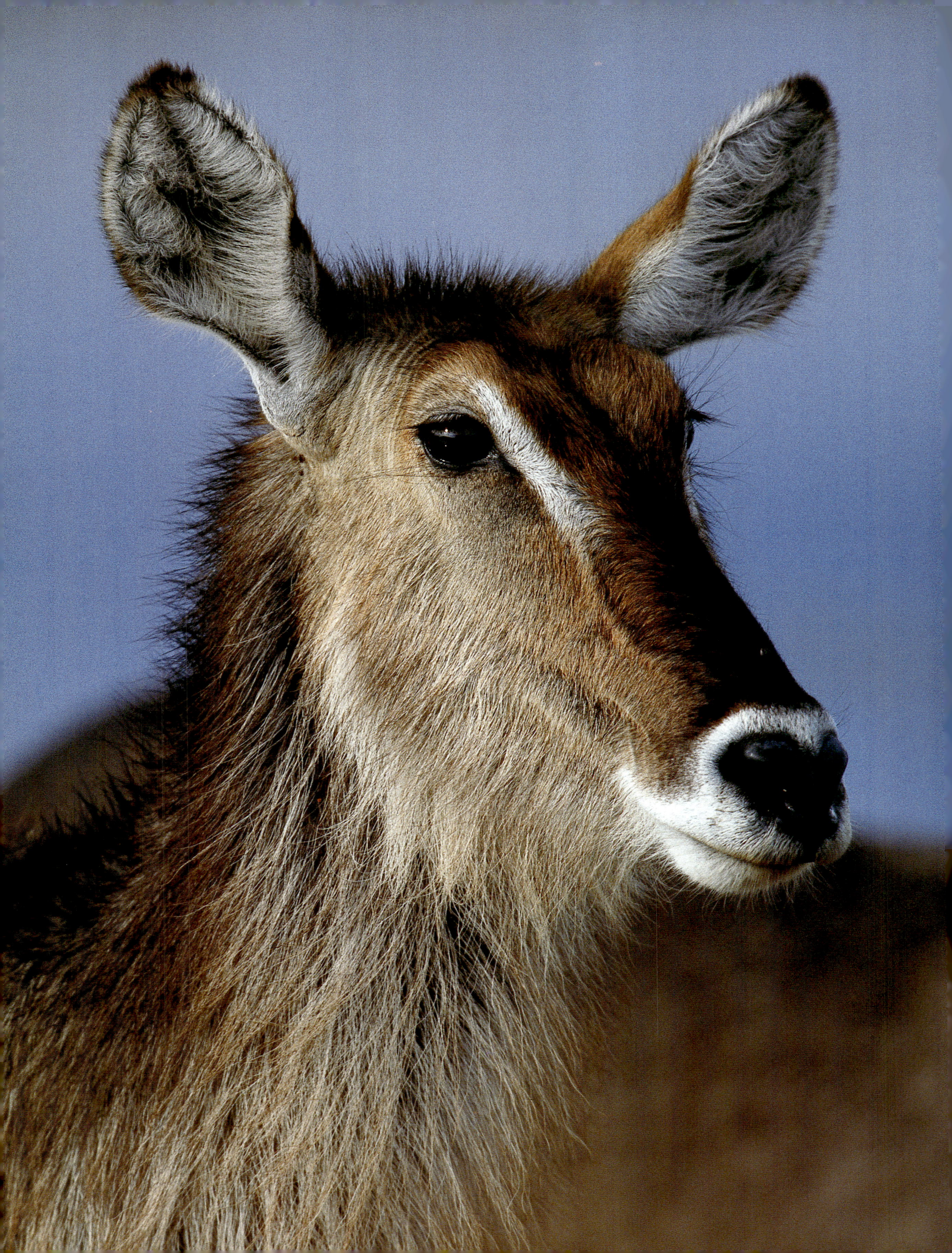

North West Province

Pilanesberg National Park
Noah's Ark

Not far from Pretoria, the Pilanesberg National Park is conspicuously absent from most of the South African tourist circuits. And yet this beautiful park, far easier to access than the distant Kruger Park, is held in high esteem by many South Africans, and offers extraordinary scope for watching animals in a majestic setting. I must admit that, of all the parks I have visited during my long stay in South Africa, Pilanesberg is one of the reserves which charmed me the most, especially when I learned about the circumstances of its creation.

In the fantastic natural setting, with its chain of dormant volcanoes, farmers coexisted with an enormous mining industry. One could have, with reason, questioned the idea of creating a natural park on such land, and yet this is what was done. At the end of ten years of effort, during which people and industry were obliged to erase any trace of their presence, the Pilanesberg National Park came into being. The curators even went as far as replanting the indigenous vegetation, after removing man-made landscapes. Then, having fenced the 50,000 hectares of park near a few villages, Operation Genesis was launched, reintroducing 19 species of animal, that is, almost 6,000 individuals. This was the most important programme of animal displacement ever undertaken, enough to make Noah green with envy!

Crossing the Pilanesberg, I admire the scale of the work undertaken and I understand the success it enjoys. In this place of simply magnificent landscapes, I am able to observe, at very close quarters and without having to travel long distances, numerous animals such as white rhinos who have found refuge here, and large elephant families. On the banks of Lake Mankwe, in the centre of Pilanesberg, I even surprise giraffes peeling young acacia buds, without worrying about the crocodiles or hippos bathing nearby. At night, I also hear the roar of a lion, and the cries of hyenas. But there is, above all, the immense pleasure of seeing that savannah sprinter, a cheetah, chasing its prey over the large grassy plains overlooked by the volcanic landscape.

The Pilanesberg Park is proof that, if he so desires, man can influence nature in a positive way, and the reserve provides an example for others to follow.

Perched on the branch of a dead tree on the edge of Lake Mankwe, kingfishers watch the waters, denying any fish the chance of escape (above).

The waterbuck is one of the many species to have been reintroduced into the Pilanesberg Park (opposite).

A village weaver occupies itself with the construction of its nest. For birds, the mating season is the occasion for keen competition among the males. He, who has built the best nest, will win the female's favour (left).

A cattle egret hunts the frogs and toads that populate the banks of Lake Mankwe (above).

The starling is one of the most common birds of Pilanesberg. The metallic reflection of its feathers changes colour depending on the bird's relative position to the sun (opposite).

Thanks to Operation Genesis, the caldera of Pilanesberg has returned to it original wild state. In the middle of these dormant volcanoes, Lake Mankwe has become a mecca for a multitude of animals (following pages).

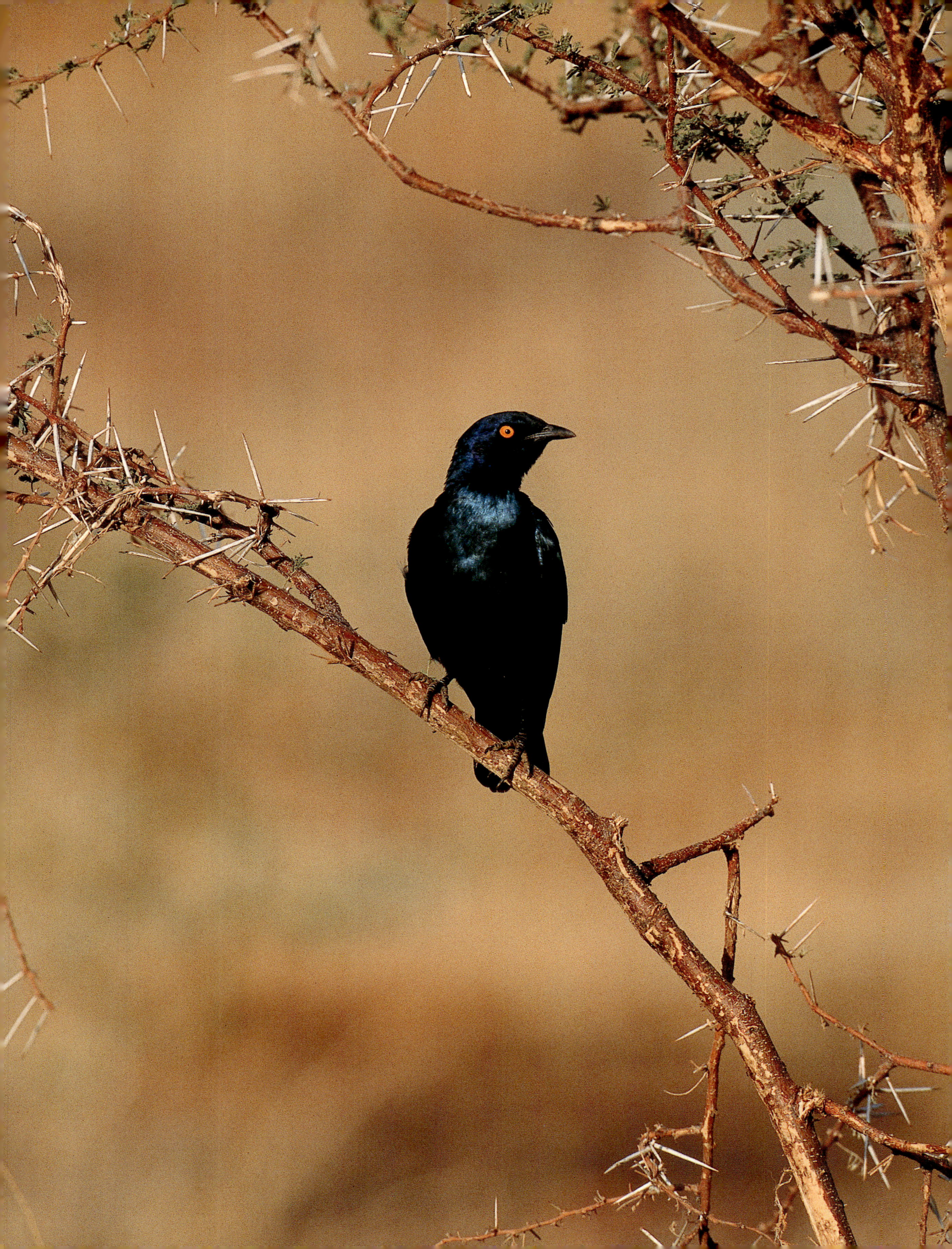

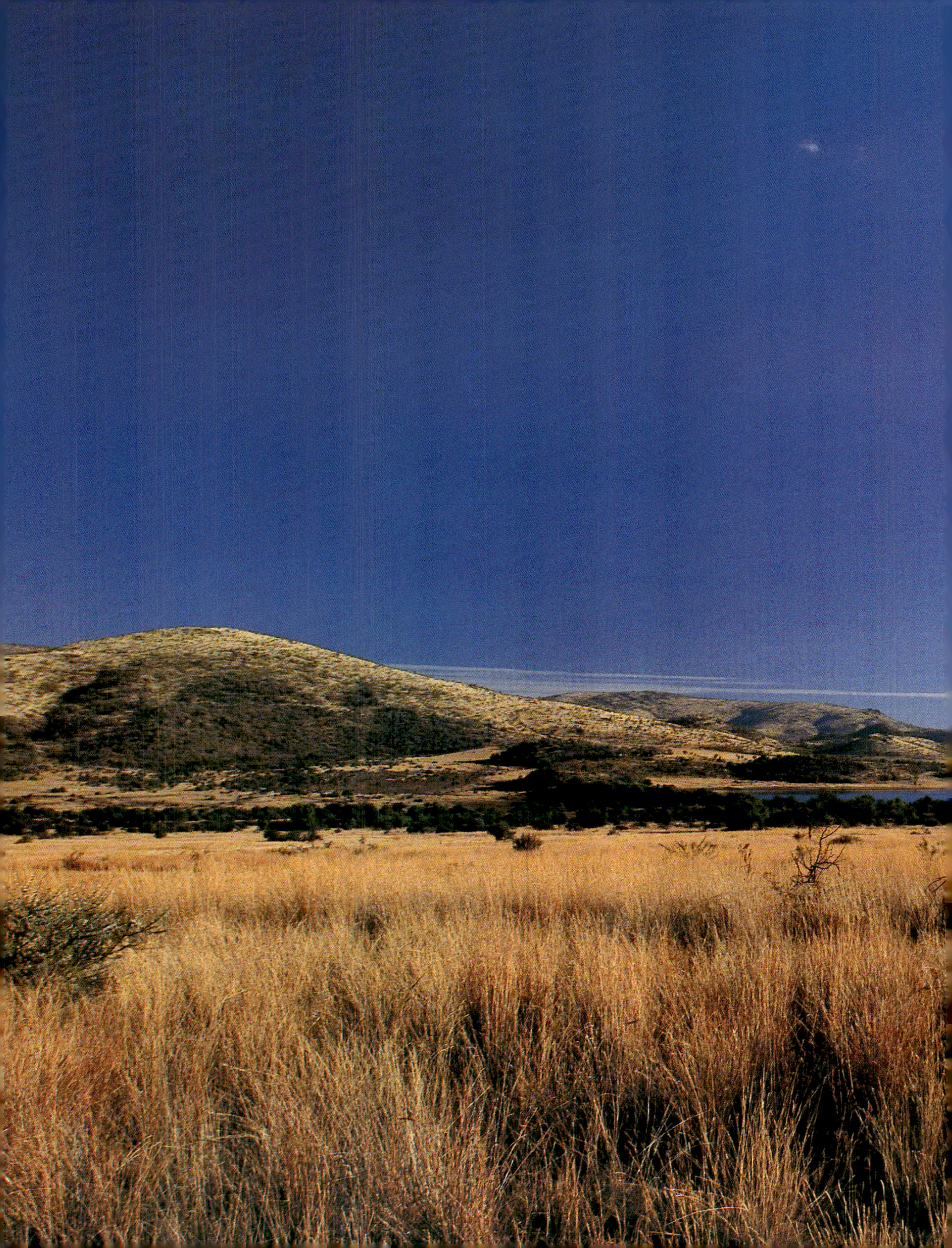

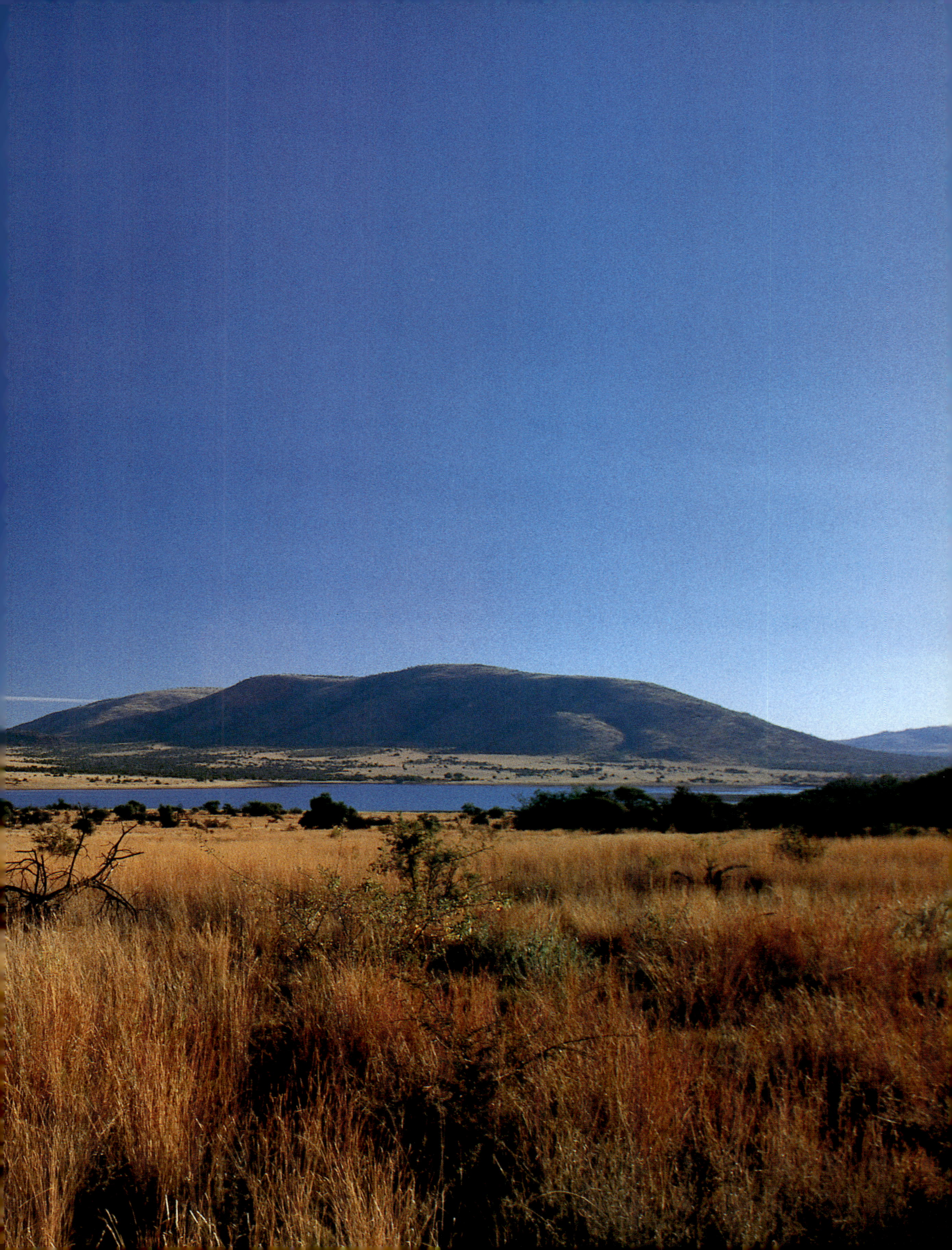

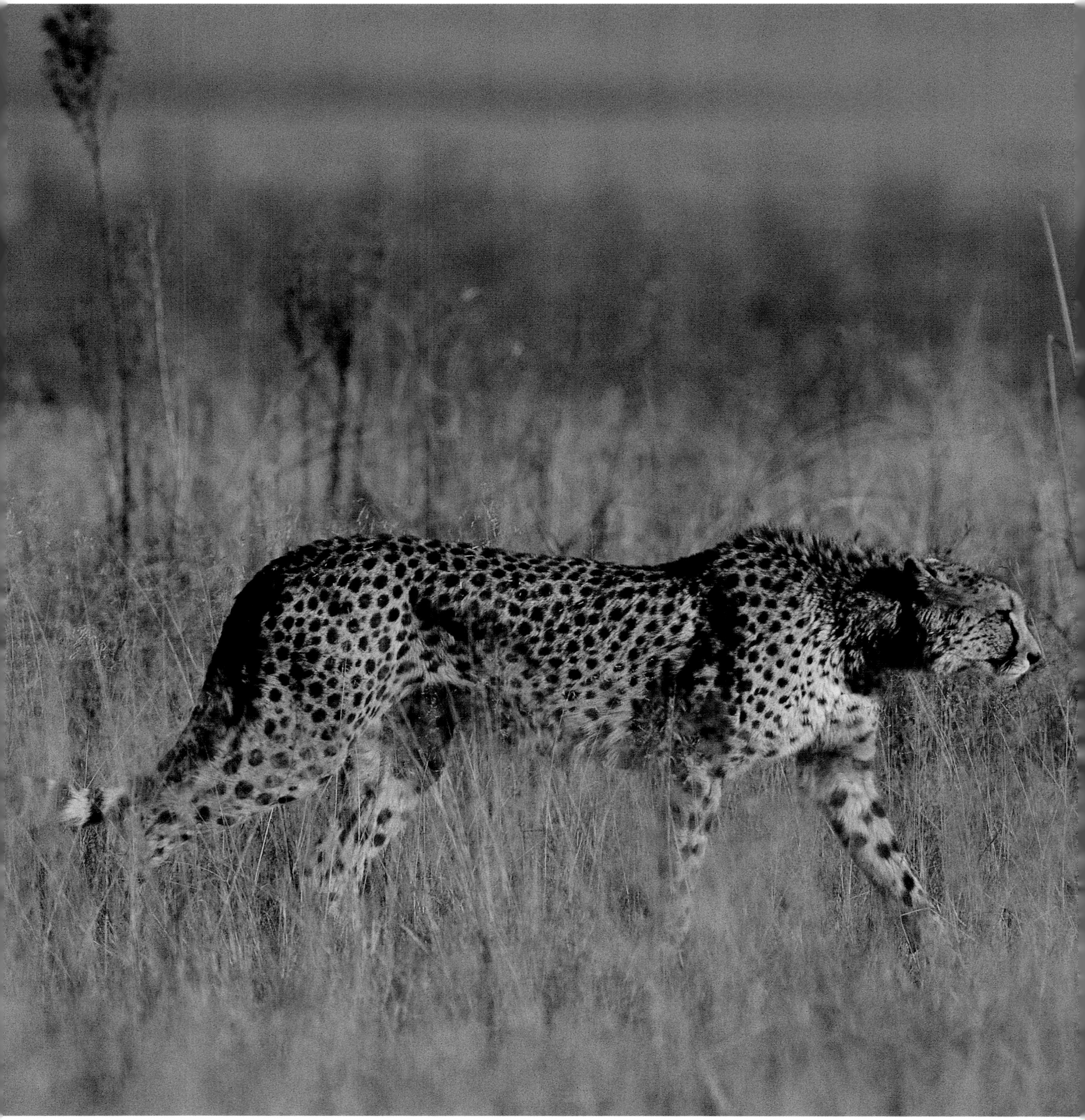

The cheetah prefers discretion.
The high grass does not help me
to observe this feline, which is able
to conceal itself and pursue its prey
at high speed (left).

Perched on the lookout upon a rock,
a springbok keeps out of the reach
of predators, while the impalas
are on the alert (top and above).

The sun sets on the banks
of Lake Mankwe, in the middle
of Pilanesberg. Night will soon
fall upon the natural world
(following pages).

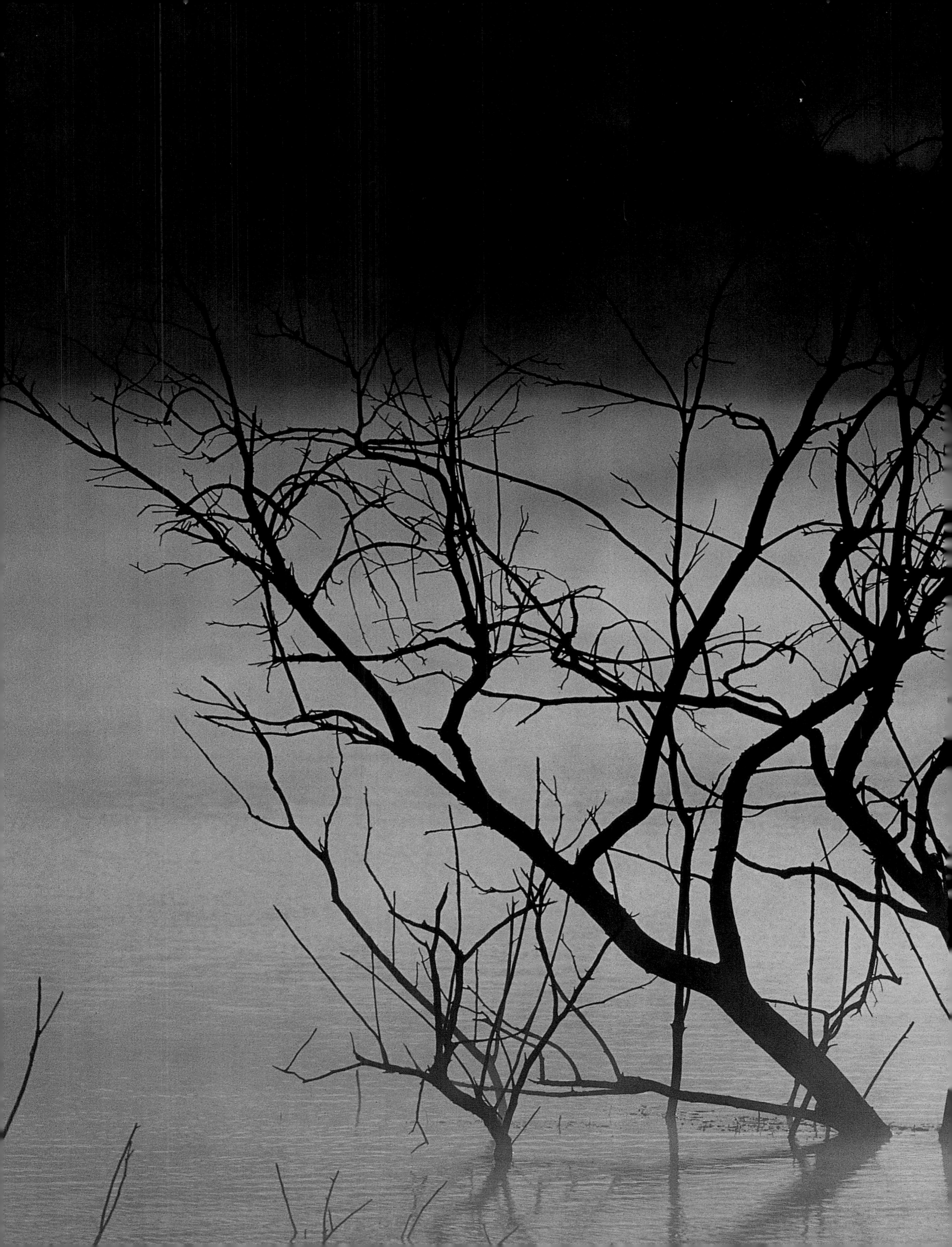

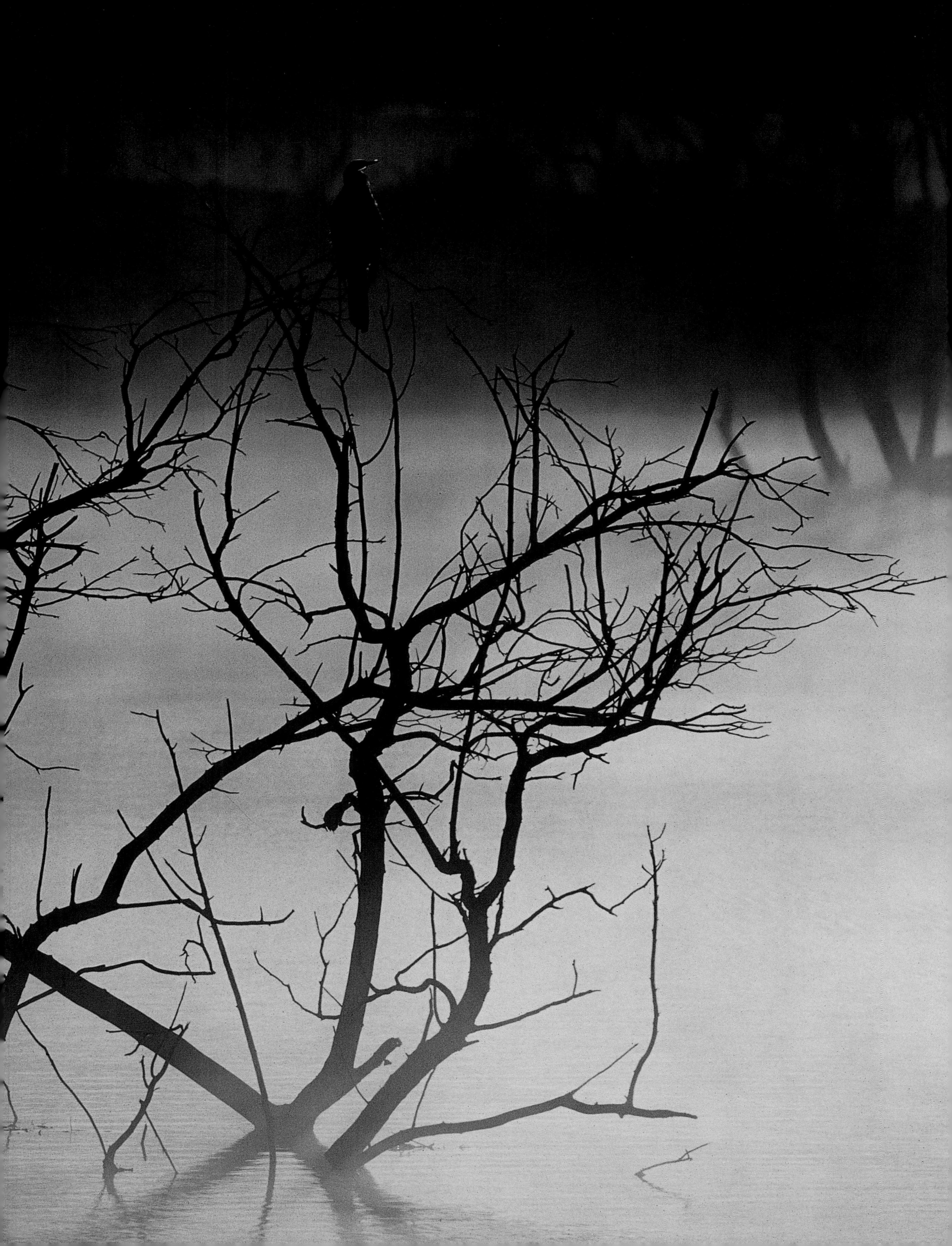

Practical Advice

Facts and figures
Surface area ▶ 1,221,037 sq km
Population ▶ 43,420,000 inhabitants
Capital ▶ Pretoria
Languages ▶ No less than 11 official languages, including Sotho, Zulu, Swazi, and Ndebele. However English and Afrikaans remain the most commonly spoken languages.
Time difference ▶ One time zone – GMT + 2 hours

When to go
It is a pleasure to visit South Africa at any time of year, but it is best to avoid the South African holiday periods – December, January, April and mid-June to mid July – because accommodation prices can double! The best time to discover the country is in the last three months of the year, because the southern spring reveals the most beautiful landscapes.

Climate and seasons
South Africa is below the equator, which means that the seasons are reversed in relation to those in Europe: summer lasts from November until March, winter from April to October. However, despite some cold temperatures, winter still offers a high rate of sunshine.
Winter temperatures range from 0°C to 25°C. Summer temperatures range from 15°C to 40°C. Rainfall is far heavier in eastern and south-eastern regions than in the rest of South Africa.

How to get there?
Airports ▶ Many airlines fly to South Africa and its three major airports: Johannesburg, Durban and Cape Town.
Airlines ▶ Air France (*www.airfrance.fr*), British Airways (*www.britishairways.com*), Emirates (*www.emirates.com*), KLM (*www.klm.fr*), Lufthansa (*www.lufthansa.fr*), South African Airways (*www.flysaa.com*).

Useful Addresses in the UK
South African Tourism
6 Alt Grove, London SW19 4DZ
Information: 0870 1550044
Tel: + 44 (0) 20 8971 9364
Fax: + 44 (0) 20 8944 6705
Email: *info.uk@southafrica.net*

South Africa House
Trafalgar Square, London WC2N 5DP
Phone: +44 (0) 20 7451 7299
Fax: +44 (0) 20 7451 7283
Email: *webdesk@southafricahouse.com*

Luxury tours to South Africa
UK: ▶ Abercrombie & Kent Ltd
St George's House, Ambrose Street
Cheltenham, Gloucestershire GL50 3LG
Phone: +44 (0) 845 0700610
Fax: +44 (0) 845 0700607
Email: *info@abercrombiekent.co.uk*
Australia: ▶ Abercrombie & Kent (Australia) Pty. Ltd Berkeley Hall
11 Princes Street, PO Box 327, St Kilda
Melbourne, Victoria 3182
Phone: 00 61 3 9536 1800
Fax: 00 61 3 9536 1805
Email: *contact@abercrombiekent.com.au*
Website: *www.abercrombiekent.com.au*
USA: ▶ Abercrombie & Kent Oakbrook, Inc.
1520 Kensington Road, Oak Brook, IL 60523
Phone: 00 1 630 954 2944
Fax: 00 1 630 954 3324
Email: *info@abercrombiekent.com*
Website: *www.abercrombiekent.com*

Health
Diphtheria, tetanus and polio vaccinations need to be up to date. Typhoid, Hepatitis A and B, and BCG may also be recommended. When you are planning your trip, check with your doctor for the latest advice. Some areas of the country are affected by malaria. It is highly recommended to take a zone 2 or 3 preventative treatment.
Further information: *www.malaria.co.za*

Money
Local currency ▶ The Rand (ZAR), made up of 100 cents. The notes are R200, R100, R50, R20, R10. The most common coins are R1, R2 and R5.
Credit cards ▶ Accepted almost everywhere, except in petrol stations, where cash is required.
Traveller's cheques ▶ Accepted everywhere, but verification may take some time. Traveller's cheques in Rand are available from issuing organisations.
Cash machines ▶ Referred to locally as ATM machines, can be found in almost all towns, even the smaller ones.
Banks ▶ Open from 9 am to 3.30 pm Monday to Friday and 9 am to 11 am on Saturday.

Formalities
Documents ▶ EU citizens require a passport that is valid for at least six months. No advance visa is required. Visitors' permits are issued at the airport on arrival. They are valid for three months and can be extended. In order to rent a car, an international driver's licence is required.

Communications
To call South Africa from the UK ▶ Dial 00 27 followed by the local area code (without the 0) and the number of your correspondent.
To call the UK from South Africa ▶ Dial 09 44, followed by the local area code (without the 0) and the number of your correspondent.
Mobile communications ▶ Network coverage is reasonable, as long as you do not venture far from the main routes.
Internet ▶ Many points of access are available, even in small towns.

Safety
Compared to European countries, South Africa is a violent place. But if you follow the basic rules of caution (avoid walking in big cities, isolated places or dangerous suburbs), you run little risk of being robbed. In general, travelling by car or on foot at night is dangerous. Seek local advice and use common sense.

National Parks and Reserves

Kruger National Park
Location ▶ 500 km east of Johannesburg, along the Mozambique border
Surface area ▶ Nearly 2 million ha
Key feature ▶ The "Big Five" (lion, leopard, elephant, black rhinoceros and buffalo) and many other animals
Entry price ▶ R120 per adult, R60 per child, per day
Accommodation ▶ From camping (R100 per person per night) to luxury hotels (R1700 per person per night, sometimes much more within the private reserves adjoining the Kruger). For information and reservations: *reservations@sanparks.org*
Our favourite ▶ The beauty of the evening light on the Olifants River and its crocodiles…
Health ▶ The park is situated in a malaria zone.
Special tips ▶ The Kruger Park authorities are not the friendliest: any breaking of reserve rules is severely punished. Pay special attention to the hours when driving is allowed.

Ndumo Game Reserve
Location ▶ 100 km north of Mkuze, on the Mozambique border
Surface area ▶ 10,000 ha
Key feature ▶ Beautiful wetlands, which resemble a miniature Okavango
Entry price ▶ R30 per adult, R15 per child, per day
Accommodation ▶ From camping (R50 per person per night) to the rental of a small chalet (R180 per person per night) There is also privately owned accommodation in the park.
Our favourite ▶ The wealth of birdlife
Health ▶ The park is situated in a malaria zone.
Special tips ▶ Ndumo Reserve is in a warm humid zone, ideal for mosquitoes! Pack a strong insect repellent.

Tembe Elephant Park
Location ▶ This park adjoins the Ndumo Game Reserve, 100 km north of Mkuze, on the Mozambique border.
Surface area ▶ 30,000 ha
Key feature ▶ The last surviving elephants from the Mozambique civil war. Some formidable individuals
Entry price ▶ R30 per adult, R15 per child, per day
Accommodation ▶ No camping in this park, the only possibility is the unique private lodge.
Our favourite ▶ The fabulous spectacle of the elephants at the Ponweni watering hole
Health ▶ The park is situated in a malaria zone.
Special tips ▶ The elephants in the Tembe park can react unpredictably. Take care to keep your distance.

Kosi Bay Nature Reserve
Location ▶ At the extreme east of the country, on the coast of the Indian Ocean, on the border with Mozambique
Surface area ▶ 4,500 ha
Key feature ▶ A rich bird fauna in a heavenly setting
Entry price ▶ R20 per adult, R15 per child, per day
Accommodation ▶ From camping (65 R per person, per night) to a small hut (230 R per person, per night). The reserve also offers private accommodation.
Our favourite ▶ The boat trip to discover the four lakes on which ancestral fish traps are installed
Health ▶ Kosi Bay is in a malaria zone.
Special tips ▶ In certain parts of the reserve quicksand is common, so it's best to take a guide.

Sodwana Bay Nature Reserve
Location ▶ On the coast of the Indian Ocean, north east of Richard's Bay
Surface area ▶ 1,000 ha
Key feature ▶ Marvellous deep sea, rich fauna and flora
Entry price ▶ R20 per adult, R15 per child, per day
Accommodation ▶ From camping (R40 per person, per night) to a chalet (R220 per person, per night). The reserve also proposes private accommodation.
Our favourite ▶ The magnificent inland landscapes
Health ▶ Sodwana Bay is in a malaria zone.
Special tips ▶ Recenty tourists visiting Sodwana Bay have been robbed, so be careful.

Greater St Lucia Wetland Park
Location ▶ On the coast of the Indian Ocean, north-east of Richard's Bay
Surface area ▶ 260,000 ha
Key feature ▶ The richness of this ecosystem, classified as a World Heritage Site
Entry price ▶ R20 per adult, R15 per child, per day (for Cape Vidal, Charters Creek and Fanies Island)
Accommodation ▶ The reserve offers camping (R50 per person, per night) and many other types of accommodation in the village of St Lucia.
Our favourite ▶ Getting close to the crocodiles and hippos by boat; observing the myriad birds
Health ▶ St Lucia is in a malaria zone.
Special tips ▶ Beware, crocodiles are dangerous animals: not a year goes by without reports of victims.

Hluhluwe-Imfolozi National Park
Location ▶ A little over 200 km north of Durban, north of Richard's Bay
Surface area ▶ 96,000 ha
Key feature ▶ Sublime landscapes, a fauna – in particular the white and black rhinos – and flora as rich as it is diverse
Entry price ▶ R70 per adult, R35 per child, per day
Accommodation ▶ No camping. The only accommodation available is in the lodge (from R425 per person, per night). The reserve also proposes private accommodation.
Our favourite ▶ Hluhluwe-Imfolozi National Park is one of the few parks to offer a network of hiking paths in the middle of the wilderness, where one can meet white rhinos. If you form a small group of travellers, an armed guard will accompany you. You can then discover nature from a new angle. Three-day circuits are proposed, and the participants are even asked to stand watch for a quarter of the night guard.
Health ▶ The reserve is in a malaria zone.
Special tips ▶ Split your visit between the north (Hluhluwe) and the south (Imfolozi): the landscapes are totally different, and rival each other for beauty.

Mkuze Game Reserve
Location ▶ A little over 300 km north of Durban
Surface area ▶ 40,000 ha
Key feature ▶ Animal life around the watering holes
Entry price ▶ R30 per adult, R15 per child, per day.
Accommodation ▶ From camping (R55 per person, per night) to accommodation in a luxury camp in the bush (R320 per person per night). The reserve also offers private accommodation.

Our favourite ▸ The incessant ballets of animals around the watering holes
Health ▸ Mkuze is in a malaria zone.
Special tips ▸ The vervet monkeys of the campsite are a nuisance, and have become masters at the art of opening tents!

Royal Natal National Park

Location ▸ 35 km from Bergville, north of the Drakensberg mountains, on the Lesotho border
Surface area ▸ 8,000 ha
Key feature ▸ Extraordinary mountain landscapes
Entry price ▸ R25 per adult, R15 per child, per day
Accommodation ▸ From camping (R50 per person, per night) to a small chalet (R300 per person, per night). The reserve also proposes private accommodation.
Our favourite ▸ The amphitheatre, a monument of power and beauty
Health ▸ Nothing to mention
Special tips ▸ Hikers, beware of extreme weather changes!

Cathedral Peak

Location ▸ About 50 km from Winterton and Bergville, in the centre of the Drakensberg Mountain Range, on the Lesotho border
Surface area ▸ 32,000 ha
Key feature ▸ A striking panorama of the Drakensberg mountains which can be seen from Mike's Peak
Entry price ▸ R15 per adult, R10 per child, per day
Accommodation ▸ From camping (R40 per person, per night) to a small chalet (R300 per person, per night). The reserve also proposes private accommodation and mountain refuges.
Our favourite ▸ The small bench on Mike's Peak where one can rest (the hike is strenuous) and admire the landscape.
Health ▸ The hikes are very strenuous. You need to be fit.
Special tips ▸ Hikers, beware of extreme weather changes!

Giant's Castle

Location ▸ About 40 km from Estcourt, in the centre of the Drakensberg Mountain Range, on the Lesotho border
Surface area ▸ 34,500 ha
Key feature ▸ Imposing Cape elands which inhabit the magnificent landscapes
Entry price ▸ R20 per adult, R10 per child, per day.
Accommodation ▸ Small chalets (R300 per person, per night). The reserve also offers private accommodation and mountain refuges.
Our favourite ▸ The superb cave paintings left by the Bushmen
Health ▸ Certain treks are reserved for people in good physical condition.
Special tips ▸ Hikers, beware of extreme weather changes!

Addo Elephant National Park

Location ▸ Around 70 km north of Port Elizabeth
Surface area ▸ 80,000 ha
Key feature ▸ The last great herds of elephants
Entry price ▸ R80 per adult, R40 per child, per day
Accommodation ▸ From camping (R100 per person, per night) to chalets (R500 per person, per night).
Information and reservations: *reservations@sanparks.org*
Our favourite ▸ Elephant games at the watering holes
Health ▸ Nothing to mention
Special tips ▸ Beware! The elephants are in on their home ground…

Mountain Zebra National Park

Location ▸ About 25 km from Cradock, on the road from Bloemfontein to Port Elizabeth
Surface area ▸ 6,500 ha
Key feature ▸ The last mountain zebras living in magnificent surroundings
Entry price ▸ R60 per adult, R30 per child, per day.
Accommodation ▸ From camping (R100 per person, per night) to cottages (R390 per person, per night).
Information and reservations: *reservations@sanparks.org*
Our favourite ▸ Meeting a young mountain zebra, a meeting filled with hope: it proves that within park this endangered species has found the land it needs to develop freely.
Health ▸ Nothing to mention
Special tips ▸ Avoid hiking during the hot hours of the day.

Tsitsikamma National Park

Location ▸ About 95 km east of Knysna on the cost of the Indian Ocean
Surface area ▸ 50,000 ha
Key feature ▸ Luxuriant vegetation which appears to tumble into the sea
Entry price ▸ R80 per adult, R40 per child, per day
Accommodation ▸ From camping (R150 per person, per night) to chalets with views over the Indian Ocean (R760 per person, per night).
Information and reservations: *reservations@sanparks.org*
Our favourite ▸ The powerful ocean waves breaking on the rocks which line the Otter Trail.
Health ▸ The Otter Trail demands physical fitness.
Special tips ▸ This park is extremely popular with South Africans during their holiday seasons.

Karoo National Park

Location ▸ About 10 km from Beaufort West, on the road from Johannesburg to the Cape.
Surface area ▸ 80,000 ha
Key feature ▸ Undisturbed nature, as it was in prehistoric times!
Entry price ▸ R60 per adult, R30 per child, per day
Accommodation ▸ From camping (R100 per person, per night) to cottages (R500 per person, per night).
Information and reservations: *reservations@sanparks.org*
Our favourite ▸ Walking in the footsteps of dinosaurs
Health ▸ Beware of heatstroke during hikes
Special tips ▸ There is a circuit for off road vehicles in the Karoo Park. For those who do not have such a vehicle, it is possible to travel with the rangers for a small fee. Do not miss out – the sights you will see are striking

De Hoop Nature Reserve

Location ▸ West of Cape Agulhas, on the African meridian
Surface area ▸ 34,000 ha
Key feature ▸ The last of the black oystercatchers, birds on the brink of extinction. They are easily approached.
Entry price ▸ R20 per adult, R10 per child, per day
Accommodation ▸ From camping (R95 per tent per night) to cottages (R450 per cottage per night).
Our favourite ▸ From mid-May to mid-December whales come to the reserve's waters. One can normally watch them from the high dunes on Long Beach.
Health ▸ Nothing to mention
Special tips ▸ Depending on the intensity of the tides, swimming can be very dangerous.

Cape Peninsula Nature Reserve (Boulder Beach)

Location ▸ Simonstown, small town on the outskirts of Cape Town
Surface area ▸ A few hectares
Key feature ▸ Cape penguins
Entry price ▸ R10 per person, per day
Accommodation ▸ No accommodation in this tiny reserve, however Simonstown has plenty of hotels.
Our favourite ▸ The clumsy walk of the adorable penguins. Be careful of your ears, these birds can screech very loudly.
Health ▸ Nothing to mention
Special tips ▸ Go to see the penguins early in the morning or in the late afternoon, because Boulder Beach is often overflowing with people.

Cape of Good Hope Nature Reserve

Location ▶ A few hundred metres from Cape Town
Surface area ▶ 7,700 ha
Key feature ▶ The world famous Cape, easy to explore thanks to its many hiking paths
Entry price ▶ R30 per adult, R15 per child, per day
Accommodation ▶ No particular accommodation in the reserve. Numerous hotels in Simonstown.
Our favourite ▶ The open sea and the spectacle of nature's brute force
Health ▶ Nothing to mention
Special tips ▶ Do not be put off by bad weather: it will help you to understand what sailors must have felt as they approached the Cape!

The West Coast National Park

Location ▶ A little over 100 km north of the Cape
Surface area ▶ 30,000 ha
Key feature ▶ Maritime landscapes, impressive tides, and the Langebaan lagoon
Entry price ▶ R30 per adult, R15 per child, per day
Accommodation ▶ In dormitories. Cottages can be reserved. A floating house on the lagoon (R800 per night, for four people) can be rented.
Reservations and information: *reservations@sanparks.org*
Our favourite ▶ The small hamlet of chalk whitewashed houses with their church – Church Heaven. From the charming little bench in front of its door, one can admire a sublime landscape.
Health ▶ Nothing to mention
Special tips ▶ Take advantage of the organised excursions to the small islands nearby to see penguins, seals and sharks.

Namaqua National Park

Location ▶ 500 km north of the Cape, not far from Kamieskroon, on the N7 between Springbok and Clanwilliam
Surface area ▶ 300 ha (not counting the surrounding area which has as many flowers, but is not classified as park).
Key feature ▶ After the first rains of the southern winter, the Namaqua Park, a desert for most of the year, is covered with a spectacular carpet of scented flowers. A natural curiosity, which should on no account be missed!
Entry price ▶ R10 per adult, R5 per child, per day
Accommodation ▶ No particular accommodation within the park, but there are many campsites, hotels and bed and breakfasts near by.
Our favourite ▶ Watching the desert transform itself into a Garden of Eden.
Health ▶ Nothing to mention.
Special tips ▶ The best time of year to view this extraordinary blooming is in September.

Witsand Nature Reserve

Location ▶ Near Volop, 230 km east of Upington on the road to Kimberley.
Surface area ▶ 3,000 ha.
Key feature ▶ An isle of white sand, surrounded by the red sands of the Kalahari, and its unique watering hole which is inhabited by an incredible selection of bird life.
Entry price ▶ R20 per adult, R10 per child, per day.
Accommodation ▶ From camping (R50 per person, per night) to chalets (R300 per person, per night).
Our favourite ▶ The roaring sands: fantastic and fascinating!
Health ▶ Nothing to mention.
Special tips ▶ Avoid the hot hours of the day at all costs, the dunes become furnaces.

Augrabies Falls National Park

Location ▶ 36 km north of Kakamas, between Upington and Springbok.
Surface area ▶ 48,000 ha.
Key feature ▶ Breathtaking scenery, a rich fauna and the famous and impressive water fall.
Entry price ▶ R60 per adult, R30 per child, per day
Accommodation ▶ From camping (R100 per person, per night) to chalets (R460 per person, per night).
Information and reservations: *reservations@sanparks.org*
Our favourite ▶ The intoxicating atmosphere around the falls
Health ▶ Nothing to mention.
Special tips ▶ The amount of water which cascades over the falls depends on rainfall. Heavy spring rains guarantee an unforgettable spectacle.

Kgalagadi Transfrontier Park

Location ▶ 260 km north of Upington
Surface area ▶ 9,590 sq km (in South Africa)
Key feature ▶ The magnificent felines which live in the park, especially the lions, supposedly the largest on the continent, and the African wild cat, regrettably an endangered species
Entry price ▶ R120 per adult, R60 per child, per day
Accommodation ▶ From camping (R95 per person, per night) to cottages (R600 per person, per night).
Information and reservations: *reservations@sanparks.org*
Our favourite ▶ The magical atmosphere in this mythical African desert
Health ▶ Nothing to mention.
Special tips ▶ The tracks are difficult to use. Make sure you leave with a vehicle in good condition, and with sufficient water and fuel reserves.

Madikwe Game Reserve

Location ▶ 125 km north of Zeerust, on the road to the Botswanian border
Surface area ▶ 76,500 ha
Key feature ▶ A great variety of wild animal species
Entry price ▶ There is no entry fee because there are no day trips. You are obliged to spend the night in one of the reserve's accommodations.
Accommodation ▶ There is no campsite, but there is lots of private accommodation.
Information *madikweadmin@wol.co.za*
Our favourite ▶ Watching lycaons, famous African wild dogs
Health ▶ Nothing to mention
Special tips ▶ To discover Madikwe, let the rangers guide you, they are among the country's best

Pilanesberg National Park

Location ▶ 150 km north west of Johannesburg and 120km north west of Pretoria
Surface area ▶ 50,000 ha
Key feature ▶ White rhinos, elephants, giraffes, lions, hyenas, and many different bird species
Entry price ▶ R20 per adult, R15 per child, per day
Accommodation ▶ From camping (R130 per person, per night) to the lodge (R650 per person, per night)
Our favourite ▶ The beauty of the site, and the knowledge, that this park was created by man, thanks to Operation Genesis – it is reassuring to know that man is not always a destructive predator.
Health ▶ Nothing to mention
Special tips ▶ If possible avoid the South African holiday periods: the park's proximity to Johannesburg means it will have record numbers of visitors at these times.

Thanks

The completion of this work would not have been possible without the support of my nearest and dearest, who I would especially like to thank. Many contributors also gave precious help: all the team at JFC Land Rover, and particularly François Xavier Constantin, who was able to answer the many questions (and there were many!) posed by a 50,000 km expedition; Land Rover France, and particularly Sylvain Toutain for the quality of his vehicles; José, Ophélia Mendés and their children, for their fantastic reception during my many visits to Johannesburg; Rob Harrison White, wildlife film director, met one day in the bush and a friend for life; Peter and Wendy Leitner; Claude Six.

I would also like to thank the South African authorities for their welcome and their help, as well as the different provinces and the authorities of the various nature reserves visited. A final thank you to the people I met during my stay whose kindness confirmed the warmth of South African hospitality.

All the photographs in this book were taken with Canon EOS digital and film equipment. The lenses used vary from 14mm to 600mm. Special thanks go to Bernard Thomas and Raphaël Rimoux from the Canon Pro Club. The panoramic photographs were taken with a Hasselblad Xpan and 30, 45 and 90mm lenses.